FORNICATIONALLY CHALLENGED

My Reluctant Return to Dating

Judi Lee Goshen

Chicago Story Press, Inc.

In Loving Memory of
Marge

And for Debbie
The Louise to my Thelma

CONTENTS

Title Page	1
Copyright	2
Dedication	3
Disclaimer	7
Introduction	9
Rethink The Celibacy Thing	12
Floozy	23
Transition Guy	30
Mambo Man	51
The Height And The Glasses	57
The Contractor	72
Boss Man	77
Moving Home	92
Law Of Attraction	99
Fornicationally Challenged	114
Ashton: Part 1	123
Wordless Farewell	134
The Puppy	139
Ashton: Part 2	154
He's Got A Room	170
Roxy	176

LA Richard	183
NY Dick	209
Jaded	235
Mr. Age Appropriate	239
WTF?!	262
A Journey Of Self-Discovery	264
Acknowledgements	269
About The Author	271
Books By This Author	273

DISCLAIMER

The stories you are about to read are true, to the best of my recollection. However, I may have taken creative license once—maybe twice.

If you are one of my two children, the sex scenes are entirely fictional. Mommy has never had sex. EVER.

If we had a relationship, your name has been changed. If you try to sue me, then you are claiming what I wrote is true.

Introduction

After a rocky twenty-year marriage, I told Steve I wanted a separation.

Steve never thought I'd divorce him. He was convinced the separation was temporary, so he didn't get an apartment. He moved back into his old room in his parents' home, where he now lived with his widowed father. And he worked overtime trying to get me back.

I'll change. I love you. I took you for granted. Let me make it up to you.

He even went as far as asking me to go into marriage counseling. I wasn't buying any of it. Then he told me a friend's sister asked him out. I'm sure he said that to make me jealous, but it worked. I realized I still had feelings for him. *Might as well go into counseling before blowing up a family*, I thought.

So I told my lawyer to stop the divorce process, and every Friday morning Steve and I went to counseling. He still stayed at his dad's but came to the house once in a while to see the kids and pick up his mail, mostly bills.

One night, after I got settled into bed, I heard a voice: "Open his cell phone bill."

I sat up. There was no one else in the house; the kids were at sleepovers. After a moment I settled back down, then heard it again: "Open his cell phone bill."

It wasn't like a voice of another person in the room or a voice in my head, and I'm not saying it was the voice of God, but

I swear, I heard that sentence. To make it stop, I went downstairs and opened his cell phone bill.

There were three pages, front and back, filled with phone numbers and the dates, times, and durations of each call. Most of the numbers I knew, but there were many I didn't, which was weird.

I called a random number I didn't recognize and hung up when our landscaper answered. Of course I didn't know the landscaper's home number. I'd let my overactive imagination get the best of me. How could I think he was having an affair when his main goal was to come home?

I trusted he meant it—but one always needs to verify. I called another number, feeling very silly about the entire venture—until I heard a perky female voice on an answering machine: "Hi, this is Lisa Miller. I'm out of the office right now..."

I felt a pain in my heart. The bones in my legs must have disappeared because I fell to the floor.

Lisa Miller? That was the woman who had asked him out.

Betrayal might have brought me to my knees, but anger got me to my feet. I grabbed the bill, got a bunch of different highlighter pens, and began to group the numbers by colors. There were three major repeaters. "Hi, this is Lisa Miller. I'm out of the *office* right now..." was number one. When I dialed the two other numbers I heard: "Hi, this is Lisa Miller. I'm not *home* right now..." and "Hi, you've reached Lisa's *cell phone*..."

I'm fairly certain the average person would have stopped there, but I made a chart. I listed the dates, times, and durations of each call, and then cross-referenced it with my calendar. The night of my father's eightieth birthday party, when Steve left early because he felt "sick," there were two calls to her: one at the time he would have gotten into his car—I knew it was to say, "I'm on my way," because the duration was ten seconds. The other call was exactly twenty-seven minutes later. The time it would take to drive into the city and pull up to her apartment building. Another ten-second duration: "I'm downstairs." But the best —every Friday morning after marriage counseling ended, there were calls to her.

I looked at the graph, solved for "X," and figured out the obvious—he was sleeping with her.

I made one more call that night. I left a voice mail for my divorce attorney: "Serve. Him. The. Papers."

I found out later Lisa was one of many.

Fast forward—on the last day of divorce mediation, we were sitting across from each other at a conference table. The lawyer, our mediator, was sorting documents in the back of the room.

Steve looked at me so innocently and said, "I never thought we'd be here."

"Seriously? You were sleeping with other women and never thought you could wind up divorced?"

His demeanor changed drastically. "It's your fault! You put me out there!"

"I never told you to sleep with other women."

"I didn't want them. I only wanted you!"

"Oh, so you thought the way back to me was through other women's vaginas?"

I heard a laugh escape the mediator.

That was a defining moment, not because it was the end of my marriage, and not because I was going to be on my own for the first time in my forty years, but because I found the comedy in it.

Sure, the betrayal, the divorce, the subsequent dating mishaps, and the losses that followed were some of the hardest times in my life, but because I saw the comedic element, I ended up having the time of my life.

Rethink The Celibacy Thing

I drove Eric to his car and shifted into park. We looked at each other and I knew what was coming. When he leaned in for the kiss, I met him halfway. His kiss was soft, tender, and quick. Then he kissed me again, holding it just a little longer. Long enough to breathe each other in. Then one last kiss, where his tongue ever-so-slightly grazed mine. It sent an unexpected current throughout my body. The kind that went straight to my lady parts and woke them up.

What the—?

I never expected to feel turned on, not on a first date, and certainly not while I was still married. But there I was, on my first date as an adult, sexually excited over a man I barely knew.

After I filed for divorce, I planned on being celibate. I only agreed to the date with Eric to make my husband jealous. Make him feel an ounce of the betrayal I felt when I learned he was sleeping around. I never expected to like Eric, or to kiss him on that first date. And I had no idea that that one kiss would launch me into my sexual prime. My forty-year-old hormones were screaming: *HAVE SEX NOW!*

Then he started to leave. *LEAVE?*

Having opened the car door, he turned and said, "I'd like to see you again, soon."

On the outside, I was calm and said, "I'd like that." But as I watched him walk away, I felt like Demi Moore in the movie *Disclosure*, when she yelled at Michael Douglas to *get back here and finish what you started!*

The whole drive home I was in shock at my body's response. Was I turning into one of those fast girls Mother had warned me about? The ones boys didn't respect?

I was baffled and in desperate need of the current "rules." But there was one thing I knew for sure—I definitely had to rethink the celibacy thing!

"There's a Jewish singles' dance at Navy Pier Saturday night," Roxy told me over drinks in a bar halfway between her city condo and my suburban townhome.

It was August 1999. I was forty and single for the first time in twenty years, though the divorce wasn't final. Everyone on earth was Y2K crazy, afraid that all the computers in the world would be so confused by the year 2000 that they would shut down completely. All that frenzy paled in comparison to the chaos inside my head. It was time for me to start dating, but dating could lead to intimacy and intimacy could lead to sex and sex could lead to an STD, and an STD, I was convinced, would lead to death, or worse—warts.

Mother's voice, in the Yiddish accent she used to make a point, haunted my thoughts as well. "Judala, why ask for trouble? Better you should forget about such things."

Roxy was right. I was driving myself crazy. I should go to that singles' event, meet a guy, and make Steve jealous! "Okay, sure. I'll meet you there."

"I don't go to those things anymore." Roxy was jaded and had fallen into the routine of work, home, eat, TV, sleep. Repeat.

"Come on, please?"

"No."

"What if we made it fun?"

She was intrigued. "Like fake jobs fun?"

Roxy and I loved the fake jobs game because when I told a new acquaintance I was an actress, I was offended when they'd reply, "Should I know you?" And Roxy disliked telling people she was a therapist because they'd ask, "Are you going to analyze me?"

"Yes!" I replied. "And I know the perfect jobs. We pick up dead animals from the side of the road." Since I commuted daily to and from the city, I saw a lot of dead animals on the road. I always wondered whose job it was to remove them.

Her eyes widened. I could see her brain working. I had her. "Splat and Scoop!" she said.

"What?"

"The name of our business. Our motto: 'You squish 'em, we scoop 'em.'" She laughed at her genius.

"No job too messy. No job too sticky," I added, and we laughed harder.

But Roxy had to top me. "And if mostly intact—dinner!"

We roared, and she agreed to go.

"It'll be like old times," I told her.

Roxy and I were best friends in high school and had been partners in crime ever since. We majored in partying and minored in boys. Roxy had not only remained single during my two decades of marriage; she remained firmly entrenched in the past. She still had long hair with bangs and still smoked Marlboro Reds, always holding the cigarette an arm's length from her body, and after every puff waved her hands frantically to dissipate the smoke. That way, no one in the room would think that she was the smoker. Spoiler alert—*everyone* in the room knew that she was the smoker.

"We'll need business cards," Roxy said.

"Why?"

"To give out a fake phone number: 1-800-Road-Kill."

When I got to the singles' party that night, I walked around the rooftop of Navy Pier looking for Roxy. I finally spotted her with Randy, a male friend from her building. She said that she had just met a friend of Randy's and they were hitting it off. "Hitting it off" was our code from high school. It meant I should get lost. Roxy didn't like to introduce me to new guys for fear they might like me instead. "Never trust a woman." It was a proverb both our mothers tried to instill early in life. That put me in the awkward position of having to fend for myself —alone —at my first singles party.

I put on my best party smile to hide my RBF (Resting Bitch Face) and pretended that I was having fun. But every man who came over to me made me want to disappear. They all asked questions, so many questions, and most of the questions I should have been able to answer: "Oh, so you're divorced?" *Well, not really.* "What's your name?" *Now or next week?*

My life was so up in the air that I couldn't answer a straightforward question. And I didn't even want to try. I felt like the sexual equivalent of Rip Van Winkle. I fell asleep in the '70s encouraged to *get it on* and woke up twenty years later to find abstinence being preached.

Roxy was still talking to the guy she was interested in, and I didn't want to give up too quickly, so I gave myself a time-out and snuck away to look at Lake Michigan. Lake Michigan had always been my Fortress of Solitude.

The party was on the eastern roof of the Pier, and the breeze coming off the Lake was chilly for late August, but in my daughter's new cream-colored jacket, I wasn't cold. However, the jacket didn't match my outfit: a royal blue tank top, black capri pants, and chunky black Steve Madden slides. But I was glad I was wearing it because it set me apart from all the other women in their tank tops, black capri pants, and chunky black Steve Madden slides. *Am I in style, or do all us single (or soon-to-be single) women look alike?*

I sat on one of the benches that faced the Lake and sent up a silent prayer. *Please, just someone nice to talk to.* After a while

I donned my smile and returned to the crowd, heading straight for the dance floor. I figured watching people dance would make me seem a little more engaged.

The problem—it was a Jewish Singles' event. With a few exceptions, we are people with little or no rhythm. Hence—no one was dancing. *Now, what do I do?*

A man came up and bombarded me with more questions: "Hi, what's your name? What do you do? Do you have kids? Are you willing to have more?"

That's when I realized: these men were on a search. They were interviewing women for a specific position: wife. I was in a marital meat market! Sure, it may have been kosher, but I had been a vegetarian far too long. Being a wife was the last thing in the world I wanted. Well, maybe death—and genital warts— those were the last things in the world I wanted, but getting married again and raising children was right up there. I felt cornered, boxed-in, and panic began to build. I had to get out of there, fast.

I quickly found Roxy, said goodbye, and left. I was angry at myself for having gone in the first place, angry with my friend for not hanging out with me in the fun-filled way we had planned, and I blamed my husband for putting me out there in the singles world. Yes, I was the one that wanted a divorce, but it was his stupidity that had forced me to file.

I was grumbling to myself as I walked off the roof, down the stairs, and through the arcade to get to the safety of my car. As I mumbled my frustrations aloud, a man from the party sidled up to me and asked, "Hey, where are you running?"

Another fucking question?!

That was the only opening I needed to vent my pent-up frustrations. To me, the experiment of the singles party was over, and I didn't have to pretend anymore. The party smile was gone. RBF reactivated.

"Where am I running?" I snapped at him, not losing my stride. "To my car, to get out of here! I can't believe I actually came to one of these things. All you men, you're all the same. You all want the same thing from a woman. All of you—same thing! Marriage and kids! Am I right?" I stopped walking and confronted him face-to-face. "Do you want to get married and have kids? Ugh? Do you?! Do you want to get married and have kids?!"

He looked at me innocently, and without missing a beat replied, "How 'bout we start with coffee?"

He made me laugh. It disarmed me. When I really looked at him, I saw this lovely man in front of me. He was approximately six feet tall, in good shape with rugged good looks, a warm smile and kind eyes. It had been a long time since a man looked at me with kindness in his eyes. I liked it. I needed it. My mood softened.

"Sorry. Guess I freaked out a little."

"Hey, I get it. These things are a necessary evil," he said *Gracious.*

"It seemed like everyone in there was fresh outta college and I got a kid starting next week," I said. "I just felt out of place."

"You have a college kid?"

"Just one. I also have one in high school. I had them early. I'm forty."

"Wow, I thought you were thirty-two," he said.

"Thirty-two? Seriously-thirty-two? For years, whenever I meet new people they say, 'I thought you were twenty-eight.' Always twenty-eight. Suddenly, overnight I get thirty-two?"

"It's still eight years younger than your real age."

"It's a four-year bump. Who wants to age like a dog?"

He smiled at me with those kind eyes, and I thought, *You should suggest we have coffee.*

"We should meet for coffee sometime."

Telepathic too.

"I should probably tell you my name."

"Makes it easier."

"Eric. Eric Abramson."

I had just written my first screenplay, a romantic comedy in which the male lead's name was Eric. It felt like an omen. *I manifested my very own romantic lead!*

"Judi."

"Do you have a last name, Judi?"

"I'll have to get back to you on that."

He smiled and didn't push it. We continued to walk and talk then found ourselves standing in front of the orange steel doors to the parking garage.

"Can I get your phone number?"

I fished out a pen and paper from my purse and wrote it down for him.

We had the preliminary talk, now ask me for a proper date.

He took the paper and said, "I'll call you about dinner."

I smiled as I left him and didn't stop smiling until I fell asleep that night.

That was Saturday. He didn't call Sunday. Monday came and went. My friend Victoria said he'd call by Tuesday. My other friend, Stephanie said Wednesday was the official deadline to ask for a date that weekend. On Thursday, Mitch, my male friend from high school, lectured me about giving out my home number. Friday I took my son to college, and Saturday Eric called. He asked me to dinner for Wednesday. I said Thursday would be better. After all, he made me wait a week.

When it came to choosing an outfit for the date, I was lost. I had been a mom for eighteen years and had been playing a mom in TV commercials for ten. All I owned were jeans, khakis, and pastel tops from Gap.

I asked Stephanie for help.

"You need hottie clothes, girl. Whatcha got?"

"You mean sexy clothes? Nothing."

"You have black capri pants, pair 'em with a tank."

"Wore that when I met him."

"Hmm, let's go shopping tomorrow," she suggested.

"I can meet you at the Gap."

"Oh my God. No more Gap!" she scolded.

We laughed but never went shopping. I didn't feel I needed to since it wasn't a Saturday night date. It was a low-key Thursday dinner. *But what the hell do you wear for a low-key Thursday dinner?* I should have agreed to Wednesday because on Wednesday you can wear business casual, but business casual on Thursday says, "I don't know how to get ready for the weekend. I got no life."

I finally decided on a long vintage sundress. It was feminine and pretty, and except for my cleavage (which had always been difficult to conceal), it didn't show off my body. This time around I wanted to attract someone to my personality first.

We had decided to meet halfway between his city apartment and my suburban townhouse. He suggested we meet at Maggiano's in the Old Orchard Shopping Mall in Skokie. Well, actually, in the bar of Maggiano's in the Old Orchard Shopping Mall in Skokie. And I wondered, *Is this a test? Does dinner depend on how well cocktails go?*

I was early, as usual. I'm always early. It came from years of carpooling the kids around, but I didn't like being early for a date. I feared it screamed desperation. Laura, my only divorced friend, said that she always arrived a little late for a date. "The man should always be there first, waiting for you." That sounded like something Mother would have suggested, so I stood off in a corner and hid out of sight. I then watched as Eric rushed in, looked around, ordered a beer, and waited at the bar. That was my cue. I took a deep breath and jumped into the dating world.

"Hi."

"Hello," he replied, somewhat surprised to see me. "How brave of you to meet a man you don't know."

His words sent me into a silent panic. *He's right. I don't know him. He could be anyone.* Before I could finalize my exit strategy (a proper city girl always has an exit strategy), I saw his face, that warm smile, and I knew he was a nice man: a nice Jewish man. A real one, not like the one I was divorcing.

We had an instant rapport, but that first comment sparked the memory of the HPV conversation I'd recently had with my twenty-four-year-old commercial agent.

"Did you hear about this form of genital herpes that's going around? It's transmitted by the slightest contact, and if you've been with more than three people, you have a one hundred percent chance of getting it. I'm considering celibacy."

I had no idea why I thought discussing herpes with Eric was proper cocktail conversation.

"Well, you have to be careful," he told me. "You have to know who you're sleeping with."

"Of course," I responded, "but do you know who *they've* been sleeping with?"

Luckily the hostess interrupted to tell us our table was ready. I guess he found he could talk to me about anything, and our dinner conversation flowed nonstop. He had majored in film and television in college; I'd majored in theatre. He went off to New York and worked as a production assistant; I became a commercial actress and relied on production assistants. He loved the city; I was born in the city and longed to move back. He enjoyed camping and hiking. *Me too!*

"What keeps a couple married for twenty years?" he asked.

"Sex," I answered. I had no idea why I was so forthcoming.

"So what broke it up?"

I didn't know what to say. Steve's cheating was just the straw that broke the camel's back, the excuse I could point to without letting people know the truth. I wasn't prepared to answer those kinds of questions. I had always been honest, but I never revealed the underlying problems in my marriage, not even to Roxy.

"He was abusive," I said, trying to be general.

"Did he hit you?"

I didn't answer, and I couldn't look him in the eyes. He changed the subject. "So how did you get into acting?"

"I was seventeen. My brother-in-law was in a play about the New York garment district. They needed models, so he asked me to be in it. I was in two scenes. In the first, I stood silently on stage in a handmade costume as two actors talked about the details of the dress. The second scene was a fashion show, and I could wear anything I wanted. So, I wore this outfit I bought for Junior Prom that Mother wouldn't let me wear because it was too sexy. It was a long, off-white matte jersey skirt with a matching wraparound midriff top—circa *The Sonny and Cher Show*. There were over four hundred people in the audience, and when I walked onstage opening night in that dress and heard the collective *oohs* and *aahs* from the audience, I was hooked."

"Bitten, they call it."

"Yep. I knew there was no place on earth I'd rather be than on stage."

I loved the way his eyes fixated on me as I spoke. Unlike anyone else in my life, he was interested in what I had to say, and I remembered: I do like men. Some of them were nice. Some of them were trustworthy. Some of them appreciated women. I felt like I was out with one of the good ones, but I couldn't help wondering aloud, "How are you thirty-five and still single?"

"It's a fair question. I guess I haven't met the right woman yet."

"Do you want kids?" I asked cautiously.

He shrugged, "If it happens, great; if not, that's fine too."
Good answer!

"What about you? Would you get married again?" he asked.

"Can't—still married."

He laughed, thinking it was a joke. When he realized it wasn't, he just said, "Oh."

"It's just a matter of time."

"But would you marry again?"

"No. I never want to get married again." I took a bite as I thought about it. "Something weird happens when you get married. It's like this preprogramming from past generations gets downloaded into your brains when you couple up. The man thinks his word is law and that his wife should do all the housework, and the woman feels guilty if she has other interests outside the home. It makes for a lot of fighting and a lot of compromises. And compromise is bullshit. It just means that thing you've always wanted to do—you can't. Do that all over again? Hell no. No way."

I looked up from my plate of shells and roasted vegetables to see his shocked face. I'd said too much. I'd forgotten to filter. How many times had I been warned by Steve to *keep the fuck quiet*?

Eric leaned back from the table. I hadn't realized we were both leaning in, which must have meant we were into each other until he leaned back. Then a smile of appreciation came over his face. "Interesting theory, don't think I've heard that before."

"I made it up."

The waiter took our half-eaten dinners and asked if we wanted them wrapped in one or two take-home bags. I stared at the waiter wondering what he meant. I had been married for twenty years and was always given one take-home bag because we went home together. I assumed that was the question I was being asked: *Are you going home with him?* I panicked and screamed at the waiter, "TWO!"

Although my scream caused the entire restaurant to pause for a brief second, I wasn't embarrassed. I leaned back in my chair, looked at Eric across the table and asked, "How's that for taking the mystery out of the way this evening's gonna wind up for you?"

"You're funny." His broad grin told me that kind of flirtation was appreciated.

It was all so new to me. I hadn't been single in my twenties and thirties and didn't get a chance to discover who I was or what I was like on my own. That night I learned I was witty and funny. *Who knew?* I was pretty pleased with those discoveries.

When the bill came, I made no effort to chip in because Mother's rules were still embedded: "The man always pays."

After dinner, we walked around the mall for a while before he escorted me to my car, and I drove him to his, where he gave me that kiss goodnight.

Floozy

I grew up during the Sexual Revolution. Mother was appalled at the very idea that women had pre-marital sex.

"Good girls don't do such things, only floozies!" she told me, warning me time and time again about the cows and how I shouldn't give away the milk for free. Born in 1918, Mother was forty-one years older than I, a two-generation difference. When she went off on a rant, I would nod respectfully, pretending it mattered.

Despite the sexual liberation of the time, Mother and her mid-century morals took root in my brain. When she told me women didn't have *relations* before marriage, part of me believed her, even though I knew what "she *had* to get married" and "bastard" meant. My head was contradiction central, but I was still a product of my generation.

As a freshman in high school, I hung out with juniors and seniors and our high school experience was exactly as portrayed in *That '70s Show.* Everyone that was coupled up was getting it on, yet no one had sex in the '70s: they "got it together" or "made it," and it was "far out."

So, a few months after I started dating my freshman crush, I decided it was time.

"Mitch's mom will be out of town Christmas Eve. Wanna make it? Spend the night at Mitch's?"

"Maybe."

Why didn't I get a more enthusiastic response? At that time in my life, I didn't know some Jewish families spent that holiday together. So I thought I was being rejected.

"Fine. I can always ask Julius." Julius was a popular hippy dude I'd had a crush on since I was twelve.

"I'll be there," my boyfriend finally confirmed.

In retrospect, the way I handled that invitation was wrong, but I realize the reader is probably more appalled at the idea of a fourteen-year-old girl having sex. Trust me, in the '70s, it was normal. Back then we matured faster, had sex earlier, left home at eighteen, and never, EVER considered boomeranging back.

At fourteen, I was cute. Not pretty, not beautiful. Cute. But I didn't like "cute." Babies were cute, puppies were cute—but still, I was grateful. I knew I was lucky to be considered attractive no matter how it was named and because I had what men thought was an eye-catching figure. I was thin, with long legs and all the right curves. It gave me confidence that my decision to have sex with my boyfriend would be mutual.

However, when he and I tried to have the sex on Christmas Eve 1973, it didn't work. He kept trying to stick his penis inside me, but it was as if my vagina was closed. Access denied.

A year later I fell madly, crazily in love with the new boy in school, and after a few months, we tried to have sex in his parents' Lake Point Tower condo. But he couldn't enter either. In both instances, their penises—or is the plural *peni?* Anyway, the damn things just didn't fit in. No matter how they tried—and believe me, a teenage boy with a willing girl underneath him will try all night. Unfortunately, the only thing they scored off me was a chafing.

As an adult, I understood why it didn't work. First, neither of them nor I knew a thing about foreplay. Second, I was so nervous that I braced myself, which tightened up the muscles. In the end, they each dumped me, writing me off as "uptight."

In college, at Drake University, I had another similar experience. I tried with a guy who was my best friend before we started dating, so I trusted him, but still, I encountered the very same issues I'd had in high school.

Then, one day, right in the middle of Econ 101, I turned around and saw the most gorgeous man I'd ever seen in my entire nineteen years. He had dark, thick, wavy hair worn brushed back off his face; an olive complexion; a perfect nose; small, flawlessly shaped lips; and ears that were close to his head and seamlessly proportioned. I stared at that face for as long as I could before I turned back around, releasing the breath I didn't realize he'd stolen.

I found out his name (Steve); where he lived (the dorm next to mine); where he ate (in my dining hall); where he was from (a suburb of Chicago); and who his friends were (JP and Vic). My primary goal was to get him to notice me. Every night before dinner I would put on blue eyeshadow, dab my lips with Clinique lip gloss, and feather my hair into the perfect *Charlie's Angels* 'do. Then I would sit with my friends while they ate in the dining hall. I could not eat if he was there. I needed to be flawless, and flawless women were not seen eating. But I would get everyone their drinks, because the soda machine was on his side of the cafeteria, a few tables away from where he routinely sat with JP and Vic.

I would sashay over to his side and fill cups with ice and Tab, while pretending to ignore him. But I could feel his eyes burning a hole in my Jordache jeans as I walked away.

Soon he started coming up to the soda machine when I was there, but all he would say was, "Hey." Just like Vinnie Barbarino (John Travolta) from *Welcome Back Kotter*, only better looking. Seriously.

"Hi," was all I could mutter.

When I saw him around campus, he began to add, "We should go out sometime."

"Sure," I responded, as if I could care less.

Mother would have been proud. "Never let a boy know you like him, Judala, or he'll lose interest."

I would see him walking around campus, at parties, in class, at dinner, and all year long he would suggest the same thing: "We should go out sometime." And I would say *sure*, but he never set a time or a place.

A week before the end of the spring term, when he repeated it, I asked, "When?"

Caught off guard, he replied, "Um, Friday?"

"Friday? Sure. I'll be putting my stuff in storage 'cause I'm moving off campus for summer theatre. But I can meet you after."

"Okay. I'll pick you up at six."

I gave him my phone number feeling very empowered.

He called me Friday at five forty-five. "Hey, how are you doing with the move?"

I was impressed that he remembered and grateful he called because all my friends had left, so I needed help lugging boxes to the basement. "I have four big boxes left, and then I'm ready." I waited for him to offer assistance.

"I'll give you some time to finish, and I'll be outside at six fifteen."

Disillusioned, I dragged the boxes down four flights of steps to the storage closet and met him outside thirty minutes later. We shared a pitcher of beers at a local bar, ordered burgers, and he paid. I was over the moon. My patience had paid off. It took almost a year, but I was finally on a date with the best-looking guy on campus.

At the end of our date, he didn't try to kiss me goodnight. I liked that. It showed respect. "I'd like to take you out in Chicago, when will you be back?" He asked.

"August. The last two weeks before school starts up again."

"Okay, it's a date, but we'll talk before then."

We didn't. Steve left for Chicago, and I stayed in Iowa. He never called and I, of course, didn't call him. "Never call a boy, Judala." But I certainly didn't wait by the phone either.

There was a guitar player interested in me. We were both working on a musical at Drake University's dinner theatre; I was an actor, and he was in the orchestra. He had just graduated and planned to head off to San Francisco at the end of our run. A summer romance seemed perfect. And it was. It was fun being a hippy with him, smoking pot in the afternoon, hanging out in the park, and listening to him sing and play his guitar with Clapton-like mastery.

Eventually, the day came to "get it on." Even though he knew about foreplay, no amount of that, pot, or transcendental meditation would have made it work with him either. The man was blessed—OVERLY blessed—in the genital area, and I was too young and inexperienced to appreciate all he had to offer. We parted ways at the end of the run, and I went home to Chicago for a short break.

Steve did call and asked me out as promised. I don't remember what we did on our date, but I do remember he was eager to see me again.

"What are you doing tomorrow night? You free?"

"Sure," I answered with a little more enthusiasm than I had previously allowed.

Tomorrow came. I got ready for our third date and then joined Mother, who always sat at the kitchen table playing solitaire after she'd cleaned the dinner dishes. Thirty minutes into our silence, and without taking her eyes from the cards, Mother acknowledged, "You've been stood up."

"No. He's just late."

Fifteen minutes later I admitted Mother was right. I was furious. I looked like a fool; spending two hours on makeup and hair, combing through my closet for the perfect jeans and top combo, then sitting and waiting for forty-five minutes without so much as a phone call.

Back at school a few months later, Steve came to see a play I was in called *Come Back, Little Sheba*. He'd been trying to apologize and make it up to me since school resumed. In the play, I portrayed a young woman who was engaged to one man but was cheating on him with another. There were lots of kissing/make-out scenes for me in the play, and when he saw me being a "fast" girl on stage, his intensity changed. He wanted me.

"What's going to be different this time?" I asked him after

the show, trying to hold my ground by not looking at that strik-
ing face.

"The difference is, I think I could really fall for you."

Taken by surprise, I looked into his eyes. Game over. Done.

A few weeks later, we were in his off-campus apartment
bed making out, and things got heated.

"Come on baby, let's do it."

"I can't."

"Yes, you can." He replied as he tried to stick his hand
down my pants.

I stopped him. "No. I literally can't.

"Huh?"

"I can't," I whispered so his roommate Vic wouldn't hear,
"*get it on*. For some reason, it doesn't work."

"I thought you'd done this before."

"Tried. I tried. Three times. See, um, a guy's- you know, it
doesn't fit." He looked perplexed, so I explained, "I'm really small
down there."

"That's fucking crazy."

At the time I thought he was a cocky, confident twenty-
year-old. It was irresistible.

We took off our clothes while Farrah Fawcett and Linda
Ronstadt watched from their respective posters on the wall
above. I then cautiously and anxiously braced myself, waiting
for him to try to stick his penis inside me. But he didn't. He gave
me what's called a shit-eating grin and lowered himself down
my body.

I didn't know what he was going to do or why. I still
knew very little about sex, even less about foreplay, and absolutely nothing about oral sex. But he did. He knew a lot. At the
time I thought he invented it. He had no trouble bringing me to
orgasm, and when his penis entered immediately afterward, it
fit perfectly. I felt like Cinderella: *someday my prince will come.*

We had a lot of sex after that, him being in his sexual
prime and me an eager-to-learn coed. He taught me everything
I needed to know about how to please a man. It was the only

subject at college in which I excelled. Maybe he was able to break through my barriers because he was Jewish. Maybe having sex with a Jewish man/boy was the perfect way to unite the beliefs Mother had instilled with the sexual landscape of the '70s. If that were the case, then what happened next made perfect sense. His Jewish programming caused him to declare, "I'm going to marry you." That fall, he did.

"Gottenyu!" Mother kvelled. Her job was over. She had raised me right; she could do her touchdown dance. She married off another daughter to a nice Jewish boy.

In the early days of dating, we didn't talk much. He wasn't much of a communicator, but I remember asking Steve if he'd ever hit a woman.

"Once," he said.

Why?"

"My girlfriend was giving me the silent treatment."

I didn't think that was a good reason, but I was raised in a volatile house, and in the 1970s, a hit, a slap, wasn't unusual, so I didn't find it disturbing. *He loves me.* I thought to myself. *He would never do that to me.*

I was wrong.

Transition Guy

I began my separation feeling celibacy was the safest option. I only went to that singles' party at Navy Pier as an act of revenge. I never expected to like someone, nor did I expect to kiss said someone on the first date, and I definitely didn't expect to be turned on! Overnight my hormones morphed into Glenn Close's character in Fatal Attraction: they were "not going to be ignored." I craved the very thing I was terrified would kill me: sex.

Still, the morning after my first date with Eric I woke up happy and filled with the wonder of possibilities. I had nothing to compare it to, but I was sure it was the perfect first date.

Steph called, and I uttered those three magic words: "I met someone." I then told her about the date and that kiss.

"That's great, Judes. You like him?"

"Yeah, I just called him."

"You what?! Oh my God, Judes, no! That sends all kinds of red flags."

"A thank-you?"

"A call, so soon."

"When you and John invite me to dinner, don't I always call the next day to say thank you?"

"It's not the same."

"It's manners."

"What did he say?"

"He wasn't home. I waited until I knew he'd be out of his

apartment. I'm not a total idiot."

All that day I felt like the phone was about to ring, but it never did. I knew he must have been thinking about calling me. That night, after he came home and heard my message, he did call. "Thank you for the thank-you call. A lot of women don't do that. I like it. It's kind of a test with me."

Apparently, I'd passed the first round of inspection. I felt comfortable enough to ask, "Did you almost call me earlier today, like several times?"

"Actually, yeah, why?"

"Because I kept getting the feeling the phone was going to ring, but it never did. I'd walk to the phone, stand there, and nothing. I almost called your cell to tell you to stop that."

He laughed, "You should have. I'd have laughed my ass off."

He asked if we could have dinner in the city next week—not this Saturday, which was two days away, but another weekday, specifically Wednesday. I said Tuesday would be better because I had a late appointment in the city.

The following night, Friday, having just shared a pitcher of margaritas at our favorite Mexican restaurant—the one where we dislike the food but love the tequila—Roxy analyzed where I stood with Eric as if she were the color commentator for the Chicago Cubs. "A first date connection, a good kiss, you'll be having sex on the second date."

Her response sent me into a whirlwind. It was 1999, not 1979. *Sex on the second date? Who does that? Does she do that?* There was no more "free love." The price of casual sex was very high. Weren't there guidelines? Tests to schedule?

I hadn't realized we'd left the restaurant until we were standing in front of a condom display. Roxy leaned in and whispered, "If you buy them, he will come."

I laughed, already knowing her joke. "What is this? *Field of Wet Dreams*?"

But she was also serious. "You can't rely on men to have protection. You need to be holding."

"I'm not having sex on the second date."

"No one plans to, but..."

"Oh, Lord."

"You need to practice safe sex."

"I know all about safe sex; thank you."

"As a married monogamous mom, not real-life shit."

That was Roxy's bull-in-a-china-shop way of being helpful and supportive, but since she remained single the entire time I was married, she was the closest thing I had to a dating expert.

Still, standing in a Walgreens condom aisle on a Saturday night in the Chicago neighborhood known as the Viagra Triangle felt equivalent to the time I was in a drugstore as an adolescent and got caught holding a box of Kotex by the neighborhood bully, David Newsome.

"Can we just go?"

"After you pick out condoms." She held firm.

"I'll buy condoms if I get serious with this guy. I promise." I had no intention of having sex any time soon.

"We're here now."

I knew she wouldn't give up until I bought the damn things. One by one I picked up individual boxes and looked for information on the back. I had studied an assortment when Roxy demanded to know, "What the fuck are you doing?"

"I'm looking for the charts."

"What?"

"You know, those charts? 'If you're this tall and weigh this much...?' The charts!"

"It's not like buying pantyhose. They're one size! You think a man's going to put anything on his penis that comes out of a box marked small?"

"You choose," I said and gave her money. "I'll be outside." I walked away from her. That was my MO. I never stood up to people when they freely advised me on how I should live my life. Sure, I usually did what I wanted; but at the same time, I avoided confrontation at all costs.

Once outside, I felt the full weight of Mother's disapproval. She must have been rolling over in her grave. "Nice girls don't buy such things, Judala." I knew how Mother felt about premarital sex; postmarital sex would be no different. "Oy vey! What you need is a new husband."

Never. Never again would I fall into the marriage trap. Though I did secretly want an exclusive non-relationship relationship with a nice, disease-free man for the foreseeable future. What guy would say no to that?

Needless to say, the day of my second date with Eric I was sick to my stomach. I was scared he was going to try something. Yes, I had been turned on by the kiss on our first date, but the idea of having sex with a new man scared me even more than STDs.

At dinner, Eric ordered a big meal: steak, potatoes, and a beer. I had a small dinner salad I pretended to eat. I couldn't eat it. I hadn't been able to keep anything down all day.

"If you're not busy next Saturday, would you like to go hiking?" he asked.

I was glad he finally wanted to see me on a Saturday, even if it was in the afternoon.

"Sounds great. You have a place in mind?"

"Yes, north of you. I was thinking of Door County. That's near you, right? There's a cute little market in town."

"Oh." I stared at my plate. I didn't know how to respond. He was describing Kettle Moraine, which was about an hour north of me, but he had said Door County, which was five hours away. Kettle Moraine meant a day trip. Door County implied a sleepover.

What are you asking me?

Then, barely looking up from his meal, he revealed, "I only live a few blocks from here."

Oh my God, Roxy's right! I flagged down the waitress and asked her to take away my food and bring me some chamomile tea. I felt nauseated. I had that awful taste in my mouth, and I could feel my face perspiring.

The waitress sat the cup of tea in front of me and gave an ever-so-slight pause. I looked up at her. Our eyes met and held. I saw compassion in them, as if she knew what was in store for me after dinner. Eric was a stranger. I wished I knew some-one who knew him. I needed a good game of Jewish Geography (translation: all Jews seem to know a Jew who knows the Jew in question).

Eric paid the bill and took me for a walk. It was a beautiful summer night in Chicago, and we walked around his Bucktown neighborhood talking.

"Where do you see yourself in ten years?"

I thought about it. "I don't. When I was married, my an-swer would have been living on a golf course. The kids would be grown and gone. I'd write all day while my husband golfed. Now? I don't know."

"Wow, you've already lived a whole life, haven't you?"

"Dance recitals, little league, carpools..."

As we walked and talked, I started to feel better until he stopped in front of a building and put his arm on my shoulder. "Well, this is where I live."

I froze. I couldn't move or speak. Finally, I peeled Eric's arm off my shoulder, took a step back, and somehow managed to find my voice. "Look, I can't sleep with you; it's too soon. I mean, I like sex. Sex is great, I'm all about the sex, but maybe in the fu-ture, just not tonight."

Taken aback, he assured me, "I don't want to sleep with you; it's only the second date. Who has sex on the second date?"

The next day when I gave Roxy the details, she admitted, "I was only fucking with ya." You gotta love Roxy. She never let friendship get in the way of a good laugh.

On that second date, as soon as I realized he didn't want to sleep with me, I was able to concentrate on my agenda: the good-night kiss. I needed to know if I'd have the same reaction.

I didn't. It just felt different, different from Steve. Not bet-ter, not worse, just different, and I realized that nothing was ever going to be the same, and I cried—in his face.

He was very understanding as he put me in my car. "Twenty years, same guy, it's got to be weird for you."

I started liking him even more. As I drove home, I thought about how lucky I was to have found such a great guy. I'd always heard that women usually ended up with the same type of man they divorced. I knew that wasn't going to happen to me.

That Saturday, my friend Laura came over for dinner. I told her all about Eric and how I wished that I could find someone who knew him. "He wants to go hiking in Wisconsin this Saturday."

"And?"

"And that means getting in a car and willingly driving into the woods with a man I barely know."

"What's his name?" she asked.

I thought it was a silly question. Laura worked, raised her children, and that was it. Also, she wasn't Jewish. She probably didn't know a Jew who knew the Jew in question. I told her his name anyway.

"I know him."

"What? How?"

"My company is building a structure next door to his building. He's the president of his condo association. We've had a lot of meetings with their board."

"So, you're adversaries?"

"Yeah. Well, no. The condo owners are just concerned. I can't blame them. Their concerns are relevant. And I respect how Eric handles himself. He's intelligent."

I was grateful. I could go hiking in the woods knowing he wouldn't kill me and throw my body parts in the dumpster behind the cute little market in Kettle Moraine.

The day of the hike I met him in a hotel parking lot off I-294 and Deerfield Road. I left my car there, and we drove to Wisconsin in his Mitsubishi convertible. I wore cutoff Daisy Duke shorts and a T-shirt with a jacket tied around my waist. We walked and talked, and he bought us lunch from the deli counter in the Elegant Farmer grocery store. I purposely hadn't packed us lunch. That's what I had done for decades as a mom. I was done with that.

We got back to my area at dinnertime, and I asked if I could buy him dinner. He graciously accepted, telling me later that I had passed another test, offering up the payback meal. I didn't realize men had expectations, other than the obvious—putting out.

When he dropped me off at my car, we had a good old-fashioned make-out session in the front seat of his sports car.

It's funny how life goes. When I separated from my husband and moved into my townhouse several months earlier, I felt lost. I knew leaving Steve was the right thing to do, but I had no road map, no real plan other than to get out. Once I was out and realized how hard the divorce process was, I feared I'd made the wrong choice and that my kids would be screwed up for life.

But then everything changed. My kids adjusted; I started seeing a nice man; I had two national commercials running, which meant income; and I was asked to write and perform autobiographical material for a show downtown. Darryl, a fellow actor, was the organizer, and he hoped it would turn into a regular storytelling show. I was very excited and a little scared.

I had always wanted to do stand-up comedy. I had even written jokes to tell at an open mic night fifteen years earlier, but I let a family member talk me out of it. "You wrote stories, not jokes," he said.

"I don't know what you mean—you laughed."

"They were funny stories, but comedians tell jokes, one after the other. You gotta keep the laughter going."

My father raised me on the BBC, so joke-joke-joke wasn't what I grew up to consider funny. British humor was sophisticated, well-executed, and not rushed. Hence, the payoff—the laugh—was huge.

I was young and not yet secure in my talent, so I listened to that family member. I always regretted not trying to perform my own material. Darryl's storytelling event would be a do-over.

I had three weeks to write and memorize a personal essay.

"What should I write about?" I asked Stephanie, since she had read everything I'd ever written.

"The stuff you've been telling me lately about what's going on in your life is some funny shit."

Meanwhile, I had only known Eric a month, but I was falling for him. He was the kind of man my children would like because he was sports-savvy and genuine—the type of man I could envision in my life. I felt ready to take the relationship to the next level: the sex level.

One night during one of our evening phone calls, I told him that Steve was the only man with whom I'd had sex.

"Why do you feel the need to tell me that?" he asked.

"The Surgeon General says we're supposed to give each other a list of all the people we've slept with."

He laughed until he realized that I wasn't joking. "Nobody does that."

"Really?" I was shocked.

"Don't you think talking about sex spoils the spontaneity?"

Even I knew that spontaneous sex was a male myth. I always knew when I was going to have sex. There's waxing, shaving, and a lady-part freshening routine that needs to happen first.

Still, the idea of getting naked in front of a new man scared me to death. The last time I had done that, I had the body of a nineteen-year-old. Twenty years and two kids later, I didn't know if I was ready to have him discover the miracle of my miracle bra.

"Men only have one requirement for a naked woman," Roxy told me. "That she be naked."

"You're probably right, but I'll keep the lights off just the same."

"Sex with a new man, that's the fun part. But he's just your transition guy. The sex to help you get over the Ex."

I didn't agree, though I did feel more confident. "Besides," I told Roxy, "I know what men like in bed."

She laughed. "No, you don't. You know what one man likes. Men are very different sexually. They like different things." In addition to having had more partners than me, she was a therapist. "I know. I've heard it all."

Great. Having to worry about being good in bed was the next fear that reared its head. But I quickly got the insight I needed in the checkout line at the supermarket. *Cosmopolitan* magazine's cover story: "His Secret Sex Spots: find them, and you'll have to peel him off the ceiling." *Hmmm.* According to the sexperts at *Cosmo*, there were several of those sex spots, and I studied them all. Unfortunately, I have always had poor retention skills. When I put the magazine down, I couldn't remember which spot needed which stroke. Since confusing them could be a disaster, I knew I'd need a cheat sheet. But how would I be able to read it if I had to have the lights off? I had visions of myself going under the sheets: he'd be anticipating oral sex, but instead, I'd be down there with a penlight and a map.

Roxy was right when she said that all I knew about safe sex was what I had learned as a married, monogamous mom. Even though I had the condoms she and I bought, I still made an appointment at my gynecologist's office. Oh my God, were my fears put into perspective!

"You must always use a condom *and* spermicide. You don't want to get pregnant, so I'm putting you on the pill. Some women only use condoms, but if it breaks, they call me for the morning-after pill. I prefer to go this way. After a month you'll be safe from pregnancy but always use the condoms. Condoms are the only way to prevent sexually transmitted diseases. STDs are your main concern because there are so many. Now, you'll need to inspect his penis for sores, but still, even people without a herpes outbreak can give you herpes because they are carriers of the virus. And you'll have to live with it for the rest of your life."

Talk about your cold shower! Who even wanted sex after that? That Saturday night—I did.

Stephanie and her husband had extra tickets to see Alanis

Morissette on her 1999 tour. A few years earlier, my daughter and I had played her *Jagged Little Pill* CD over and over again, singing along during long car rides. Eric and I went with them to the concert, but we sat in a different section from my friends. When Alanis sang *You Oughta Know*, I stood on my seat and screamed the words of the song with all the other wronged, angry women in the crowd.

> *And I'm here, to remind you*
> *Of the mess you left when you went away*
> *It's not fair, to deny me*
> *Of the cross I bear that you gave to me*
> *You, you, you oughta know*

Eric loved how crazy and free I was. During the evening he kissed me frequently, sweet little kisses that really got me excited. At the end of the evening, we were dropped off at his apartment since I had left my car there earlier in the day.

"Do you wanna come up?" he asked.

Knowing the three-pack of condoms was in my purse gave me the confidence to say yes. Still, I was a bit apprehensive about seeing his apartment. What if he was sloppy? What if it smelled? That could be a deal-breaker.

When we got upstairs, he gave me a quick tour. The apartment was a beautiful loft with a fireplace in the bedroom and e.e. cummings on the coffee table. It was clean, organized, and had an extra bedroom where he kept most of his books.

"You sure do have a lot of travel books."

"Yes, I love to travel. I think I've been to every part of Europe by now."

"Wow, I've always wanted to go. Whenever we had a little money to spare, Steve would say, 'Why waste money on a memory when we can have a couch?'"

"So you never even got to travel after college?"

"There was no 'after college.' I quit. By the time I was twenty-two I had a toddler. I don't even have a passport."

"Well, we'll have to get you one."

He *we'd* me. He said *we!* I could see a future with him, and apparently, he saw one with me too.

"Listen, I need to tell you something."

"Okay," he replied as he put his hands on my hips and looked at me with those kind eyes.

"I'm performing in a storytelling show in a few weeks—"

He cut me off. "Can I come?"

"Sure, of course, but I want to ask you. I'm thinking of writing about our first date. Would you be okay with that?"

"You're not going to say anything bad, are you?"

"Oh God, no. All good. It's mostly the crazy thoughts that go on inside my head."

"Alright, sure."

"Great."

"I appreciate the consideration. I can't wait to see you."

He gave me another little kiss that got my juices flowing and then walked into the kitchen to get us beers. I stood there, alone, my body on fire, my veins surging with electricity, and at that moment I had an epiphany: I was horny. I had never experienced being horny before. For twenty years, sex was readily available. I never had to wait for it. All I had to do was tap Steve on the shoulder, and he was ready to go. But it had been nine months since I'd had sex, and I hadn't gone nine months without sex since I was nineteen.

Eric and I spent the next two hours on the couch, but he sat on one end with me on the other. All he seemed interested in was conversation, while I was so randy, I was willing to reveal all of Victoria's Secrets.

Given that he didn't seem to have a clue, I tried to suggest one. "I have so much freedom these days; one kid in college, the other at her Dad's—all weekend."

No response; so much for subtlety. I remembered Alicia Silverstone's advice in the movie *Clueless*: "Anything you can do to draw attention to your mouth is good." Maybe it would work for my body. I took a deep breath, causing my chest to rise as I faked a tired stretch, indicating it was time for bed—still, no response. Okay, I needed something more hardcore, like Madonna in *Truth or Dare*. I wrapped my hand around the long neck of my beer bottle, and strategically brought it up to my lips and took a long, deep swallow—nothing.

Are you stupid, or not interested?

I gave up. It was time to leave. "Well, it's getting late."

That worked. Eric came over to my side of the couch and kissed me with a passion he hadn't shown before. His body pressed against mine as he gently lay me down on the couch and got on top of me. I had forgotten how good it felt to have a man's weight on top of me. We continued to kiss, and I used telepathy to tell him to put his hands on me. But I must have dialed wrong because instead, he jumped up and off me. "Okay, I'll take you to your car now."

What the hell happened?! I had to sit up and collect myself like an eighteen-year-old boy caught with a hard-on. He didn't even have the decency to pretend that it was hard to stop!

That's exactly what I felt like: an eighteen-year-old boy. I had freedom for the first time in my life, and I thought about sex all the time. It was the first thing I thought about in the morning when I woke up and the last thing I thought about before I went to sleep. Occasionally, it would wake me and then I'd be up all night thinking about sex. Was it hormones? Withdrawal? *I didn't know!*

My friend Victoria kept telling me I needed to stop going out with a "loaded gun." She meant, don't date horny. Take care of yourself first. But I stopped "taking care of myself" on purpose. Steve knew me intimately for twenty years. He knew what I liked and how I liked it. How could a new man compete with that? I wanted to give the new man advantage by being ready, albeit, in this case, more than ready.

I thought Roxy's take on it made sense: "Men today, at least the good ones, are waiting for a clear signal. They don't assume and attack as they did in the '70s. Women have to be more aggressive."

41

Worrying about how to undo Mother's programming and become more aggressive made me even angrier with Steve. It was his fault that I was dating during my sexual prime instead of home in bed getting laid. I was there for his sexual prime. He was supposed to be there for mine!

I could hear Mother's judgment from the great beyond: "Sooo? Who told you to get divorced?"

Eric called during the week and asked me to meet him at Northbrook Court for a movie and dinner that Friday night. It was only a twenty-minute drive for me, so that revealed his commitment to making what he dubbed our "long-distance relationship" work. As I lay across my bed enjoying the sound of his deep voice in my ear, he said he was going to Scottsdale next month. He was going to be using the family home. "I'd love to ask you to come with me," he said.

I didn't know how to respond. Had Eric asked me or merely revealed a thought? And if I did go, that certainly meant we'd have sex, and I didn't want to be so far from home the first time I had sex with a new man. What if it was awful? How could I run away? (A proper city girl always has an escape plan.)

"My ex-father-in-law has a home in Scottsdale. I love it there." I thought that was a safe answer, and he didn't expand on the subject.

Friday came, and I met him in the mall in front of the theatre. He gave me a quick kiss hello. "I always forget how cute you are," he said. I blushed.

We saw *The Sixth Sense*. We both loved it and had no idea that Bruce Willis' character was a ghost.

"Let's only see great movies," I said. Eric laughed.

We went to a restaurant in the mall where he was very affectionate, holding my hand across the table. At one point he stood, leaned over the table, and kissed me. I had never experienced that form of affection. It felt like tonight was *the* night, except for the fact that we were closer to my place than his and my daughter was with me that weekend. After dinner, we got in his car, and he drove me to the side of the mall where my car was parked. We made out in his car like were high school kids, something I hadn't done since, well, high school.

Finally, I pulled away and asked the question that had taken up residence in my brain: "Can I ask you what you meant about going to Arizona with you?"

"Just what I said, that I'd love to ask you."

I waited, but there was no clarification. "Are you asking me to go?"

He took a breath before he answered—never a good sign. "I'd love to, but I can't."

Can't? Can't why? Can't, because your parents will be there? Can't because you don't want to pay for me? I have miles I can use. I can—

"I can't ask you to go away with me because I don't think we should see each other anymore. But I'd like us to stay friends."

Excuse me?

I didn't realize I was staring at him until he said, "Say something."

"I don't know what to say."

"What are you thinking?"

"I'm thinking about all the affection you lavish on me. It doesn't feel like a man who wants to break up."

"I'm very attracted to you. I'm conflicted."

"Oh." I didn't know how to take that.

"Aren't you going to try to change my mind?" he asked with a smirk, so I kissed him as hard and as passionately as I could. I needed that kiss to be full of promise, that if he changed his mind, he wouldn't be sorry.

I stopped abruptly. "I don't want to try to change your mind. That's the sort of thing I did as a teenager. I know by now it doesn't work in the long run. I gotta go," I said, and I got out of the car quickly because tears were forming in my eyes.

I cried all the way home. I had no idea that people broke up when things were going so well. I was hurt and confused, and I had my show that Monday. Fuck him for fucking with my head a few days before a performance!

The piece was written and memorized, so I gave myself all day Saturday to feel bad. I sat on the couch, watched television, and consumed mass quantities of junk food. I had seen movies where women did that to get over a guy, so I tried it. Hell, it worked!

On Sunday I was done feeling bad. I practiced my piece and felt ready for Monday.

Of course, he called my home line early Sunday night. "I'd still like to see your show tomorrow. I was serious about being friends. Are you okay with that?"

I appreciated his asking rather than just showing up. I thought about it; I did like him, and I needed friends. I'd lost custody of all our couple friends in the divorce.

"Sure, I'd love for you to come."

"Great, I'll have my cousin drop me off after dinner." It was the second night of Rosh Hashanah, so he'd be at his parents' home.

"I'll save you a place at my sister's table."

"Great, see you there, and break a leg." I loved that he knew not to wish me luck.

The night of the show, the place was packed. I reserved a four-top for my sister, her husband, Eric, and me. Darryl told me I'd be going on fifth. I was happy not to be one of the first two. Eric joined us a little after eight and was relieved he hadn't missed me. He ordered a beer and fit right in with my sister and brother-in-law. As I waited for my turn, it became evident that Darryl was not sticking to the lineup. I knew he must have changed things up for a reason, but the not knowing added to my performance anxiety. After a while, I got up and went to the bathroom. Always good to empty your bladder before going on stage.

When I came out, Eric was waiting for me in the hallway between the bar and the restrooms.

"You okay?"

"Yes, why?"

"I don't know. I thought maybe you were throwing up."

I laughed. "No. I'm good. But thank you."

So this is what a supportive partner does. I like it.

When we got back to the room a comedian was performing, so we took a seat at the bar near the stage. When the set ended, Darryl went up to MC. He caught my eye and raised an eyebrow. I nodded.

I leaned into Eric and whispered, "I'm next."

"Really? Okay, I'm going to run back to the table."

I was touched that he wanted the best view of the stage—of me.

I was delighted to follow a comedian because the audience was warmed up and primed to laugh. Onstage I was nervous and afraid to look at the faces in the crowd. Looking at the audience was something I had never done as an actress. It's called breaking the fourth wall. As a comedian and storyteller, however, that's what you do. You talk to the crowd. I feared it might throw me to see their faces, so I looked at the top of their heads as I told the story of my first date with Eric.

My performance could not have gone better. The audience laughed a lot. Several times I even had to wait for their laughter to subside before I could continue. They laughed in the places I thought they would. They even laughed unexpectedly hard when I stated the fact that my husband dated while we were in marriage counseling. I guess that was funny. Who knew?

When I got back to the table, Eric was grinning and said, "I knew you'd be good." I appreciated that he didn't gush. It was the perfect compliment.

At the end of the evening, I drove him home. We'd had such a lovely time together that I hoped he'd ask me up. As we neared his building, I hinted, "Wow, your street sure has a lot of open parking spaces." But he didn't catch on. *We're broken up; why would he ask me up?*

I pulled up to his building and put the car in park, and he kissed me goodbye. It was not a friendly kiss. It was the way he'd been kissing me all along.

I stopped him. "Is this how you say goodbye to a friend?"

"Yeah, how about we forget about breaking up." He kissed me again, and I could feel a new intensity from him. "You wanna come up?"

I panicked and said, "I can't. I gotta get home."

Roxy once told me that "cooking a man dinner" was code for sex. "Your birthday is next week. How 'bout you come to my place the following weekend and I'll make dinner? My daughter will be with her dad, so Friday or Saturday, either works for me."

"I'll let you know," he said and got out of the car.

I drove off agonizing over the evening. Was it too soon? Steve and I might have been living separate lives, but the lawyers had not finalized the papers. We were still married, and I didn't want to still be married when Eric and I had sex—if for no other reason than to be able to hold it over Steve that I was faithful the entire time we were married. But my hormones were impatient, and my daughter would be away for that whole weekend, and, bottom line, I really wanted *it*.

I hoped I was subtle. I wanted Eric to feel spontaneous. But during the long drive home I wondered why he hadn't made a move yet. I thought men were always up for sex. I remembered back to our first date. When he had asked me how I fell into acting in TV commercials, I gave a witty response: "Because I'm really good—for thirty seconds."

He laughed and said, "Yeah, me too."

Maybe he had nice Jewish boy programming too. I was being silly and overthinking it all; Eric was a good man. He was waiting, patiently. He was a true gentleman. I just wasn't used to that.

Weeks ago, I made it clear to him that I would want a sexual partner to get tested. He said he knew he was healthy but would get tested to ease my mind. There was no longer any doubt. We would have sex after his birthday dinner in my condo, providing he passed the STD tests.

I didn't hear from Eric for almost a week. He didn't call Sunday. Monday came and went. Victoria said Tuesday was respectable, and that's the day I bought sexy smelling cologne for his present. I also started planning the meal. We would eat by the fireplace and have my fabulous chocolate mousse for dessert. But he didn't call Tuesday. Wednesday, Steph said, was pushing it, so I exchanged the cologne for a book and decided we'd go out to dinner. On Thursday I returned the book and bought a card. That night while I was soaking in a hot bath, he called.

"Hi." I tried to sound casual and not at all like a woman who'd been waiting by the phone all week.

"Hi. Look, I'm sorry I haven't gotten back to you sooner, but—"

"Hey, don't worry about—"

"We must have a bad connection because you sound like you're in a tunnel."

"Sorry, I'm in the tub." There was a pause. "Hello?"

"I'm here. You're in the bathtub?"

I smiled at the thought of him picturing me naked. "Yes. You caught me in the tub."

"Shit, this is hard."

"Excuse me?" I asked playfully. "What's hard?"

"Look, I've thought a lot about dinner at your place and I just can't."

Oh man, here it comes again.

"I really like you. I'm attracted to you, but it would be a mistake to have sex with you."

"Oh." It was the only verbal response I could muster.

"I date two kinds of women," he continued. "Nice Jewish girls I can see myself marrying and other girls for fun. You told me you don't want to get married again and that you don't want more children."

Marriage and kids? Did I miss a meeting? On our first date, he said he was good either way, having kids or not having kids. But I had been the decisive one. I told him in no uncertain terms that I did not want to get married and I did not want any more children. He took me at my word. Yes, I knew what I wanted, but I was always prepared to be talked out of it. Steve always got what he wanted: suburbs over the city, furniture over travel. Eric was a great guy, the whole package. If we had continued to date, I'm sure I would have married him and had a baby for him. I didn't have my independent sea legs yet.

I finally found my voice and told him I could be the other type of girl he dated. "I like fun."

"Judi." His tone said that I wasn't that kind of girl.

"Roxy says I need a transition guy."

"You're the type of woman I could fall in love with, and I'll just end up hurt."

"Can't we just see where this goes?"

"You're forty years old. I want to date my wife for a while before marriage, then travel before we have children. By then you're what, forty-four? Forty-five?"

Shut up, just shut up; you had me at goodbye. You had me at goodbye.

"Ironically, I did get tested for you." He added, "Funny, huh?"

"Hysterical."

When Eric and I got off the phone, I immediately called Roxy.

"So what night are you having sex?"

"We're not. Eric won't have casual sex if it's not leading to marriage and children." Roxy was silent. I continued, "I can't comprehend his turning down a no-strings-attached invitation to have sex."

But Roxy understood. "Thirty-five-year-old men are the new women."

"Figures. I'm finally attracted to a guy with character and integrity, and it comes back to bite me in the ass."

"Just not literally."

I didn't laugh. I thought back to the last guy that broke my heart. I was sixteen. What did I do? Ah yes, I did regular drive-bys down the street where he lived, went to places I knew he'd be, and called his house regularly only to hang up when he answered. I didn't realize until years later from watching *Oprah* that my behavior had a name: stalking.

I decided to go with what I knew, but with caller ID you couldn't make anonymous calls anymore, and I didn't have a clue where he liked to hang out. So I settled for a good old-fashioned drive-by. One afternoon, after an audition and before heading home, I decided to drive down his street. What harm could that do?

Plenty. He busted me on the first pass.

See, I didn't drive a beige Honda Civic or a black Toyota Camry, something that blended into the rest of the cars on the street. I drove a bright yellow Volkswagen Beetle with my name, JUDI, on the license plate.

He was getting out of his car and spotted me immediately. He was alone, thank God, and as he walked over to talk to me through the passenger side window, I started to panic. *Think. Think. Think.*

I came up with a lame excuse. "I just wanted to return your book and get mine from you."

I caught a lucky break when he said that the book he gave me was a gift, because I didn't have it with me in the car. We ended up talking like that for thirty minutes. Finally, he reiterated that he'd still like to be friends, and did I have time to see a movie?

I did. I went. I thought for sure Eric would realize that he wanted me back.

It was weird, sitting so close to him in the movie theater like we had done weeks before, except he wasn't holding my hand or kissing my neck. After the movie, he dropped me at my car, and I said goodbye and got out without a kiss. Usually, our goodbyes lasted longer than our dates.

It was nice seeing him, but I still wanted more. He had broken it off when we were at the stage of becoming intimate and wanting to touch each other all the time. I couldn't switch gears that fast. His change in behavior toward me was confusing, overly affectionate one minute and then, only a week later, nothing, nada, zilch.

Admittedly, I had a lot to learn about dating, about men,

and myself yet, I was delighted to learn that, although I had been in a bad marriage, I wasn't jaded. I decided to remain friends with Eric. His honesty and integrity would become the benchmark for which I would evaluate future men. He would provide the inside scoop on the male dating perspective, and I could trust him to tell me if I looked fat in jeans.

In the meantime, dating him had ignited desires, desires that demanded gratification. What was I supposed to do with all that pent-up sexual frustration?

Mambo Man

My divorce was final on December 29, 1999. Instead of changing my name, I changed his. The man formerly known as Steve would henceforth be referred to as The Ex-Hole.

The marriage had lasted twenty years, one month, and four days. I could finally give myself freely to a new man, but there was no new man. Eric, my would-be transition guy, broke up with me several months earlier, and that breakup left me frustrated, sexually *and* mentally. I'd put weeks into getting to know him, getting to trust him, and ended up with nothing. All that time I was gearing up for sex, and now what? I had to start over? Starting over meant more time: time to get over Eric, time to find a new man, and time to get to know the new man.

Roxy chimed in, "Yeah, it's called dating."

"Well, dating sucks!"

I didn't know what to do with my pent-up sexual frustration until I went to a nightclub. The ladies at my talent agency took me to a club's opening night, where one of their other clients was the General Manager. He was slightly older than I and was either Latin or Italian. He was good-looking in a mafia-movie way: olive complexion, dark, slicked-back hair, and a face that looked like it had taken its fair share of punches. He wore black pants with a fitted black T-shirt, a black belt, and black shoes.

My agents might have been trying to set us up, but I was

more interested in dancing. It's common practice for newly divorced women to go dancing. That night, as the Latin Pop invasion took charge of my hips, I understood why. Dancing was a safe and fun release of my sexual energy, made obvious because my dance moves morphed from the white chick shuffle to pole dance stripper.

The following week I dragged Roxy to the club and made her dance with me. "Judes, you exhaust me. I did this in my twenties."

"Well, I didn't."

We became semi-regulars at that club on Ontario Street in Chicago. The crowd was mid-thirties and up, and the GM always let us in without paying cover. He put us at the best table and even sent over a round of drinks on the house. Roxy didn't mind coming with me if it didn't cost her anything. Besides, we weren't there to pick up men, so we danced together.

One evening, as Roxy and I danced near the edge of the floor, the GM walked by and made a playful comment in my ear: "You dance very well—with women."

I pulled him onto the floor to dance with me. I thought he'd feel silly and beg off, and I'd gain the upper hand by showing him I was a good dancer with any partner. Instead, he took my hand in his and put his other one on the small of my back, pulled my pelvis to his, and expertly led me around the dance floor as if we were starring in 1940s movie.

Never in my life had I been able to follow a man's lead, but my body was not my own. It was under his control and moved at his every command. When the song was over, he went back to work, and I was the one left bewildered on the dance floor.

Roxy and I would go to the club once a month, and the GM and I would always have at least one dance together, it was so much fun! Roxy called him Mambo Man.

One night, everything changed. I saw Mambo Man whisper to the DJ, and then he came to collect me as a slow song began to play. This time our bodies moved gently and rhythmically to the music. It felt more deliberate, intentional, and very intimate.

"I'd like to take you to dinner," he whispered in my ear.

My hips made me say yes.

We were to go out that Wednesday. Of course, I freaked out all week.

"You're making too much of it. It's just a date," Roxy said.

"Dates are made based on good conversations and mutual interests. The only thing we know about each other is that our bodies move very well together. So, he's expecting sex, right?"

"Maybe."

"Well, I can't. That's not me. I can't have casual sex." Or could I? Was that my rule or Mother's?

"Be a good girl Judala, or you'll get a reputation."

And then what, Ma, I won't get married at twenty years old? Madonna didn't have a mother's influence growing up, and she made a fortune not denying her sexuality. So what was I afraid of?

I was afraid of catching something—*that* was what I was afraid of.

"You need to have a mindless affair. Mambo Man looks like he can teach you a few things."

"Teach me what?" I demanded, feeling as if my sexuality was being questioned. "Has sex changed? I've had twenty years of on-the-job training. Thank you."

"Fifteen-minute married sex is not enviable."

She had a point. Still, I didn't think I could have a "mindless affair." I wanted to wait for the right guy.

Wednesday came, and as I dressed for the date, it just felt wrong. Who goes out on a Wednesday night? I should have been at a PTA meeting. What was happening to me? I was acting like I was in my twenties. But at least I was smarter than the real twenty-year-olds. I had recently watched reruns of an MTV show, *Sex in the 90's*, and those twenty-something women had all kinds of STDs. Why? Because they thought they were safe on the pill.

They should have tried being a housewife for twenty years, doing dishes three times a day, and cleaning toilets. Then they would have learned about the power of protection. My hands were still gorgeous. *It's called latex—keep it covered, girls!*

The original plan for the Wednesday night "date" was dinner. That was what I agreed to. Instead, he called that afternoon and asked me to meet him at a nightclub in the northwest suburbs called The Living Room. That was my first solid confirmation that "dinner" didn't mean dinner.

He was not waiting for me at the door when I arrived at the club, so I paid a cover charge in exchange for a free drink ticket. Since my dance attire was sexier than how I usually dressed for a date, I decided to make sure he knew where I stood.

"I hope you don't think I'm some club-going hoochie mama," I said when I found him sitting at a table.

He said no but laughed—at me or in spite of me; I wasn't sure. "What would you like to drink?" he asked.

"A vodka martini, three olives. Slightly dirty."

He smiled at me and motioned to the cocktail waitress. When she came over, he told her what I wanted, and then said, "She'll need your drink ticket."

I gave the waitress my ticket. Nothing about the evening felt like a date: I paid for everything so far, and there was no dinner in my belly.

The music was loud, and he didn't talk much. Clearly, he didn't want to get to know me, so we danced. When we sat at the table for our first break from dancing, he said, "After my divorce, I truly learned how to please a woman."

Ew!

"Do you have kids?" I tried to change the subject.

"Three. They live with their mother in Florida."

"That's gotta be hard on you."

"Let's dance."

We danced to a slow song on the floor, our body parts perfectly aligning, and I considered what he said about pleasing a woman. I needed sex. He was offering the sex. Every divorced woman I met had a similar story of how they purposely chose a one-night stand as their first sexual experience. I was sure

Mambo Man had serviced many women like me, and I considered using him as a palate cleanser.

As if on cue, he looked into my eyes. "If a woman knows how to respond to my kiss, I know I have it made."

Then he kissed me. At least, I assumed it would be a kiss. He just stuck his tongue in my mouth and left it there like a wet tuna. *Gross!* His last statement was replaying in my head—*if a woman knows how to respond to my kiss*—and I got what he meant. It was a test, a penis test. He probably wanted me to suck it.

Sorry, Charlie. This girl wants tunas with good taste.

We both felt that it was time to leave the club, me because I wanted nothing more to do with him, him because he wanted sex.

"My parents have a house in Arlington Heights, not too far from here. They spend the winter in Florida, and I need to check on the house. Why don't you follow me there?"

Fuck no!

"No, thank you. I need to get home."

He walked me to my car, and I prayed he wouldn't kiss me again. Another dead-fish kiss would surely induce vomiting of the two martinis and no dinner. I had my keys ready in my hand, and when we got close to my car door, I gave him a quick preemptive kiss on the cheek, said thank you, and got into my Bug. I pretended to check my mirrors as he walked to his car, but I was waiting, watching him get into his car. I wanted validation that I was right.

He got into a white Camry and turned on the engine. When he started driving, I slowly pulled out of my spot and followed several car lengths behind. (A proper city girl knows how to tail someone.) He drove onto the main street. If he went straight, that road would take him to Arlington Heights. When he turned onto the I-90 East ramp to Chicago, clearly going back to the city, I knew that checking his parents' home was a ruse. All he wanted from me was sex.

Working in a nightclub gave Mambo Man a keen insight into divorced women. He knew what they wanted, how they wanted it, and, I was sure, despite that disgusting kiss, how to give it to them. He wasn't wrong about me. I did need to have a sexual experience, and sooner rather than later, but the nice-girl programming Mother had instilled would not let it be just any-one. Even though I didn't want a permanent relationship, I still wanted a relationship.

The Height And
The Glasses

T he date with Mambo Man may have been a bust, but the introduction to that nightclub, The Living Room, was a lifesaver.

It was early 2000, and my union, the Screen Actors Guild, was on strike. It was the longest commercial strike on record. I was unable to audition or work for six months. During that time, the two national contracts that had been paying me residuals for the last few years both ended. Overnight I lost half my income, and from there it steadily declined. Making ends meet became an intricate game of writing checks to pay bills before my unemployment compensation arrived. The Ex-Hole paid the minimum on child support, but no alimony, thanks to my bargain-basement divorce lawyer. I had one kid in college who needed tuition money and another at home I needed to feed.

Without an education, I was only qualified to work at low-paying jobs like reception and retail sales. Waitressing at that nightclub would provide good money and also keep my days free when the strike ended. I also knew it would embarrass The Ex-Hole, make him look like he wasn't taking care of his family. *Win-win!*

Mother would have agreed with him. "What am I supposed to tell people?"

I applied to be a cocktail waitress. Sol, the General Manager, a slight man in his early fifties, told me he needed a server for the fine dining restaurant upstairs, but I could cocktail after the kitchen closed when they were busy.

At first, it felt like any other waitress job: learning the ordering system, getting to know the clientele, and figuring out how to hold a tray with a dozen drinks in one hand—a feat I never mastered. And of course, at any nightclub, recent divorcées were the chosen delicacy. Given my history, the staff hit on me regularly.

John, a thirty-eight-year-old married waiter, imparted his thoughts one slow night. "There are secrets you have yet to learn. I'd almost like to show you."

"You'll *almost* get the chance."

"I feel sorry for you," Ben, a twenty-eight-year-old bartender, added. "You haven't experienced the real deal."

"You all think that because I was married so young and for so long that I'm this inexperienced, outdated, oral-sex deprived, missionary-position freak?"

"I'm convinced of it," Ben said.

I smiled coyly at him and got closer. "It's true, I may have had only one partner, but he knew exactly what to do to please me, how to drive me wild with desire. After that, why would I want to fall into bed with some young wannabe?"

John laughed. "I'm up for the challenge. We can hook up anytime."

I stood there staring at him.

"'Hook up' means have sex," Ben said, clearly getting me back.

"I know that." I didn't know that.

"John, you're married."

"Which means he wouldn't have intercourse," Ben explained.

They were all recent graduates of President Bill Clinton's School of Adultery, Class of 1998.

"You can make more money waitressing at a Gentlemen's

Club," a pretty, young cocktail waitress told me one night. I was intrigued but knew that bigger tips meant revealing bigger cleavage. In other words, tip-for-tit. It was a slope too slippery to entertain. Besides, I was the mother not only of a teenage daughter but also of a college boy who could someday show up at a club like that. I couldn't risk the loss of home cred. They knew I served dinner and occasionally stayed late. Because my daughter was with her dad every other weekend and had an active social life, my job didn't seem to interfere with motherhood.

Once I got the lay of the land, I enjoyed working at The Living Room. I liked watching people on dates and others trying to "hook up." It made me feel like I was part of the scene, albeit on the sidelines, a safe, judging distance away.

"You're not going to meet a nice guy in a bar," Roxy warned me over and over.

"I'm only there for the money."

"Yeah. Right."

One Friday night, I was standing at the bar when Sol informed me he would be seating a gentleman for dinner who also had reserved a table at the nightclub downstairs afterward. I was to update Sol as to the timing.

A few minutes later, I watched as the man came upstairs. Sol sat him at one of the tables overlooking the dance floor of the club below. He was handsome and professional-looking: short dark hair, well-built, and he wore those modern rectangular glasses with thick black frames.

I walked up to greet him. I had been working there for about a year and had developed a sense about men. If I felt self-conscious around a man, he was a player. If I felt shy or intimidated, he was mean. If I felt at ease, he was a nice guy. By the time I arrived at his table I was very comfortable.

"Welcome to The Living Room. I'm Judi. I'll be your server. May I offer you a cocktail?"

"Hi, Judi. I'll have a martini with blue cheese olives."

I smiled at him. "Coming right up." I turned to leave with such a snap that my hair bounced.

I went to the bar and relayed his order to Rhonda, the only female bartender at the club. She was in her late forties, pretty, but tough. She had enviable thick blonde-streaked hair that she teased into the perfect sexy quaff every night—it had to be every night because the smoke was so thick it stuck to your clothes and hair. Hair and makeup were crucial to all the female servers, as our uniforms were unbecoming and bland. We all wore black pants, long-sleeved white-collared shirts buttoned up with a bolo tie, and a black, white, and silver paisley vest. The men wore the paisley print on a cummerbund.

"He's cute," Rhonda said. It had become her mission to find me a man.

"I know. Right?"

I brought him the martini and rattled off the specials. "We have Lobster, T-Bone, Porterhouse, and Prime Rib. Or, if you can't choose, Surf and Turf."

"What's your favorite?" he smiled and slightly tilted his head.

"I'm a vegetarian. I can tell you that the roasted corn, garlic mash, and the asparagus spears are my favorite sides. But the Prime Rib is extremely popular, especially with our regulars. The filet is a close second."

"You don't eat meat?"

I thought about giving him my stock answer that got me big tips, *I don't eat dead meat*, but I wanted to keep it real. "Nope."

"I'll have the petite filet, medium rare, twice-baked potato, the asparagus you spoke of so highly, and a Cabernet to be brought with dinner. Thank you, Judi."

I smiled and stood there longer than I needed to, then, "I'll put your order in—"

"So?" Rhonda asked as I typed his order into the computer at the bar.

"He's a meat eater."

"I know. He's at a steakhouse. I mean, what's going on? You're flipping your hair; he's looking at you sideways."

"He's being polite." But I was already imagining myself on

his arm at the many charity functions we would attend as a couple.

Rhonda prepared her bar for the later crowd, and I pondered my next move as I watched him from the corner of my eye. I decided to walk by his table as if I were going into the backroom, to see if he'd stop me.

He stopped me. "Judi."

I smiled. "Yes?"

"Where is everyone?"

"We're not that busy in the summer on Friday nights. The college kids scare away the regulars."

"But the club won't be empty?"

"No."

"Okay, sorry. I kept you from doing something."

I smiled. "Not a problem." I walked into the back room and stood there with nothing to do—no need to fill salt and pepper shakers; they weren't empty. I waited a bit and then walked back out.

He stopped me again. "Judi?"

"Yes?"

"I'm expecting friends to join me after dinner."

"I'll keep a lookout."

"Thanks."

His food arrived, and I served him. "I'll just go and get your wine now."

Rhonda poured the glass as I told her, "He's got that look I like. Clean." She looked confused. "You know, when you can tell a guy takes pride in his appearance? I bet it means he keeps his apartment neat too."

"That's maturity."

"Yeah, I definitely want a mature guy."

Rhonda had been trying to get me to be bolder when I met a man at the club that I liked. She said that when we were in uniform, we could get away with being forward.

"I'm going to give him my card," I told her.

To my surprise, she said, "No. Wait and see what happens."

I brought him his wine.

"Thank you. Good tip on the asparagus, by the way."

"I'm glad you're enjoying it. Your friends live around here?"

"No. We all live in the city. I work near here. It didn't make sense to go home."

Perfect. I want a man that lives in the city.

"They're sick of seeing the same people when they go out, so they wanted to hit this place."

Oh no, he's a club regular.

"I don't normally go with them. It's not my thing. I'm divorced."

"I'm sorry." I wasn't sorry. "How long?"

Please don't be under a year.

"It's been a year."

We are so in sync.

His friends started coming in as he finished his meal and I brought them their drink orders. He introduced me to them like I was someone, not just a waitress. The guy had class.

Before he went to his table downstairs, he stood up and pulled me aside. He was well over six feet tall. I loved feeling consumed by his height. He leaned over and asked, "What time do you get off of work?"

Why can't I stop smiling?

I responded with the perfect combination of acting skills and Mother's training. "On Fridays? Around 11:30, 12:00."

"Can I buy you a drink?"

Oh, hell YES!!!

"Sure, I'll look for you when I'm done up here."

It was not only playing out exactly like Rhonda thought it could but somehow as I had foreseen when I first greeted him. When he was out of sight, I looked inside the check folder to see how he had tipped: ten dollars on a thirty-five-dollar bill. Class.

The rest of the night sailed by. I was on Cloud Nine. I was even nice to the Friday night loud, rude, techno-loving, Gen X crowd. I saw the height and the glasses come upstairs a couple of times during the evening, and I played it cool, looking very busy. But there was definitely something igniting between us.

I always brought a top to change into on the weekends in case I wanted to stay for a drink or go out with the other servers after work. At the end of the evening, I changed into a violet cashmere sleeveless turtleneck. It was girl-next-door cute as opposed to what the twenty-something girls wore—or rather, almost wore. They sported halter tops that were tied together in the back by one string. From behind they looked naked. I was still young-looking enough to have gotten away with that look, but my breasts needed far more support than a handkerchief offered. Besides, I'd always heard that men liked to have a little something left to the imagination.

When I went downstairs, I didn't see him anywhere. I felt hurt and abandoned. I couldn't believe it. I went back upstairs to tell Rhonda that he'd ditched me, and she said, "No, he couldn't have. He really liked you. Look again."

I did, and he was there. I spotted the height and the glasses over the crowd. He must have been in the men's room earlier. He had taken off his jacket and was wearing a short-sleeved silk T-shirt. He had nice arms with just the right amount of hair, which looked soft. I knew what it would feel like against my skin. "There you are. I thought you ditched me."

"Oh, no, I wouldn't do that." And I believed him. One of the great things about a new relationship is that it's a clean slate. You have no reason not to believe.

We spent the next two hours talking. I felt present with him, in the moment. During the conversation, he'd invade my space from time to time by getting too close or touching my arm or leg as a gesture, and it amazed me that I didn't care. I knew it meant that I liked him—in that way.

I've been waiting so long for this, and it's finally here!

Because his friends were there, I felt like I'd passed the friends test. His brother was there too, so I passed the family test as well. They liked me: I could see in their faces how glad they were that he had met a nice woman. They were probably worried about him going through a divorce. Mostly, though, we just talked to each other. And when we did, it was like we were the only two people in the club. And this was where I worked! I didn't even care that my co-workers were probably watching. We seemed to have so much in common. Both our spouses had cheated on us; both our mothers died recently.

"I'm sorry, how long has your mother been gone?" I asked.

"Six months. She had a massive coronary and was dead within minutes."

"That's tough. I had a two-year warning. Two years to make peace with her. I can't imagine the suddenness of your loss."

He touched my arm and looked deep into my soul. "Thank you."

We had similar spiritual beliefs, attitudes, and neither of us could tolerate deception of any kind. His friends left one by one, and at two thirty in the morning I told him we should go. I didn't want to be one of the pathetic people still at the club when the lights were turned up.

We walked outside. He asked if I wanted to go for breakfast. I said I was tired, but I wasn't. I didn't know if "breakfast" meant going for bagels or back to his place for sex and a schmear.

I knew he'd ask for my number.

"Can I get your number?" As he waited at the valet station for his car, I wrote it down for him. "I'm going to call you tomorrow."

"Well, I'm going to answer." I rolled my eyes at my response as I walked to my car.

I got into bed that night—morning, and imagined what that height would feel like draped around my body.

The next day at my brother's house I joked to my sister-in-law, "He's got everything on my list. Even things I didn't know I wanted, like glasses." When she looked confused, I explained, "You know, when things get intimate, I won't have to worry that he sees my flaws or cellulite, because he'll have taken off his glasses."

He didn't call the next day. I couldn't believe it. It didn't seem possible. Had I experienced that whole romantic comedy meet-cute by myself? No. There were two of us there! I couldn't help but feel let down. I thought he was something special: I had already told all my friends "I met someone."

He called two days later. "I thought I lost your number! I didn't know where I put it. But today, I'm in my car, I put the visor down, and it falls on my lap."

I forgave him instantly. It sounded genuine. He asked me when I'd be in the city that week, and I told him Saturday. I had a print job for a magazine ad in the afternoon, so I wasn't going into work that night. We made a date for Saturday night.

I had a date that Saturday night! It filled me with eager anticipation all week. We liked each other and had so much in common. That 'didn't happen often. He'd even met me when I wasn't looking my best, wearing a conservative uniform. The gentleman had scored major points. I would reward him by wearing a slinky dress.

I assumed he'd call a few days later with a specific time and place to meet. I assumed wrong. He never called. He never canceled our date. He left me hanging.

Hmm, who does that remind me of?

Now when a guy does that, yes, it makes you mad, and yes, you know HE is a jerk. But some small voice in your head still tells you that it's because you're not good enough. Something's wrong with you. No matter how much *Oprah* you've watched in your lifetime, it still taps into adolescent insecurities.

What's wrong with me? Does he want someone younger? I'm a forty-one-year-old waitress. He doesn't want me. I'm not pretty enough. I revealed too much of myself. I should have played harder to get. I was too nice. I should have been more aloof. I should have gone to breakfast with him.

It's quite messy, *should*-ing on oneself like that.

I called Roxy and told her what happened, hoping she would offer some insight. But she wouldn't venture a guess. "What do you expect?" she asked. "You met him in a bar."

Four weeks later I was at a charity benefit, dressed to kill because charity events had become the new singles' scene. I wore a velvet Cynthia Rowley flowered slip dress and matching jacket trimmed in purple faux fur. My young manager at The Living Room said it was the perfect combination: fur and cleavage. Paired with black go-go boots, I was gunnin' for bear.

I was a bit tipsy as I surveyed the room, but it wasn't long before I spotted the height and the glasses in the corner. I made a beeline for him. *We can't let these guys get away with this shit.* Mother used to tell people off regularly, and I had always been embarrassed by it. I had vowed never to do that myself, but seeing him made me change my mind. As I got closer, I wasn't sure if it was him.

"Hi Judi."

"It *is* you. I just wanted to tell you that you're very rude."

I turned around with such force that I felt my hair flip him off as I walked away. He didn't follow me, and that made me angrier.

I had gone to the party with my friend Laura, but she and I had split up for a while. I went to the dance floor alone. Leaving the dance floor later, I saw him in my peripheral but kept walking away to look for my friend. Then I felt someone touch my waist from behind.

I turned. It was him. He tried to talk to me, but I couldn't hear him over the music. I said, "Let's take this outside and finish it."

I stormed to a quieter area just outside the room. I was still upset. My brain wanted to do the thing that would save my pride, but as I turned around and watched him walk up to me, every part of me hoped he'd give an acceptable excuse.

He apologized several times. "You're right. I was rude." I stared at him. "I lost your number."

"I'm in the book, and you knew where I worked. So-"

"You're right: there's no excuse, except that dating is so new for me."

We talked for a while before his friends whisked him away

to another room in the venue. As he walked away, he asked me to meet him later, but instead, I found Laura and left.

When I got home that night, I looked in the mirror and cried. I couldn't understand why I didn't meet anyone at the event. *Why didn't anyone talk to me? What's wrong with me?*

He called the next day. "How'd you get my number?" I asked immediately.

"You said you were in the book."

"I did."

Pause.

"Listen, let me take you to dinner. I want to make it up to you."

"Look, I'm a straight shooter. I don't play games." Pause. "But IF I were to consider it, you have to tell me what happened."

"You're looking for me to give you an excuse, but there isn't any. I screwed up."

He was straight-shooting right back at me. My initial reaction to him was so strong, and I had felt so comfortable that I decided to give him a second chance. Sadly, the truth was that as soon as I had heard his voice on the telephone, I already knew I was going to give him a second chance. I just had to make it look like I needed convincing.

I insisted we set a specific day and time before we got off the phone. He asked about the following Saturday. It was a Jewish holiday. My kids were going to be with The Ex-Hole, and I was going to my brother's house in the north suburbs, but I knew we'd be done with dinner early because my brother and his wife had three young children. I said I could meet him, but it had to be in the north suburbs. He agreed to come out my way and called the next day with a restaurant choice in Glencoe. I asked for his phone number in case I had to cancel but told him not to worry. "When I have to cancel, I call."

He called the day before to confirm. I liked that. I had him on his toes.

"That's my Judala." I knew Mother was happy.

After not eating much of the dinner at my brother's house,

I followed his wife upstairs. I had on a flower print skirt with a white T-shirt and sandals. She put me in a shimmering silk knit tank top with a matching sweater.

"But don't wear the sweater, your tan arms are sexy," she said and tied the sweater around my shoulders. I am not a woman who wears sweaters tied around her shoulders; that's for blonde country club women with thin lips and no hips. I was a tie-it-around-your-waist girl, but for that night, with him, I wanted to be seen as something more than a waitress.

I met him at the restaurant. We had several glasses of wine and great conversation at the bar. I don't remember what we talked about, but I'm sure I shared with him my taste in music, how I still loved Led Zeppelin or that I had every Chicago and Jim Croce album.

The restaurant was empty because that area had a high concentration of Jews who were all either having dinner with family or were still at a temple, so the staff was very accommodating, almost too much so. They could tell that we were on a first date and that it was the beginning of something special. They seemed to want to be part of it. "May I recommend the fish? How about I top off your wine?"

He ordered for both of us, just like in the movies. I'd never had a man do that for me, and I ate it up. He seemed like such a gentleman. I knew we'd go to nice places. Everything I learned about him, from his kind interactions with others to the tales of his upcoming trip to Africa, made me like him even more.

After dinner, he walked me to my car a half block down from the restaurant. He stood there, so tall, and bent down to kiss me. He kissed the way I like on a first date: soft and tender, not demanding, not leaving his tongue in my mouth waiting to see what I'd do with it, like Mambo Man.

"Can we get together during the week? I know you work on weekends. I could even come out to The Living Room." His eagerness told me everything I needed to know. He was all in.

"Yes. I can get together during the week, and we can make a plan for the weekend. I don't have to work both nights." I liked the money, but it was time to stop watching from the sidelines and have my own dating life.

He kissed me again when we got to my car door and again after I opened it. "You're dangerous," I said softly, looking deep into his eyes. I had no idea why I felt the need to behave as if I were in a romance novel.

He walked back toward his car, and I drove away with that excited glow of a new relationship. He didn't make me guess how he felt about me. He stated his intentions to see me that week and the next weekend.

It never happened. I never heard from him again.

It was a Friday night, a year later. I was still working at The Living Room, but I'd stopped cocktail waitressing after dinner because I wasn't good at it. My wrists weren't strong enough to balance a tray full of drinks, so Sol was desperate when he asked me to stay that night. It was midnight and the techno music was pounding. There were wall-to-wall twenty-somethings, and it was hard to maneuver my shaking tray through the crowd. I only had thirty minutes left on my shift when I spotted the height and the glasses. He didn't see me, so I turned around and headed back to the bar, which put me out of sight. I needed to collect my thoughts, even though I had not distributed the drinks from my tray.

"What balls!" I said aloud.

"What?" Ben, the young bartender, screamed over the crowd noise, but I shook my head to indicate I didn't need anything.

I considered my options. I couldn't run away; I was at work. *He came to my work! He probably thought I didn't still work here a year later. I'm so pathetic; I'm still working here a year later.*

I stood there near the bar wondering what to do. *Should I ignore him? Tell him off? Act like I don't care?*

Then calmness washed over me. Probably Mother's spirit

coming to guide me, because suddenly I knew exactly what to do. I picked up my tray and began to distribute the drinks. Out of the corner of my eye, I saw him making his way over to me. As I emptied the last drink from the tray, I started to walk back to the bar, allowing him to overtake me.

"Judi?"

I turned around and looked at him furrowing my brow as if trying to place him. I let out a long, bewildered, "Hiii."

"Hi." He acted very normally.

"I'm sorry. You look so familiar." I stood there assessing him. "I know I know you, but I just can't remember where."

He told me his name, as if that explained everything.

You arrogant asshole. We had one date and one kiss. I pretended to be confused, "Okay."

"We dated?"

"We dated?" I asked as if that were impossible, but I didn't want to overplay my hand and quickly portrayed recognition. "Oh my God, yes. We had *a* date, yes. Hi."

"Hi." He looked deflated.

Good.

"How've you been?" Small talk was all I would allow.

"Good. Thanks. Listen, I'd like to, can we—"

I had no interest in anything he had to say and interrupted him. "I'm really slammed, can't talk. You have a great night," I added over my shoulder as I walked away.

It was the first time in my life that I played it perfectly. I didn't say too much. I didn't say too little. I wasn't too nice. I wasn't too mean. Yes, I put him in his place, but he deserved it. I was wrong about him, judged him from the outside in. He only had the appearance of class.

I called Roxy on the way home, wanting validation that I'd done the right thing. She would only reply, "What did you expect? You met him in a bar."

"But—" She knew that part of me hoped she'd tell me to go back to the club and give him another chance, so when I started to speak, she cut me off, reiterating louder, "A bar, a B-A-R!"

Case closed.

Shortly after that, I quit working at The Living Room. Residual checks had started coming in again and doing anything to spite The Ex-Hole no longer appealed to me. But I mostly quit because, as Roxy so eloquently put it, "You need to stop watching life and get a life!"

The Contractor

Roxy was right when she told me not to go out with men from the nightclub. So when a waitress from work offered to set me up, I was open to the idea.

"He lives in Indiana but loves coming to Chicago. I think you two would really hit it off."

"Why, because we're both single?" It irritated me that people thought a relationship status was a common interest.

"Because his wife cheated on him and she was the only partner he'd ever had."

"Oh."

I met him at The Living Room just before I quit. He came in exclusively to meet me. He sat at my station, and we talked sporadically during the night as I served dinner.

"This place is outstanding."

"How do you know our mutual friend?"

He rattled on about how they'd gone on a date once but decided to be friends instead. He helped her when her furnace needed repair, her roof leaked, or she got a flat tire. He was a rescuer.

"You're a fix-it guy?"

"I'm a contractor."

Bingo. I had a bathroom in desperate need of renovation.

"Would you like to go to dinner next Saturday night?" He asked.

"Sure."

"Outstanding."

The Contractor loved the word *outstanding*. The date was anything but. He drove all the way from northern Indiana to my northwest Chicago suburb, then, with me, he drove back into Chicago for dinner, where he proceeded to talk about his ex-wife during the entire meal.

"How long have you been divorced?"

"Two years, but separated longer."

"And it's still painful for you?"

"Not at all."

Then why the fuck are you going on and on about her?! Especially because I was sitting across from him in my faux-fur-and-cleavage getup.

After dinner, he wanted to take me to Pops for Champagne, a popular live jazz place on Sheffield. I had always wanted to go but told him I wasn't feeling well. He took me home.

As we pulled into my driveway, I was nervous about how I would say no to a second date.

"How "bout I come in next Saturday morning and we get started on your bathroom?"

"I'd love that."

Over the next few weeks we spent countless hours ripping out tile and picking out new fixtures. He trusted me with his tools, let me do most of the demo, and did all the dumpster runs. I smelled cigarette smoke on him when he'd return, but since we weren't dating, I didn't care.

He revealed that his eleven-year-old was not his biological daughter. He adopted her a few years after he married her mother. When his wife left him and moved several states away for a man she'd met on the Internet, he generously offered to keep their daughter until she and her new man got settled.

"That was very big-hearted of you."

"No," he replied with a cunning smile, "I knew they'd never get settled and the years would go by quickly. By then, my daughter would be old enough to tell a judge she'd rather live with me."

"Sneaky."

"I am the only stability that girl has ever known." It was obvious how much he loved his little girl.

After five weeks, when it was time to turn the project over to the tile guys, he asked me to a play I'd been dying to see at the Apollo Theater. I hesitated before responding.

"Look, I know our first date didn't go so well," he said during my silence.

"Don't say that—"

"Please, I talked about my ex the entire night."

"Yeah, what was that about?"

"Nerves. You were across from me, the most beautiful woman I'd ever been out with—in that dress—"

I happily agreed to go out with him again. Spending those weeks working with him was a great way to get to know each other without the pressure of dating. I learned he'd been the overweight audio-visual geek at school, completely afraid of the pretty, popular girls.

That night after the show, I invited him in. We began kissing on my couch right away. Even though he hadn't had a cigarette all night, I still tasted the ones he'd had on the drive up earlier in the day. It was a turn-off, but when I mentioned it to him, he promised to quit.

As we kissed, he slid his hand in between my legs. Even though it was over my jeans, it was odd. There was no warning, no lead-up. It confused me. I'd never played the field, but when had it become okay to go for third without hitting second? In my head I was thinking, *I should stop him*, but then it occurred to me: he'd just taken me to see *The Vagina Monologues*. Maybe he was inspired.

After that, I figured there'd be sex on the next date. And you know what? I wasn't scared to have sex with The Contractor. Maybe it was because I knew he had been tested for STDs after his ex-wife cheated. Either that, or the five martinis I had at dinner, but whatever the reason, we did take matters into the bedroom.

I went into my bathroom and slipped into a silk bra and

panty set. I put a robe over it and walked into the bedroom, where he was sitting on the edge of the bed. I then slipped the robe off my shoulders, letting it fall to the floor. It was similar to a move I used to do for The Ex-Hole: come out of the bathroom wearing only a towel and let it slip to the floor as if unwrapping a present for him. It would turn him on so much that we would get right to business.

It didn't have the same effect on The Contractor. When he saw me standing there, performance anxiety swept over him and he lost his erection. "That's okay, I'm sure you can coax it back," he said, trying to save the moment.

But I had never done that before. Penises—or is the plural *peni?* I still hadn't looked that up. Anyway, in my experience, they always came ready to play. I had no clue how to coax a flaccid penis, and I didn't want to try. It looked like an old elephant trunk: wrinkled, shrunken, and shriveled.

I did the best I could, and then he tried to work on me. That's where I learned we had a communication problem. We didn't speak the same language. Apparently when I said, "Oooh, right there," he heard, *try something completely new and really painful.*

I finally understood what Roxy meant when she said that the key to sex with a new man was to be verbal in bed. I not only had to tell a man *what* I liked but also exactly *how* I liked it. I had been dreading that moment. I was fine doing the acts, but I just didn't feel comfortable discussing the specifics. But I had to coach The Contractor because he was literally rubbing me the wrong way.

I tapped him on the shoulder. His face looked like a player called out of the game. He lay next to me and listened as I spoke. He was open and patient with me as I tried to find the words to communicate my needs. I kept my eyes down, looking at and playing with a string on my quilt, and finally, I blurted it out. I told him how I liked to be touched.

When I looked up, he was asleep. I knew people fell asleep after sex, but we hadn't gotten through the foreplay.

The three-pack of condoms Roxy and I bought a while ago remained unopened in my nightstand. They weren't going to make it to the show, not tonight anyway, because I was too angry to wake him up. As I lay in the bed next to him, I thought of a story Mother told me about her first time with my dad.

"When he finished, he rolled over and went to sleep, and I thought, 'This is what everyone is talking about?'"

As I wondered if Mother had ever enjoyed sex a day in her life, The Contractor started snoring like my father. When he boxed me out by taking up the entire bed, I realized that's probably why my parents had twin beds pushed together. Strike three came when he kicked me so hard that I fell to the floor.

A smoking, snoring, restless sleeper was a deal-breaker. I spent the rest of the night on my couch. I didn't see him again after that, and in the end, the only thing that got laid was the bathroom floor.

Boss Man

"**R**ox, I met the man I could sleep with!"
"Hall-a-fuckin-lu-ya. Who is he?"
"My new boss."

"Oh no. You can't date Boss Man. It's against the rules. You'll have to stay away from this one."

I'd always planned on going back to school, and the fear of becoming a sixty-five-year-old waitress inspired me to enroll at Columbia College Chicago. They accepted all my Drake University credits from 1979, and I received grants to cover most of the cost.

In the spring of 2002, I was one semester away from graduation and had a part-time job as an assistant in communications at the City Hall in a nearby suburb. I helped program the message display and wrote news reports for the cable access channel nobody knew existed. It paid eleven dollars an hour, but I wasn't there for the money. I was building a resume with *real* jobs. I'd worked all my life but never had a corporate job. However, since I played the role of "businesswoman" in many industrial films (in-house training films used as learning tools for employees), I knew how to fake it.

My boss at the City Hall soon moved up the corporate ladder, and his replacement started on my day off. When I got to work, I walked into the new boss' office to introduce myself.

"Excuse me, I'm your—" The sight of him silenced me. He had dark brown eyes, dimples, and short, neat, full, grab-able hair. He was six feet tall and stood so erect that Mikhail Baryshnikov would've looked like a slouch. I heard he'd been a cop in a small Ohio town for the past fifteen years, and after seeing him, I wanted him to serve and protect me.

I stood frozen in the doorway, with every cell in my body at full attention, as our eyes met and locked. Sparks flew and ricocheted off the walls; the lights dimmed, stars twinkled above us, and I swear, Barry White was singing a sultry song in the background, encouraging me to make love to the man right there on the desk that separated us.

"You're my what?" he asked, breaking the silence.

The sound of his voice summoned me back to reality.

Talking, he's talking. Oh, my God. How long have I been staring at him? Can he see what I'm thinking? Speak, Judi.

I finally found my voice. "I'm your Judi, I mean, your assistant, Judi."

Oh Lord, I'm a blubbering idiot. Okay, Judi, you're an actress, just look like you're listening. I furrowed my eyebrows and continued to stare.

"It's good to meet you, Judi."

"Yes, yes, good to meet you, Judi. I mean—that's my name. I was told your name. It's not Judi."

As soon as I could get away, I ran outside and called Roxy from my cell phone. That's when she told me I wasn't allowed to date him.

"What rules?" I asked her over the phone. I had acted in sexual harassment industrial films, but they didn't cover *dating* a co-worker.

"You don't shit where you eat," she stated.

I figured Roxy knew more about workplace etiquette, so I complied. But how was I going to stay away from my boss?

The next day we had a one-on-one meeting in his office so I could explain to him what we did in his department. I sat in the chair facing his desk, and he got up and began to pace as we spoke. When he turned his back to me, I couldn't help looking at his butt. It was round and high and hard. I lost track of my thought process. When he turned to see why I'd stopped speaking, he caught me red-handed checking out his ass. He smiled a knowing, boyish smile, and I turned several shades of crimson.

The next time we had a meeting in his office, I lucked out because he asked his boss' secretary to sit in and give her input. She and I sat in the chairs facing his desk. To concentrate, I looked at anything in the office other than him: the top of his desk, the picture of President Bush—

Wait. Bush? Why Bush? Red flag. Disengage.

Too late. Hormones overruled.

I looked at my writing pad, then his hands... *His hands.* His hands were beautiful; long, thin fingers, short, clean nails. I knew his hands would feel soft on my body.

Stop it, Judi, look at his hair, look above the dimples, those gorgeous big brown eyes, look at his hair!

There, too, I started daydreaming, imagining myself grabbing hold of that thick hair and bringing his face into mine. I must have gotten lost in that thought because suddenly they were both staring at me as if someone had asked me a question.

"I'm sorry. I must have drifted off."

Boss Man smiled that knowing smile at me, and I wanted to disappear. My desire for him was palpable and not something I was able to hide. I couldn't even rely on my acting skills. Hormones superseded talent. I couldn't stop thinking about having sex with him. They weren't explicit sex dreams; I just imagined touching and kissing him—in bed.

To make matters worse, he had all the equipment I worked on moved into his office. "I'd like to see how you do it," he told me. "As the boss, I need to know how to do everything."

So began our working in the same small office space. Even though my back was to him as I worked, my body still swelled with his presence.

I didn't know what was wrong with me. When I was with

Eric, I'd felt like a horny teenager, but now I felt like a horny teenager on steroids. I was with The Ex-Hole when he was at that stage, so I'd experienced his sexual prime firsthand. That's when I recognized what was happening. I wasn't just in my sexual prime; I had hit my sexual *peak*. And being single and sexually cautious meant the desire wasn't getting satiated. Logically, it was escalating.

It's not fair! I was there for Ex-Hole's prime. He was supposed to be here for mine! I hated him all over again.

When I was given tickets to a charity ball, Roxy suggested I ask Boss Man.

"Really? Can I? I can date him now?"

"It's not technically a date. He's just a co-worker. He's new in town. You'll just be showing him around."

I didn't care what the reasoning was. I was excited to get the green light! But I had never, EVER asked a man out. I'd never needed to; if I liked one, I'd wear something cute and sexy and make him notice me, then he'd ask me. But sometimes it took months; I needed a date by Saturday. I was going to have to ask him out.

Mother would not approve. "In my day that was unheard of! Better you should stay home."

Hormones overruled Mother too. I planned to call him at the office on my day off. I practiced all morning what I would say and the casual tone I'd use. I even memorized the points I wanted to hit: *free tickets to this charity; you should see downtown... It's not a date.*

I dialed his number. Before it rang, I hung up. And repeated the behavior a dozen times. I'd never realized how hard it must be for men. If he said no, I'd have the humiliation of facing him every day at work. But if he said yes, it could be the start of something. My mind kept spinning out of control. *But if he is interested and I make the first move, then he'll know I like him and he'll have the upper hand, and then I can't play aloof and hard-to-get like Mother taught me.*

I finally grew a pair when I realized Roxy was right. He was new in town. He didn't know anyone. If I didn't ask him, he'd probably sit home, alone. I'd be doing him a favor.

I dialed. He answered. "Hi, it's your Judi—assistant, Judi—from work. I have tickets to this charity, and since you're new in town, I thought you might like to ball—go to a ball, a Charity Ball. Anyway, it's formal. And it's not like a date or anything. I just thought that since you don't know anyone here, and you haven't—but you don't—or maybe you have a girl—"

"Judi!" he interrupted, saving me from myself. "I'd love to."

I grinned like the Grinch after he stole Christmas.

He was wearing a tux when he picked me up that Saturday. Gorgeous. His bow tie perfectly accentuated his dimples. I wore a long, clinging, black sequined dress with a low back, and when we got to the ball, I swear to God, the band was playing "At Last" by Etta James. I didn't want to ask him to dance, so I swayed back and forth until he got the hint.

"I don't dance," he confessed.

"Everyone can dance slowly," I said, looking into his eyes. He nodded.

I loved the way he led me through the crowd onto the dance floor with his hand on the small of my back. It said, "You belong to me." Once we got to the dance floor, it felt awkward, like preteens at a Bar Mitzvah not knowing how to engage. Slowly we got comfortable; he pulled me closer to him, and I put my head on his chest. I could feel his breath on my neck. I liked that. Every part of the front of his body was touching every part of the front of mine. *It's a good thing women don't get erections.* I prayed I didn't say that out loud.

"Pardon me?"

Oh Lord, I did. "It's a good thing women can follow directions," I said.

Needless to say, we didn't dance together for the rest of the evening. I didn't trust myself, and I was nervous. I was always nervous and constantly smiling around him. We left after dinner. There was nothing else to do at the ball, but still, I didn't want the evening to end.

When we were back in his car, he read my mind, "Tell me the longest route to take you home."

He didn't want our non-date date to end either. On the drive home, he reached over and rubbed the back of my neck. Normally, I didn't like a man to invade my space so quickly, but with him it felt right.

When we got to my place, he insisted on walking me to the door even though it was just a few feet from my driveway. I couldn't ask him in for coffee because my teenage daughter was at home and, raging hormones aside, I wasn't going to introduce her to anyone unless it was serious.

"Well, I guess there'd be no harm in the boss giving you a hug," he said as he held out his arms.

A hug? You're an ex-cop, throw me against the wall and force me to spread "em. Thankfully, I didn't say that out loud, even though it was front and center in my brain. I gave him a quick hug without letting any part of my body touch any part of his.

As I pulled away, he said, "You know, I saw you at my second interview and was instantly attracted."

"Really?"

"Yes. I was in the outer office filling out paperwork, and you came in to ask the secretary a question. I heard her say something about you being single and I smiled. I even told my mother that there was a woman at the new job I was interested in."

I vaguely remembered a man sitting at a table, but I never saw his face. I had no idea men played out scenarios in their heads too. "You told your mother about me?"

"Yes, but..."

Oh man, why is there always a but?

"But then you came in that day and said I was your boss and I was disappointed. I had hoped we'd date."

I was never able to sleep on the days that I saw him because I was so jazzed up. That night as I lay awake in bed, I weighed my options: one hundred dollars a week or a sex life. *I mean boyfriend.*

82

That Monday morning, I gave my two weeks' notice. When I handed him my resignation letter, he gave me a sly smile.

"You what?!" Roxy demanded. "You don't quit your job for Boss Man!"

Maybe not in her family; her mother was twenty years younger than mine. She was also a feminist and a very successful real estate agent. Roxy's mother told her to get an education and be self-sufficient. Mine instilled the importance of marrying well. Besides, it was just a day job. It wasn't a career.

"You're judging me?" I responded to Roxy. "You try two years of celibacy in your sexual prime, then get back to me."

During those last weeks at work, Boss Man and I started to get together outside the office. He had just bought a home a few towns over from mine, and I offered to take him to Bed Bath & Beyond. We weren't dating yet, but his nearness still drove me crazy. One evening, we were in the parking lot of Best Buy going over his shopping list. The radio was on, and suddenly Barry White began outing me, telling him all my secret thoughts. I had to stop him. I reached over and abruptly silenced Mr. White by turning off the radio. Boss Man laughed as if he knew why.

That last week at work, I started to feel more of my sassy self. He told me that he was going back to Ohio that weekend. "My house finally sold. Now I can pack up the rest of my things and bring back the cat."

"You have a cat?" *Deal-breaker.* I'm extremely allergic.

He shrugged. "When I was on the force, I got the call one night during a terrible storm. A woman saw a kitten in a tree outside her window. I came with a ladder and got the cat out of the tree. It was wet and shivering, so I put it under my coat, and my partner and I took it straight to the vet. In the squad car, my partner kept saying, 'Don't look at its face.' When we dropped it off, the vet asked, 'You keeping it?' I sneered at her."

"So, how did you wind up taking the cat home?"

"I looked at its face. But I never told my partner. I went back alone the next morning and picked him up. Named him

Storm."

Greatest cat story ever!

My hero sat back down at his desk with a sigh. "I hate packing," he complained. "It takes forever."

I smiled and rolled my eyes. "What's the big deal? I can pack up a house in the time it would take you to make a frozen dinner."

"Come with me." I thought he was joking, but since I still didn't know how to respond, I didn't. "I'm serious," he continued. "Come with me."

I smiled and said, "I would if I could, but I can't. I have an audition this afternoon." I didn't mean it. I wouldn't have gone if I could.

I went downtown that afternoon, ran a few errands, got home at dinnertime, and when I figured he'd be halfway to Ohio, called to tease him.

"Hey, where are you? I thought you were picking me up?"

"Really? I can be there in thirty minutes."

"Wait. What? I thought you left hours ago."

"That was the plan, but no, I'm still at my hotel."

He assured me we'd have separate rooms, but I tried to talk my way out of it. Yet while I was telling him all the reasons why I couldn't go; I was packing a bag. My daughter was spending the weekend at her dad's, so there was no real reason to stay home. Besides, I trusted my ex-cop. We hadn't kissed, held hands, or dated for that matter, yet I went away with him for the weekend knowing full well I am extremely allergic to cats.

What can I say? Hormones made me do it.

It was a seven-hour drive that sailed by quickly. He touched my hand a few times in the car, and I felt like a schoolgirl on her first date. Finally, we pulled into a gravel driveway with a "sold" sign. I wondered what would happen in that house when we were finally alone.

Nothing. My cat allergy flared up. I started sneezing the minute we walked in the door, so I had no qualms as he made up the bed in the spare bedroom, even though for the past month

I had longed to feel his body against mine. But I was sneezing and blowing my nose, needing two tissues per blow—not very romantic for a first encounter. He gave me an allergy pill, and I went to my room.

A little while after I settled into bed, there was a knock on my closed door. I liked that. Boss Man came in offering to open a window. He thought it might help to have some fresh air. The sight of him startled me. He was barely dressed, wearing only sweatpants. His hairy chest left me speechless. Up to that point I had only seen him in starched white shirts buttoned up to the neck. I checked out his body as he opened the window, and then he was gone.

"Thank you," I murmured to the closed door.

I wished he had climbed into bed with me. *Was I supposed to ask him to stay?* But it didn't matter because my eyes started itching. I knew if I rubbed them, they would swell and become as red as my nose, so I lay on my back and concentrated on keeping them closed.

I awoke three hours later, at 5 a.m., clear and dry. The medicine and fresh air had worked. I thought about Boss Man sleeping across the hall from me in those sweatpants, his chest bare. I knew if I walked to the hall bathroom it might wake him up. So I did. He awoke.

"Hey, feeling better?" he called from his room.

I went to the doorway, and when I saw him lying there in his bed, something inside me snapped. With no warning or planning, I jumped into his bed, got under the covers, and swung into position so he could spoon me. He did, and we fit together fine.

"What took you so long?" he asked, and finally, we kissed for the first time.

The kiss didn't ignite the passion I'd dreamed it would, but I loved the story I would tell friends: "Where were you when he first kissed you?" *Well, we were in bed...*

We kissed for a while, and though I never got totally into it, I had done enough love scenes to know how to fake it. I let my hands wander down his back, expecting to feel the band of his sweatpants. I got dangerously close to where his butt should have been, so I moved my hands to his sides and lowered them until I discovered—

"You're naked!"

He smiled at me sheepishly. "I know. That's how I sleep."

"The last time I saw you, you were wearing sweatpants," I said as if my words would magically put them back on.

"Are you okay?" he asked when he saw my anxiety.

I was wearing sweatpants, a tank top, socks, underwear, and my bra, so I thought I'd try to lighten the mood. "I'm just feeling a little overdressed." And I tossed off my socks.

It was supposed to be funny, but then he started kissing me again and got on top of me. I thought, *holy shit, this isn't what I had in mind.* Not that I'd had anything in mind. Spontaneous actions by their very definition are not thought-out. And where had spontaneity gotten me? I was seven hours from home, in Ohio, in—I didn't even know which town. And there was a naked man on top of me!

I had just wanted us to hold each other. Yes, it would have made an even better story: "Tell me about your first kiss?" *Well, he was naked...* but I couldn't think about that. I wanted to give up writing stories about the men in my life in hopes of actually having a man in my life.

I stopped him and said I wasn't ready. He was cool with that because, after all, we still worked together. I had one week left of my two-week notice. Still, I was worried about myself. After being married for twenty years and having regular sex for all that time, you'd think I would have wanted it, especially after a two-year dry spell. I always thought of myself as a woman who loved sex, yet there I was, lying in bed with a man I was supposedly sexually attracted to and feeling nothing.

The next day we packed up his house. He was working in the kitchen and sent me to the spare bedroom with a giant trash bag to fill up with miscellaneous things. When I opened the closet door, I saw a shotgun in the corner. That was a first for me.

Nice Jewish girls don't know people with guns, let alone rifles.

I stood there in a daze. *How do you pack a rifle?* I went downstairs to speak to him in person.

"There's a rifle in your closet."

He looked concerned and ran upstairs. "Only one?" He opened the closet, moved a few things and found another one. Relief washed over his face. "My dad gave me this when I was little."

"Oh." I didn't know how to respond.

"I'll take these." He took the artillery back downstairs.

I didn't know how I felt about dating a man who had guns —plural. I knew he had a pistol because as a cop he didn't like his service-issued firearm and had bought a Glock 9mm. But two rifles as well? What did that mean?

I used to have a fascination with guns, but The Ex-Hole always said we could never have a gun in the house because I'd shoot him. He joked, of course, but jokes are funny because they contain elements of truth. I could see my younger self, waving a .22 at him to make him stop lying or to show him he'd pushed me too far. You know, just for emphasis. But the day his frustration escalated and he slapped me hard across the face, causing tears to well up, then asked, "What? You're gonna to cry now?" Exactly as I would see Ritchie Aprile do to Tony's sister Janice years later in an episode of *The Sopranos*, I would have done what Janice did—shot him. Dead. On the floor.

Who's the fucking cunt now, biatch?

When Boss Man and I finished packing up, we went to a small, quaint place for breakfast where he introduced me to the locals. The owner of the restaurant, a large woman who looked like Aunt Bee from *The Andy Griffith Show,* pulled me aside and told me how happy she was that he had met someone who was "their kind." I wondered if she if she knew I was the Jewish kind.

"They're good people," He said as we drove away, and I wondered if he knew I was Jewish. Would that matter to him?

"Oy Gevalt! My baby's dating an armed Nazi!"

We dropped the keys off at his realtor's office and made

our way back to Chicago. This time we held hands in the car. When he spotted the Chicago skyline, he said, "At first that view frightened me, but now it feels like coming home. Coming home to you."

Wow.

On Monday we went back to work, but we started hanging out more. We had a few "work" lunches, and one evening when my daughter wasn't home, I had him over. I asked him to do something I needed desperately: fix things in my apartment. He fixed my leaky faucet, rewired the light in the hall, and programmed my thermostat. I'd never known a man who could fix things around the house, and I loved it. It may be a stereotype that Jewish men aren't handy, but it's one based in truth.

The day after my last day of work, we had our first official date.

"How "bout a movie?" he asked as we left the restaurant.

"How "bout we go back to your place?" That I did say out loud, on purpose, and I wasn't embarrassed because it was time, time to have sex. Besides, it wasn't like a real first date. I had known him for months. And work put him through extensive medical tests for insurance purposes, and I'd snuck a peek. He was clean as a whistle.

"Great, my place it is. I just rented two movies."

I thought maybe "movies" was code for sex, but when we got back to his place he actually put a movie into his VCR, and we sat on the couch and watched it.

Two years into dating, I was no longer afraid of having sex. I was worried I'd never have sex.

As he got up to put the second movie in, I realized he might have thought from our trip that I wanted to take it too slow. I was going to have to take control. But I couldn't initiate anything. I was old-school. As a man, it was his job to make the first move. My job was to make him *think* he was making the first move.

Okay think Judi, you have to manipulate a cop. A cop. His gun! And he probably keeps it where he feels most vulnerable.

"Um, could I see your gun?" I asked, so innocently it verged on overacting.

"Sure, I keep it in my bedroom."

God, I'm good. I followed him to his bedroom. He went to the nightstand, took out the pistol, removed the clip and handed it to me. I held it in my hands and examined it. It gave me a sense of power and control. I loved it.

And he must have liked the way I stroked his Glock because he started kissing my shoulder, making his way to my neck. He pulled my head back gently and kissed me. This time with the cool, hard, gun in my hands, I felt something when he kissed me.

As the kiss grew in passion, he took the gun from me and put it on the nightstand. He gently guided us so that we were lying on the bed. He was on top of me, but I could see the gun in the moonlight that shone through his window. So sexy. Soon our clothes were off, and when I touched his penis in the darkness, under the covers, it didn't feel anything like the gun.

Now, I may have only been with one man, but I'd attempted to have sex with several others, and I don't mean to generalize, but all those penises—*or is the plural peni?* Hold on while I look that up... penises! The plural of penis is, in fact, penises. Anyway, the damn things were all pretty much alike.

His, however, was a bit thin. When he put it inside me, I remembered Tom Arnold's response when Roseanne publicly announced he had a little dick. He stated, "It's like landing a 747 in the Grand Canyon." I wondered—was he Tom or I Roseanne?

Obviously, I was spending too much time in my head and not living in the moment. I emitted a few moans. He finished. I smiled and said I needed to get home. What I needed was to call Roxy from the car.

"Pencil dick," she said matter-of-factly.

"That's a thing?" I asked.

"Oh yeah. You had a short fat one yet?"

"You know I haven't." And I never wanted to.

"They come in all sizes." And we laughed at the unintended "come" pun.

"Seriously," she continued through the laughter, "the first time is always weird. He may not have been fully erect, and besides, you can make anything work with the right positioning."

Roxy was right, so right. I bought the Kama Sutra and studied it for new position ideas, and soon I was eager to try again. Later that week, I got the perfect chance. His air conditioner broke, and it was in the high 90s. My daughter was at her dad's, so I invited him to sleep over.

"I'm sorry. I need to be careful how I spend my time," He responded.

"What does that mean?" I knew he had some work to do in his house, but it was very livable; nothing was pressing.

"I need the house ready for my sister when she comes to visit." She wasn't due for another three weeks. I was extremely insulted and got off the phone quickly.

I sat and thought about him turning me down, and then I thought about all the times that The Ex-Hole had disappointed me, choosing anything and everybody over me. Slowly, as if coming out of a dream, the spell I was under began to lift. I came back to reality, and back to my real self.

I called Boss Man.

He answered. "Hi, I'm so glad you called. You sounded funny on the phone, and I didn't know why."

"Listen, I didn't get out of a twenty-year marriage just to be last on someone else's list."

He was surprised and said he was sorry I felt that way, but I still broke up with him. I didn't feel as bad as I thought I would when I hung up the phone. I felt like I had grown. I knew what kind of relationship I wanted, and I wasn't going to settle. Besides, all signs pointed to the fact that he was a conservative, gun-toting Republican. And Mother would haunt me till kingdom come if I took up with a Republican.

Sadly, the three-pack of condoms remained in my nightstand.

I did regret having sex with him. I wanted to keep my

numbers low so as not to get HPV. I felt I'd wasted a punch on my "get out of HPV free" card.

"It don't count," Roxy told me.

"How so?"

"If it ain't bigger than a tampon, it don't count."

"You're awful!"

"Me? I'm not the one with Glock envy."

Moving Home

After yet another failed relationship, with hormones still raging, and about to become an empty nester with my daughter going off to college... what was the next logical step? Any guesses?

I'm sure many come to mind, but I did the exact opposite. I moved home. Not just home to the city of Chicago, but home to the house where I grew up. *Back* home, where my father still lived.

Here's how that happened. It was the fifth anniversary of Mother's passing: September 11, 2001. I awoke earlier than usual. I had an audition in the city, so I needed to get out of the house soon. I didn't have time to watch *The Oprah Show*, but I turned on the television anyway. In place of Oprah was the horrific news that a plane had crashed into one of the Twin Towers in New York City.

I sat there on the couch with my green tea. I couldn't move. I was in that state of confusion when you see something you've never seen before and don't know how to process it. There's no point of reference stored in your brain to tell you what's happening. I couldn't take my eyes from the screen and watched live TV as another plane flew into the remaining tower and exploded. It was intentional. I realized America was under attack. I accidentally spilled the hot tea, and it burned my chest. It left a red reminder I hoped would never fade.

I never got dressed that morning. I never went downtown.

I watched TV all day until finally, the President spoke. I've never been a political person and certainly not a Republican, but before I could turn off the television and go to bed, I needed reassurance from the President of the United States. He took far too long to address the nation.

Sitting alone in my suburban townhouse, I thought of my elderly father sitting alone in his city townhouse. Since my divorce, he'd repeatedly asked me to move in with him. He gave all the right arguments: his house was paid off, free rent, living downtown closer to school and auditions.

I dismissed the idea. I was a grown-ass woman. I was not going to move in with my father. But that afternoon, as I watched the Twin Towers fall into a sea of ash, my reasoning dissolved as well. Moving in with my father no longer felt like the desperate act of a divorcée. It felt like family being there for each other. Every part of my being told me to do it, even if it looked pathetic to others.

Six months later I put my condo on the market and got the price I wanted. Everything seemed to fall into place, perfectly timed, with the move happening after my daughter's high school graduation and before my last semester of college. That's when I heard about a program in the Film and Television Department called "Semester in LA."

It was a screenwriting class on the CBS Studio lot in Studio City, California. Given that all I had left in my last semester were elective courses, I applied to that program and was accepted. Had I not sold my townhouse and planned to move in with my father, I would not have been able to afford an LA sublet that August. Following my instincts paid off.

In June, I packed up my three-bedroom townhouse in Buffalo Grove and moved into my dad's four-bedroom townhouse in the East Lakeview area of Chicago. On top of the packing and the moving, I had to clean out all the stuff my parents had accumulated over the past thirty-eight years before I could do the unpacking of my things.

My father didn't mind the piled-up boxes and extra

couches and artwork strewn about his living room, nor did he mind the piles and piles I stored in the basement until the Salvation Army van could pick it up. The man loved his basement; he watched TV down there while he smoked his beloved cigars, so I expected him to feel a little put-out. He didn't.

When I finally got the house almost settled, I asked him if I could put his baseball caps in the hall closet. He said, "No, I need them there."

There meant in the dining room, on the spindles of four of the six chairs. Eight hats.

"Okay," I said, respecting his wishes. Of course, I thought my eighty-four-year-old father was a bit eccentric. But calling my father eccentric was putting it mildly.

Since I was a little girl, I'd always explained my Dad as being a cross between George Burns and Walter Matthau. He mostly looked like Matthau (big nose, thin), but he smoked cigars and was contemplative like Burns, *except* when he was dramatic for emphasis like Matthau. However, at eighty-four, he'd morphed into Mr. Magoo.

Dad was a character. I always thought that if Hollywood discovered him, they'd have tried to make him a star—well, a character actor. I say *try* because it wouldn't have interested him. He was a simple man with simple needs. "I have no use for that."

He was a man with a routine: when he woke up, he went straight to the toilet, then down to the living room to stretch. After that, he had breakfast, went to the toilet, and jogged—if you could call what he did jogging. He ran so slowly that you'd swear he was merely bouncing. Then he'd come home, go to the toilet, bathe, have lunch, toilet again, watch the stock market reports, toilet, ride his bike, toilet, smoke again, have dinner, toilet, watch the news or sports, have a ten p.m. snack, then to bed an hour later. Of course, going to sleep for the night did not negate going to the toilet a half dozen more times.

He also had *no use* for anything extraneous, like answering machines and call waiting, though he did have a computer my brother bought him so he could access his stock portfolio.

He neither remembered birthdays nor cared if you forgot his. He said things that sounded hurtful: "You can't write anything funny that Henny Youngman hadn't already thought of," or "I didn't care for your pea soup this time." But if you truly knew him, you knew he didn't mean it cruelly; he just stated the facts as he saw them.

However, he was quick to recant when challenged. "Sure, Dad, but did Henny ever write dating stories from the point of view of a forty-year-old divorcée?"

This was not the father I had known as a child. The father I grew up with worked all day, came home at seven, had dinner, watched TV, and went to sleep. He maybe gave us attention once a week—on Sunday—*if* the Bears won. He was stern and unapproachable. The father I grew up with never cooked a meal, made a bed, did laundry, emptied the dishwasher, or went grocery shopping. Ever.

The father I moved in with did all of that. He ran and emptied the dishwasher, did his laundry, and parked his car on the street so that I could have the allotted space in the alley. I awoke late one Sunday, Pancake Day, and he had the table set for me with a half-grapefruit. When I came downstairs, he made me fresh pancakes.

It was actually the best living arrangement I ever had. Never—in college, in marriage, or living alone with my adult children—had I ever been treated with such care and respect. He trusted my instincts and accepted that I needed to go to Los Angeles, even if he didn't understand it.

One night I went into the living room to close and lock the windows. He was watching television, lying on the couch in his usual position with his head on a pillow and his body stretched toward the set. No one ever alternated the cushions, so there was a permanent imprint of him in the couch.

"This is my favorite show," he said as I closed the windows behind him.

I looked at the TV, fascinated that he watched anything other than sports, news, or stock reports and that he had a favorite show. "Is this *Star Trek: The Next Generation*?" I asked.

"Yes, I love this show," he answered as I sat on the chair next to him. "It's on every day at seven p.m. and all night on Friday." It was Friday.

Pause.

"I like Worf, and I like Data. I love what comes out of his mouth."

We watched for a while. At the commercial break, I spoke. "I want to ask you a question, not as a person wanting to clean," I gave the disclaimer, so he wouldn't think I was pushy, like Mother, "but as a writer." I continued, "I have to know. Why eight hats?"

"Are there eight?" he asked, his eyes never leaving the TV.

"Yes, two floppy and six baseball caps. Do you wear them all?"

"Yes."

Another pause. Dad continued to stare at the TV set.

"I don't particularly wear one more than the other," he finally said.

"What determines why you wear a hat?"

"Well, I'm not going to wear the hat I wore yesterday or the day before, and by the third day I forget."

Pause.

"I wear hats for the sun." Did I mention he was bald? "On hot days I wear a floppy one so I can fold it up and put it in my pocket when I'm in the shade. That way I don't get too hot."

I'd seen him do that very thing the day before while he was riding his bike. I was walking to the park to attend a Fourth of July picnic, and he generously offered to store the beer and guacamole I was bringing in his tricycle basket and escort me there. Mr. Magoo rode a big, adult-size women's three-wheeled bicycle around town. He bought it in his mid-fifties as a gift for Mother.

"What do I want with such a thing? You like it? You ride it," Mother told him.

Years later he confessed that he'd really bought it for himself. He rode it on the sidewalk. It took up the entire sidewalk, but he didn't care. He let everyone else worry about getting out of his way.

It's against the law to ride a bike on the sidewalks in the Lakeview area. There were signs written on the pavement of every street corner in my father's neighborhood telling you so, put there, no doubt, because of pedestrians complaining about my father. Again, he didn't care. "Forget them. I'm not riding in the street." Growing up not knowing how to ride a bike, he loved that thing.

On the way to the park that day, I saw him take off the hat and fold it into his pocket when a building shaded us. Then he put it back on when he was in the sun again, off seconds later when shaded—then on, then off, et cetera, but I didn't ask why at the time. I was too busy watching the faces of the people who were watching him riding a large tricycle on the sidewalk of Lake Shore Drive while putting on and taking off his Gilligan hat.

"So not wearing the same hat, is that like not wearing the same outfit?" I asked him during the next commercial break.

"No."

Pause.

"The hat will get insulted if I don't wear it once in a while."

Pause.

He didn't smile so I asked, "Are you serious?"

"Quite."

Pause.

"Not insulted, left out," he continued.

Pause.

"I didn't know I had eight hats. I knew I had a lot."

My father spoke with many pauses, and in a fast-paced world, it was no wonder that family members never understood him. I think it was because they didn't know to sit still and wait through the pauses.

We were still watching the same episode. "I've seen this one, but I can't remember what happens."

"So it's all new again," I said in jest, but remembered I'd said that when Mother had Alzheimer's—but this was different.

His forgetfulness was nothing like Alzheimer's.

The episode ended, and I decided not to watch the next. I went upstairs. The master bed and bath were my room now, and thanks to The Contractor, beautifully remodeled. My father had moved into my old room when I got married and stayed there even after Mother died.

As I closed my eyes to welcome sleep, I realized how lucky I was. There was already a man in my life who loved me unconditionally.

Law Of Attraction

C arl Jung said, "What you resist persists." Along the same line of thinking, the principle behind the Law of Attraction states that what you focus on, manifests. By that logic, if you are focusing on what you do not want, the universe will respond with more of what you do not want.

I did not contemplate those theories during the two months I lived with my father in the summer of 2002. Those days were mostly filled with unpacking and finishing up summer classes. I loved being back in the city. I took out my old ten-speed racing bike, and as I rode along the lakefront, I couldn't wipe the smile from my face if I wanted to. I was in sweet home Chicago.

Living in the city made it possible to hang out with my fellow fiction-writing classmates. One evening, as we walked through a local street fair, we came upon a vintage car on display. I excused myself and went to take a closer look. I circled the vehicle, taking in every detail. Two men standing off to the side were also interested in the car. One of them spoke to me, "She's a beauty, isn't she?"

I continued circling as I answered, "1957 Chevy, two-tone, seafoam green—my absolute favorite. Although I wouldn't kick a "65 red-and-white Corvette outta my driveway."

He smiled and walked closer to me. "You like vintage cars?"

"Love," I responded, not looking at him.

"Do you have any?"

I laughed, "Not yet. I plan to start my collection with an old Beetle bug. But living in Chicago with this weather, it's probably not a good idea."

"You live in the city?"

"I do," I was happy to reply.

"My brother and I live in Indiana," he said, and the man standing with him nodded before wandering away, "I'm—"

I knew Roxy would call him Indiana Boy, so that's what I heard. He was five foot ten, had short brown hair, brown eyes, and a wholesome face like the Beaver, sans freckles. He looked very trustworthy.

"Judi."

"You here alone, Judi?"

He was clearly interested in me. Since every relationship I'd started since the divorce had an average lifespan of six weeks, and I was only in Chicago for another six weeks, I figured it was a sign.

"I'm here with friends," I said and looked over to where I had left my school chums. Several of them were staring at me, and I grew self-conscious.

"Do you think they'd mind if you and I talked for a while? How about a corn dog, my treat?"

"I'm sorry. I don't feel comfortable ditching them." I still felt awkward in those situations, so I dug into my purse to get out one of the business cards I had made for my LA trip. The cards were double-sided. One side said "writer" with a caricature of me holding a pad of paper and pen. The other side had my headshot and said "actress." "Let me leave you with my card," I said, rehearsing the role of LA Screenwriter.

As I walked away, he said, "I'll call you."

My classmates heard, and as we started walking away one of the girls leaned in and asked, "Did you just pick up a guy at a fair?"

I shook it off like I hadn't. *But oh my God, I had.* Roxy would be proud.

He called the next day. I liked that. No games. He asked

me to have dinner with him on Saturday night. He said he came into the city often. He loved Chicago, and there was even a reggae club in my neighborhood that he attended regularly, so he was very familiar with my area. He was thirty-eight years old, never married, no kids, and worked in the family business that he now owned with his cousin: a funeral home.

"A funeral director?" I asked.

"Yes."

I had to be careful. I couldn't judge Indiana Boy for taking over the family business; after all, I was a forty-two-year-old woman living with her father. I didn't ask him any more questions, though several were in my head: *Have you been around dead people all your life? Do you do the embalming? Is it spooky?* I didn't know how I felt about dating a funeral director, so I asked him how he felt about being one.

"The baby boomers will be dying soon. It's going to be very lucrative," he replied, and I knew that must have been the sales pitch his father used to get him interested in the business. I didn't have the heart to tell him that he was a baby boomer, albeit on the young side.

He called again during that week before our date, but I let it go to voicemail. I called him thirty minutes later. "I'm sorry, I was watching my favorite show, and I don't allow anyone or anything to interrupt it."

"That's okay," he responded. "I appreciate you calling me back. What were you watching? What's this favorite show?"

"Sex and the City."

"Learn anything?" he asked.

His words hung in the air like a cloud of bug repellant. I didn't know how to respond. What did he mean? *Learn anything?* Was he one of those sex perverts Mother warned me to avoid?

"It's always the quiet ones, Judala," she used to say, and I knew now what she meant.

He was a stranger. We had no friends in common. He wasn't vouched-for, and he wasn't Jewish, so Jewish geography wouldn't apply. As my mind raced with all the reasons why a per-

JUDI LEE GOSHEN

son would respond like that, I decided not to take a chance. "Listen, I don't think dinner is a good-"

He cut me off. "It was a joke, a bad joke, yes, but a joke. Please don't cancel dinner. Get to know me. I'm a great guy."

"A great guy with a bad sense of humor?" I asked, because I fancied myself a quasi-expert on funny and decided it was unfair to think that everyone else was too. I decided to give dinner a chance. We were going to meet at a restaurant in the Gold Coast, one of Chicago's nicest neighborhoods. I'd be safe.

We didn't go to one of the higher-end restaurants. We met at Gino's Pizzeria on Rush Street, the very same location where I had gone on dates as a teenager. Back then we used to carve our initials on the tabletops: *John loves Judi*; a year later, *Judi + Kevin 4-Ever*. Being out on a summer night with a new guy in my old haunt made me feel like that schoolgirl again.

After dinner, we walked to Oak Street Beach and sat on the sand. It was mid-July. I hoped he wouldn't put his arm around me or hold my hand. Just because it was a romantic setting didn't mean we were ready for that.

We watched the waves crash to the shore in silence, and then I spoke: "Mesmerizing, isn't it?"

"Yes," he agreed as we both continued to stare at the water.

"The waves crash in hard and then meekly retreat, followed by another and another—they don't let up, they just continue coming."

"Always nice to continue coming," he said.

I heard a record scratch in my ear, the sound of a double take. *What?* I looked over at his smirking face. "Is that your idea of a joke?" I asked.

He smiled that innocent smile that told me he didn't know any better. "Sorry, I guess that wasn't funny."

I certainly did not have an overly sophisticated sense of humor, and I was not above a good fart joke. But there's a vast difference between Mel Brooks and Beavis & Butthead. "Huh huh huh, you said *coming*."

Then it dawned on me. Indiana Boy's sense of humor had

not evolved since junior high. But I could fix that. After all, the rest of him seemed nice and normal.

The following week, we went for a bike ride. We rode from my house—my dad's house—to Navy Pier. We laughed and talked while we rode. I showed him all the places along the lake that had special meaning to me.

After the ride, we locked up our bikes and walked into Wrigleyville. We stopped in an ice-cream parlor, got two large cones, and ate them on the steps of our townhouse complex. My father came home carrying Jewel grocery bags and walked right by us without stopping. "You're destroying all the good you did with the bike," he said as he walked past, clearly not interested in meeting Indiana Boy.

"Oh, Daddy," I giggled as I licked my ice cream.

"That was your dad?" He asked.

"He's a man of few words," I told him so he wouldn't take it personally.

Indiana Boy's brother was single, and we fixed him up with Roxy during the Air and Water Show. We watched the jets flying in formation from their friend's high-rise apartment.

Afterward, we went to Ranalli's on Lincoln Avenue for pizza and beer. Roxy knew the owner, and he graciously comped our entire check. Indiana Boy and his brother thanked the waitress and then left the table without leaving her a tip. Having both been servers, Roxy and I were horrified. She looked at me with big questioning eyes. I nodded back, and she understood, "I'm going to the ladies' room, I'll meet you guys on the street," I said as Roxy led them out of the restaurant. I then found the waitress and slipped her some money.

It's hard to stump Roxy, but they had. "I'm fucking done with these Hoosiers," she whispered to me.

"They're small-town. They probably don't think you tip the owner."

"It wasn't the owner who served us."

"You're right. Just hang out a bit more. Please."

"Fine."

We walked over to Lincoln Park by the zoo and farm. Indiana Boy began to lag, and I stayed back with him. I noticed him gasping. "Are you alright?"

"Yes, sort of. I'm having a panic attack. I don't know why I get them. It's so random. Luckily, it's a mild one."

I didn't know what a panic attack entailed, but I did have a tachycardia issue. Sporadically, my heart would race for no apparent reason, and when an event occurred, I would need to sit and wait for it to pass. Episodes could last anywhere from thirty minutes to several hours. I once had one that lasted twelve hours. I took his hand to show my support, and we strolled along slowly until he felt better.

"How sweet," Roxy commented when she turned around and saw us holding hands. It didn't sound like she meant it, but it *was* sweet.

Because I lived with my father, I never asked Indiana Boy into my home. Our dates always ended outside on my doorstep. It was very old-fashioned and innocent. *Who knows, maybe there is a future with him,* my overblown imagination wondered.

The following Friday, I drove out to his place in Indiana. We walked around the water near his house. He was very proud of it, but it paled in comparison to my beautiful, ocean-like Lake Michigan. He put his arm around my shoulder to keep me warm from the night air.

He took me to his house, a very small two-bedroom bungalow. I was not impressed until he said, "I bought this when I was twenty-one, then got a roommate who paid me rent."

We spoke on the phone a lot since he lived and worked in Indiana. I would lay on my bed, wrapping the cord of my old princess phone around my finger as we talked into the night. Occasionally he would let a childish pun slip, and I'd correct him. One night, he dropped the hint that every four weeks he took one week off; "The perk of owning a business with your cousin." We still didn't discuss the details of what he did at the funeral home. I didn't want to know, but I figured he brought it up because he was willing to drive with me across the country to LA.

"Do you want to come with me?" I asked before I had time to consider what I was asking. We hadn't been intimate. We hadn't even had "the talk" yet. But he didn't make a joke out of the fact that I asked him to "come." *Progress!*

He responded immediately to my question. "Yes, I'd love to. Let me check schedules, and I'll get back to you."

"Great!" I responded. "My original plan was to drive alone to San Francisco. I'd love the company."

"Why only to San Francisco?"

"I'm meeting my friend, Victoria, there. She and her husband live in New York but will be in San Francisco then. Victoria and I planned to drive down the coast together. You can fly home the same day her husband goes back to New York. Sound good?"

"We could go to Napa first," he suggested.

"I've always wanted to do that, yes! How fun." *And romantic,* I thought as we hung up the phone.

He called a few days later. "We haven't discussed the sleeping logistics," he said, and I was so happy he wanted to have "the talk."

"Nobody has 'the talk,'" Roxy told me over and over, but she was wrong. Indiana Boy was a responsible, clean-cut, small-town boy.

"Yes, we should," I affirmed, happy that we were on the phone so he couldn't see that I was blushing.

"Are you thinking we might sleep together?" What a perfect gentleman, a man who understood the importance of health and safety.

"That's a possibility," I said coyly.

"We need to talk first."

"Okay, well, I'm pretty simple. One guy in the last twenty-two years." It wasn't a real lie. Roxy said Boss Man didn't count. "I was tested when we first split and then again six months after. I'm good."

"Well, I've had chlamydia before."

Wow! Right off the bat. Take a breath. Okay, not so bad, I thought to myself, *it's curable.*

"Twice."

"Twice?"

"Yes, and gonorrhea."

Oh, my God. That's a little more threatening.

"Twice."

"Twice? How? How twice with two different STDs?" but as I asked the question, I knew the answer.

"Don't like condoms," he said.

Or finding out with whom you're sleeping. I recalled the clubbing he said he did. My imagination played a pornographic montage of him having casual sex in bathroom stalls, back rooms, his car, dark alleys, and nearby trashy apartments.

I tried to stop the images in my head and wrap my brain around the possibility that he might be ready to leave his sordid past behind. Penicillin cured those diseases; he got a do-over.

Then he lobbed over strike three. "Now all I have is genital herpes."

Genital herpes? Genital herpes? What did I fear worse than death? *Oh yes, genital herpes!*

If we weren't on the phone, he would have seen my eyes pop open, and my jaw drop to my waist. My head was spinning, and my inner voice screamed like the Robot on *Lost in Space. Danger, Danger, Will Robinson!*

"I'm sorry. How did that happen?"

He told me about a sketchy girl and how he thought he was safe by just getting a blowjob.

"I'm really glad you told me but—"

"I know," he said, making it easier for me to break up with him—which I did.

I was stunned but grateful he'd told me long before anything physical started between us. I wasn't in love with him. There was no reason to try to make it work. I was leaving for LA. It was all too much for me to take in, and I needed a Roxy talk. Now!

It would be over a decade before I could say to an iPhone, "Call Roxy." So I dialed her number as quickly as possible on my rotary relic, which was slower than shit.

"Fort Knox Security," she replied when she heard my news.

"I'm not going to sleep with him! Are you fucking nuts?!"

"I'm just sayin'.' He didn't have to tell you."

"Yes. Yes, he did."

"Exactly, he's a good guy."

There was a pause. I was thinking.

"Fort Knox Security," she said again as if she thought I would go there.

"What does that mean?" I finally asked.

"Two condoms."

I laughed. Roxy's response reminded me of an old Rodney Dangerfield joke: "She was so ugly that she was known as a two-bagger: one bag over your head in case the one over hers breaks."

Over the next few days, I wondered if I'd done the right thing in breaking it off. When I was at my dermatologist appointment, I casually brought it up. "Is it possible to be with a man that has genital herpes and not get it?"

"Of course, if you use a condom," she responded, but before I could feel better she added, "I seem to treat women that have it on their rear ends." *I knew it!* Just like my twenty-four-year-old agent told me when I was getting a divorce, it's *transmitted by the slightest contact,* obviously from snuggling. I was right not to be intimate with him.

If what you resist persists, it made sense that I was facing my biggest fear—not wanting it created more of the not wanting it. I manifested genital herpes in my mind, but at least it didn't manifest on my body. I needed to think positive thoughts. I needed to think about what I wanted. I wanted a relationship, but not a relationship-relationship. I wanted a clean, healthy man who didn't want to get married and have children, but who wanted to be in a monogamous non-relationship for the foreseeable future.

"Good luck with that," Roxy said sarcastically.

"If I could manifest my biggest fear, I think I can manifest my deepest desire."

After Indiana Boy's news set in, I felt terrible that I reacted harshly. Clearly, we weren't going to be lovers, but why had I cut him out of my life as a friend? I always believed that people showed up in your life when you needed them. Maybe he showed up in my life to drive across the country with me. Why was I letting that rational, conventional side that I'd fought against my whole life make the decision? I grew up on movies like *Sweet November*—the story of a terminally ill woman who moved a new man into her bohemian apartment on the first of every month to help the guy learn to relax—and *I Love You, Alice B. Toklas*—a young lawyer falls for a hippy chick and runs out on his wedding. I was a hippy at heart. I didn't believe that the people in your life needed to stay in your life. We met. We liked each other. We could hang; go to Napa. My best friend, Mitch, took me to visit a college in Miami, Florida when I was eighteen. We shared a hotel room but didn't sleep together. Was the situation with Indiana Boy any different?

I called him and asked if he wanted to be travel companions.

"Separate rooms?" he asked.

Yes, please.

Both my children were attending colleges in Chicago, and mom was the one loading up the car and going off to school.

The Semester in LA was a six-week program. I told family and friends that I would be home for Thanksgiving to either pack or unpack.

Roxy, never one for sentiment, chose her parting words carefully: "Fort. Knox. Security."

I got to Indiana around lunchtime, and Indiana Boy and I made our way to Iowa City, where his sister lived with her husband. The plan was to say a quick hello. However, the quick hello turned into "let me show you the house," which turned into "my husband will be home soon, we want to take you to dinner," which turned into an evening with delicious wine and a lingering dinner, which turned into "just sleep in our guest room and leave in the morning."

All in all, I enjoyed myself. They were part of the literati at the University of Iowa. They rented out their cool attic space to a visiting writer every term. Since I didn't believe in accidents, I thought maybe I would come back and study writing there one day.

Everything was going well until his sister led us to the guest room, gave us towels, and shut the door, leaving us alone with one queen-size bed. We stood, staring at each other across said bed. He obviously hadn't told them we weren't a couple. Finally, he broke the silence. "I can sleep on the floor."

Leprosy was an incurable disease in the Middle Ages that caused parts of the body to rot and fall off. It was thought to be highly contagious, and people with the disease were rounded up and quarantined into colonies. I felt bad. Had I made him feel like a leper?

My empathy got the better of me, and I said, "No, that's silly. We can share the bed." After all, he wasn't contagious if we didn't have physical contact. I excused myself and went to wash up for bed.

When I came back into the room, he was under the covers on the right side of the bed, with his back turned away from the door and me. I crawled into bed and faced his back. At first, it felt awkward to be in bed with a new man, but since it was strictly platonic, it lacked that pressure to perform.

As I relaxed and tried to settle into sleep, my hormones, having a mind and independent will of their own, began stirring: *There's a man next to you.* I tried to reason with my hormones and explain to them how contagious herpes was, but they had zeroed in on his sexual prowess and didn't care. *Come on,* they called to me; *it's been three years since we've had sex.*

My entire body was tingling with the anticipated touch of a sexual partner, and I was helpless in suppressing the hormonal desire. I still had the three-pack of condoms Roxy and I bought when I was dating Transition Guy. I didn't leave them at home for fear they could be found by my dad or the cleaning lady. *Where did I pack them?* I wondered. *In the suitcase buried in the trunk of my car, or my overnight bag at the foot of the bed?*

I didn't know which part of me was contemplating the condoms, but I needed the rational side to take control. I turned my back to Indiana Boy, cuddled myself into the fetal position, and forced myself to think about my sexual future. I needed to stay healthy. I was waiting for the non-relationship relationship guy, and when I found him, I wanted to be able to give myself freely.

The next morning, we awoke, had breakfast, and got on the road by ten a.m. We took turns driving and picking music. I vetoed reggae music, and he refused to let me play the sound-track from *Rent.* At first that made me mad, not being able to pass the time singing along to my favorite car music, but when we stopped for gas, he was the one who checked the engine and cleaned the windshield. It was a fair trade. That night at a motel, he asked the clerk for two rooms.

"One," I corrected him.

He was surprised. "Are you sure?"

"Listen, we shared a bed last night. I think one room with two beds is fine." I didn't know if that was frugal Judi proposing an amendment to the plan or my hormones sneaking in their two cents, but from then on, we shared one room with two beds.

That night, as I tried to leave a wake-up call for six a.m., he stopped me. "Why don't we just sleep until we wake up, have breakfast, and then start out?"

Car trips with my family growing up were regimented, my parents woke us up so early our eyes hurt, and you had break-fast according to Dad's rule, "One hundred miles down the road." Indiana Boy's loosey-goosey style was a whole new way of travel-ing, but I was game to try it. I took a swim in the hotel pool, and we turned in early.

The following night we were even more comfortable with each other and lay in our separate beds facing each other. We talked and giggled like two girls at a sleepover. I don't remember the benign conversation that preceded the sex talk, but some-how we got on the subject of oral sex. He described what his previous girlfriend called "climbing the wall."

"It was her favorite position. I would lie on the bed with my head at the headboard, and she would straddle me. I would go down on her as she stretched her arms up along the wall to steady herself." I can't remember if he added, or I imagined, "While I gently pinched her nipples."

I didn't know my vagina had ears, but that's the part of my body that heard the story. I could barely eke out my response: "Goodnight." And I turned away from him for emphasis. No more talking, and I prayed sleep would find me.

That morning, I found brochures for Napa in the lobby. As he drove, I scoured them and found the perfect place: a cabin-like suite with a fireplace, Jacuzzi tub, and two large beds. It was the perfect room because it lent itself to two different scenarios: romantic and platonic. I hadn't made up my mind as to which I would choose. I made the reservation from my flip phone.

When we got to the outskirts of San Francisco and saw the Golden Gate Bridge, tears of joy came to my eyes. "I feel like I'm finally on the right coast."

We dropped off our bags that afternoon at the hotel in Napa and went to a few vineyards.

Feeling a bit tipsy later that day, we started holding hands as we walked, just like we had in Lincoln Park when it had all seemed so innocent and promising. It felt like we were a couple even though I was fully aware that it was a sham. An elderly woman on a bench commented as we walked toward her, "You two look so good together."

He made a reservation for a nice dinner, and shortly after ordering, our wine poured, he looked at me. "We have to go. Now."

"Why?"

"I'm having an anxiety attack." He stood up like I was supposed to follow immediately.

"People needed to be notified and paid," I pointed out.

He stared blankly at me. "I'll be outside."

I found the waitress and explained we wouldn't be staying.

"Your food's almost ready."

"Okay, could you bag it up along with the rest of the wine?"

I watched TV from my own bed that night. I ate my dinner and drank my wine, grateful that I was not in the least attracted to the man cowering under the covers.

The next night, we met my friends at a hotel in San Francisco. That night at a downtown restaurant, Indiana Boy's seventh-grade sense of humor did not go over well with Victoria and Michael. If I prided myself on knowing funny, Victoria and Michael were the experts on funny. Over dinner, Victoria explained that she was so busy with work that she hadn't been able to cook a decent meal in ages. Michael added, "Yeah, we eat out a lot."

To which Indiana Boy chimed in, "Eating out is great. But what do you do for dinner?"

His words silenced the conversation. Finally, Victoria tactfully changed the subject, but Michael shot me a raised eyebrow across the table. I nodded in agreement, feeling vindicated that it wasn't just me.

As dinner ended and we talked over the remnants of our meals, my tachycardia acted up, causing my heart to race up to 140 beats per minute. When Indiana Boy saw the vein in my neck rapidly throb, he took me back to the hotel immediately. As I said, it's not a serious condition, so no one had ever been concerned before, but it still felt nice that he was so considerate.

We got back to the hotel, and he ordered a movie. Then he spooned me on my bed, on top of the covers, in our clothes. I felt his hand and concern across my clavicle, monitoring the beats. It was a kindness I had never experienced from anyone. Yes, Mother was a worrier, but from a distance, not up close and personal.

By the time the movie was over, my heart rate had resumed its normal rhythm. We were still in my bed, neither of us wanting to break the connection. I turned my head toward him, and we were kissing. His hands found their way to all the right places on my body, and finally, I surrendered to my hormones. They were stronger than me.

"Let me see it," I demanded softly. Indiana Boy pulled down his jeans, revealing a beautiful penis. It was exactly what I remembered they looked like, only slightly larger. It was the perfect size and shape. *It figures!* "I want it. I want you."

He looked hard and long into my insisting eyes. "No." He then pulled up his pants to keep me safe from myself and began to pleasure me manually. It didn't take very long, and I felt minimal guilt over not reciprocating.

The following morning, just before Indiana Boy and Michael got on the shuttle bus to the airport, Michael pulled me to the side. "Judi, the guy told me last night he wants kids."

I smiled, "I know, Mike. He was just my Sweet November."

I said goodbye to a confused Michael and sent Indiana Boy back to Indiana. Then Victoria, my three-pack of condoms, and I started off for Los Angeles.

Fornicationally Challenged

"**I**'d like to go to LA for pilot season. See if I can get cast in a sitcom," twenty-something Judi told Steve during the early years of our marriage.

"Who's gonna watch the kids?"

I asked Mother if she'd help Steve, to which she replied, "What's wrong with you? What kind of mother does such a thing?"

Steve added, "I'm not moving if you get a job. So, basically, you'll be leaving me and the kids."

Without Mother and Steve telling me what I could and couldn't be, do, and have, the possibilities were endless. And, FYI, Disneyland is not the happiest place on earth. The CBS Studio Lot in Studio City, California is the happiest place on earth! I loved it there. Everyone, from the security guards to the maintenance workers, loved it there. Even the actor Eric Roberts, driving by in his BMW convertible while checking out my ass, loved it there.

I knew LA was the place where my dreams would come true. One day television credits would roll; Carsey-Werner-Mandabach and me, Judi Lee.

I stopped telling people I was an actress. When I said I was a writer, I saw respect in their eyes that I never got from acting. Besides, actors are to LA what cockroaches are to New York.

I went to classes by day and was assigned covers to write at night. A cover is a short synopsis of a script. Being able to write a good cover is a very useful skill because most LA producers do not read full scripts.

On the weekends, I took in the sights. I wanted to see all the places I'd heard about—Venice Beach, Beverly Hills, the Hollywood Hills, Laurel Canyon, Mulholland Drive, Brentwood, Bel Air, the Palisades, the Hollywood sign, and Canter's Deli—and I wanted to be driving on Santa Monica Boulevard while Sheryl Crow sang "Santa Monica Boulevard" on the radio. And I absolutely loved Venice Beach, Beverly Hills, the Hollywood Hills, Laurel Canyon, Mulholland Drive, Brentwood, Bel Air, the Palisades, the Hollywood sign, and Canter's Deli. And I drove on Santa Monica Boulevard while Sheryl Crow sang "Santa Monica Boulevard" on the radio. I shopped at the Beverly Center and bought expensive designer sunglasses; walked up and down Rodeo Drive; got my hair cut and colored in one of the salons frequented by celebrities; and had drinks at the Four Seasons among the visiting East Coast players.

But soon those pesky hormones caught up with me and began waking me up in the middle of the night, reminding me: *you haven't had sex in three years, you haven't had sex in three years, you haven't had sex in three years!*

"The not having sex is perpetuating the not having sex. You need to have a mindless fuck," Roxy bluntly stated over the phone.

"I can't do that."

"Fine, keep on doing what you're doing, and you'll keep getting what you're getting—a whole lot of nothing."

She had a point, but a one-night stand? That meant sex with a stranger. Strangers had diseases. I needed the safety of really knowing someone, like a friend. And as synchronicity would have it, an old friend was visiting LA.

"Roxy! The guy I did that play with is in town!"

"Edgar Winter? Hal-a-fuckin-lu-ya!"

As most romance tales go, our relationship began with my annoyance of him when we first met six years ago. We portrayed lovers in a play I was doing in a suburb near the home I shared with my husband and kids. He was twenty-eight, nine years younger. He was a very talented and funny actor, but immature and not good-looking—think of an albino Philip Seymour Hoffman. His skin was so pale it was almost translucent, and the long, thinning, white-blonde hair that hit his shoulders was an interesting balance to the bald spot on the back of his scalp. Hence the reason Roxy called him Edgar Winter. (A popular rock star from the '70s with pale skin and long white hair. Google him. I'll wait.) As a mature professional working actor, I couldn't imagine how I would get through a love scene with him.

It was the spring of '96. I had a successful career as a commercial actress, kids I carpooled, a house with many chores, and Mother was entering the third stage of Alzheimer's disease, as was my mother-in-law. Still, I needed to do something for myself. But adding one more to-do to the already strained to-do list proved to be extremely stressful, especially since I simultaneously booked a trade show, which included memorizing fifteen pages for live performances occurring every hour at McCormick Place.

At six a.m., I'd travel downtown and work the trade show; at five p.m. I'd go straight to the theatre to rehearse until eleven p.m. Then I'd get up the next morning and do it all over again.

I was overworked and overtired, and both my day and night directors complained that I was not performing at my best.

Having to depend on Steve to help with the kids always brought out the worst in him, making him more thoughtless and abusive than usual.

"Is there anything I can help you with?" EW asked one night.

"Can you rehearse the trade show lines with me?"

"Of course. Happy to."

We made plans to meet at my house the next afternoon. He was so helpful. He was kind and understanding when he didn't need to be, considering I judged him so harshly when we met. He even ate the raw-food lunch I prepared for us.

"Wow, this is delicious."

I was used to hearing, "This tastes like crap." Praise was a welcome change.

EW quickly became a friend and confidant, the only one in my life who knew the pressure I was under. Slowly but surely, the kissing scenes became the parts in the play I looked forward to the most.

One night, our kiss ignited that part of my brain that told my body to get ready for sex. In other words, I got wet—while fifty pairs of eyes watched!

Roxy was in the audience that night and called my house the next morning. "What the fuck did I witness?" Others may have believed I was a good actress, but Roxy knew better.

"I'm totally having an affair with him."

"What?"

"In my head."

"Well, be careful; that's a lot harder on you and much worse on the spouse."

I wasn't worried about it. The play was ending in two days. "It'll all be behind me soon."

I was wrong. After the play ended, it was difficult to put it behind me. I missed EW. I called him, and we met for lunch.

"Do you think we could be friends?"

"That's all we can be," he replied. I didn't know how to respond, because I knew I wanted more from him, so I stayed quiet. "As your friend, can I ask you a favor?" he continued.

"Sure." I thought he was going to ask me to introduce him to my agent.

"Could you take your breasts off the table? It's a bit distracting."

I looked down. I had been leaning over the table, unaware

that my breasts were resting there. I sat back, embarrassed. "As you wish."

He smiled mischievously.

The next time my husband made plans to go out with the guys on a Friday night, I met EW at the local movie theatre to see *Michael*. After the movie, I sat in his car, lingering long after it was time to go.

"Are you waiting for me to kiss you?" Usually, I loved his bluntness.

"I don't know what I want."

"I can't. I'd love to, but I can't kiss you. It's like the song says: 'a taste of love is worse than none at all.'"

Love.

I knew better than to break up a family for a struggling younger man, but I still wanted, needed to see him. The following week my husband and son went to a wrestling match, so I made dinner plans with him.

"We're saying goodbye again, aren't we?" he asked over hummus at Reba's in Andersonville.

"Yes. It's probably best."

"I get it."

Afterward, we went bowling. Even without my ball and shoes, I won every game. He would then trash-talk me into playing another and another and another until I realized he really was an awful bowler. It wasn't an act.

"You keep saying you're going to beat me."

"And you keep buying it." He smiled.

"Why would you purposely humiliate yourself over and—" Then I knew. EW didn't want the night to end. He had used my competitive nature to prolong the evening and keep me out way too late.

I knew my husband would be asleep, so I decided I would stay downstairs as if I'd been there all night. But when I stepped into the house from the garage, I saw my husband's face over the pony wall watching television. He turned to me and asked coolly, "Where've you been until three in the morning?"

My sixteen-year-old son's faced popped up and looked at me, waiting for my answer too.

"Bowling," I said as nonchalantly as possible. My son and I were very competitive bowlers, so I figured he'd understand. Instead, he looked at me with a disappointment that told me just how far I had fallen off the pedestal.

"Bowling until three in the morning?" his father asked.

I answered as my son went up to bed. "Yes," I said, hanging up my coat. "Time just got away from me."

I wasn't concerned about my husband's forgiveness. I was upset that he'd let our son wait up with him. A more considerate man would have made sure his son didn't witness his mother's entrance of shame, but a more considerate mother would not have been out with another man.

Six years later, I was 2400 miles from my children, divorced, and hormonally desperate. I could take Roxy's advice. I could have a "mindless fuck," because EW was the perfect sexual candidate. He was a good friend, I felt safe with him, and our friendship was strong enough to withstand any awkwardness we might feel afterward. When we said goodbye all those years ago, he said, "I'll always love you." Who better to pop my born-again, virginal cherry?

During the two weeks, he was in LA for work; we saw a lot of each other. We had dinners, shared wine, saw movies, and every night ended with a kiss—but nothing more.

They say a woman always knows the night she'll have sex. I knew that EW and I were going to have sex on Wednesday, his last night in town.

I cleaned my apartment, shaved my legs, and he took me to a karaoke bar where he introduced me to his LA friends. It felt good walking in on his arm like he was showing me off.

He sang "Ballroom Blitz," and the crowd went crazy. I got drunk and sang Wynonna Judd lyrics to him:

I shivered once; you broke into my soul;
The damage is done now,

I'm outta control.
How did you get to me?

I'm not a good singer by any stretch of the imagination, but I belted it out with feeling, and he got the message.

We were barely inside my studio apartment when he pulled me close, kissed me, and slid my sweater off my shoulders so that it fell to the floor. I'd seen enough movies to know what that meant. *We're gonna have sex!*

Then I made a fatal mistake. I spoke: "Look, this doesn't have to be anything more than what it is."

I'd like to say I said that to be straight with him so as not to lead him on, but I was just being theatrical, like bad soap opera acting, raising the stakes of the scene to make it more dramatic. Still, I was stunned by his response.

"I'm not staying." That's what he said, but he kissed me again passionately and pulled me down to the floor and got on top of me.

Wanting to be more comfortable, I got up and pulled down my Murphy bed.

"I'm not getting in there," he said as though I was way out of line.

I thought he was joking. "What? We spent two months together in bed."

"We were in a play," he answered, and I didn't know what to say. "What is it that you want?" he continued.

Oh my God, is he really making me say the words? Fine, I'm a grown woman. "I want us to have... You know..." And I pointed to the bed.

"Sex? Is that all you want?"

Apparently, he'd needed confirmation. "Yes?" *There, I said it.* I was a grown-up, sexual woman who had just asked for what she wanted, what she so desperately needed. I was very proud of myself, *and* I was about to have sex!

"Well, I can't be casual. Not with you."

We stood, staring into each other's eyes. It felt like we were playing a game of chicken. Did EW want me to tell him it was going to mean something? An eternity of seconds passed. He then turned and left without another word.

I stood there in shock. Just stood there. I thought for sure he'd do the comeback, like in all those romantic comedies where the guy comes running back in and sweeps the woman off her feet. So I stood there. Waiting.

He didn't come back. I heard his car start and then the fading sound of the engine as he drove away.

I stood there quietly, my senses so keen that I swear I heard a disappointed moan from the still unused three-pack of condoms in my underwear drawer.

I was still standing in that spot when I called Roxy. "What the hell happened? He was here. He was peeling off my clothes. What changed?"

"He cares about you, Judi."

"So wouldn't that make him a sure thing? Tell me, when did men start turning down sex? Or do they just turn down sex with me?"

I could hear her take a drag from a cigarette. She was contemplating my question, and I knew to wait for the exhale. "You're right," she finally said. "It is you. You are fornicationally challenged." And we laughed. She loved making up words.

"What does that mean?"

Through her laughter, she added, "You can't even get laid by a sure thing."

"Hey, I could get laid if that's all I wanted." And I reminded her of what I wanted. I wanted a relationship, not a relationship-relationship, but a relationship. I wanted a good man with character and integrity, someone I could trust, laugh with, and have fun. I wanted love without necessarily being *in love*, exclusivity but not seriousness. I didn't want to get married and have more kids, but he had to be someone my kids would like.

"Then why are you spending so much time in the baby pool?"

"Are you implying that I date younger men?" The age

differences never felt like an issue. I never considered it.

"Do the math."

I did the math. Transition Guy was almost five years younger, big deal. Boss Man was eight years younger, and EW was nine years younger. She was right. I was dating younger men, though it wasn't intentional. Those were the men who pursued me.

At the time, many celebrity women were dating younger men, so I went for the joke. "Look at me, I'm so hip!"

"It's a self-preservation thing," she analyzed. "It makes you feel safe."

She might have been a trained therapist, but I had taken enough psychology classes in my recent college experience to know what she meant. Freud believed that two major instincts influence a person's life: self-preservation and sex. I had the knowledge to intellectually argue my point.

Instead, I said, "Fuck you."

And of course, we laughed.

However, her comments haunted me all night. There definitely was an age difference theme that had dominated my dating life thus far. Why? I didn't know, but I promised Roxy, and myself, that I would stop dating younger men.

The following night at a networking meeting, I met someone. Someone even younger.

Ashton: Part 1

I saw him sitting at the other end of the table.

It was the week after completing the Semester in LA program. I had already decided to stay on in LA, and I was at a weekly networking meeting I'd been invited to by one of the guest lecturers. There was this guy at the end of the table that kept pulling my attention, and I didn't know why. He wasn't my type. He had wavy light red hair and fair skin, but I found myself drawn to him. Most times when I looked at him, he was already looking at me.

The meeting was at the IHOP on Sunset Boulevard in Hollywood. The group had the entire back room, and there must have been about forty or so people in attendance. I didn't know anyone. Over dinner, we went around the table and introduced ourselves. We stated our name, what we did, and what we needed. In my case, I needed to find a storytelling group. The leader hooked me up with one that met weekly in a coffee house a few minutes from where I lived in the Valley.

The meeting lasted four hours. Afterward, as we all got up to stretch our legs, the guy from across the table made a beeline toward me. Despite my tired state, as he got closer, every part of my being woke up. He was well over six feet tall and lanky, with an infectious smile.

He stuck out his hand to shake mine and told me his name.

His touch shot electricity through my veins. "Ju-"

He cut me off. "Judi, looking for a story group," he said with that smile.

"Yes, and you're making a movie with your brother?"

"Writing one. Hoping to move to production by the end of the year. As an actor, writing your own stuff is the best way to get work."

As he spoke, I felt his baritone voice vibrate inside my soul. I looked up and into his blue eyes, silently reciting the thirteenth step of Roxy's program: *Lord, grant me serenity. Please make this one over thirty-five.*

He continued, "You're a writer. Maybe I can pick your brain?"

"Oooh."

"What?"

"I'm a literal person, so when you say, 'pick your brain,' I get an awful visual."

"Like, 'sitting on pins and needles?'"

"Yes! Painful. But the worst, the absolute worst, is when people say, 'keep your eyes peeled.'"

He laughed. There was a connection, but it didn't render me stupid like with Boss Man. I was witty and funny and in-control, just as I had been with Transition Guy. He even looked at me like Eric had, really zeroing in. We talked about everything: favorite movies, comedians, what we did, our hometowns. His nearness generated an energy inside me that I had never felt before. We exchanged cards in the parking lot.

A few days later I got an email: *Hi, remember me? 6'3" strawberry-blonde hair?*

I emailed back immediately: *Of course.*

I waited at my laptop for a response. Instead, my cell phone rang. "I'll be in your neighborhood today running an errand. How 'bout lunch?"

"I'd love to."

"I'll pick you up. Where you at?"

"The Oakwood Apartments in Toluca Lake. The building next to the Leasing Center. Park there and I'll meet you."

"I'll see you at eleven thirty."

I was excited. I had a date! *Wait, do I? Is lunch a date?* Dates had always been dinner. Sure, there was the meet for coffee or a drink thing, but that was the audition for the date. *So, what's lunch?* I wondered, clueless. *Maybe it's just part of the networking.*

At lunch, he examined his swan-shaped napkin. "Now, how do you think they do that?"

"No idea."

He then asked the waitress for two unfolded napkins and handed me one. "Let's try to figure it out."

Being a city girl, born and raised, left me a bit judgmental, but surprisingly I wasn't with him. I found myself joining in the fun. In spite of his tall stature and deep voice, he had a childlike innocence and a curiosity that was enchanting. As we concentrated on our napkin-folding skills, I learned that he lived with his brother and a friend of theirs in a two-bedroom loft apartment near Venice Beach. His room was in the loft. He had done a few episodic television shows; *Charmed* was one of them.

"Very cool. So, do you have a commercial agent?" I asked.

"No," he responded. Which meant there was nothing left for me to "network."

"What do you write about?" He asked as he looked at me earnestly.

"Dating mostly."

"I bet you have a lot of material."

"I do. I'm just not sure what to do with it yet. But I know there's something. I have visions of myself in front of an audience."

"Like a one-person show?"

"I think so."

"Well, you got yourself here. You're certainly brave and resourceful."

Out of a different man's mouth, it might have sounded like he was using a line on me. He didn't know me well enough to have made that observation, but I still believed his sincerity. I had a feeling that he was incapable of cheesy lines. I smiled at him across the table, our eyes taking each other in for longer than is *friend* appropriate. I noticed his shirt was a little baggy, but it still clung to the curve of his chest, outlining his right pectoral muscle. I wanted to reach across the table and touch him. It took every bit of willpower I could muster to fight the desire. It wasn't a fantasy, like with Boss Man. It felt more like a vision: a vision of the future.

"So, what breaks up a twenty-year marriage?"

I'd heard that question before, but this time answered, "Genital warts."

"You have them?"

"No, but he was out there looking for 'em."

"He was cheating."

"I should have known. He started acting differently in bed and wanted to do *it* in public places."

"I never got that. Who's comfortable with the fear of being caught?"

"I know, right? Give me a healthy man and a locked bedroom door and I'm good to go."

I froze. I had gone too far.

He broke our gaze by picking up the check and reading it. "I'm glad you feel you can talk to me." Then he put the check back on the table and gently pushed it to the middle. That action screamed friendship because Mother always said, girls don't pay on dates.

I picked up the check, looked at it, and threw down a twenty.

He stood up. "Will you come run my errand with me?"

I wasn't the slightest bit ready to say goodbye to him. "Sure."

The conversation in the car veered toward my kids. When I told him they were in college, he couldn't believe it. "If you don't mind my asking, how old are you?"

"Whatever age you think I am, add ten years." I didn't mean to be evasive. I'd always told the guys I was dating my age, but I wasn't sure if this one was a date or a fellow actor with whom I was "networking." Besides, actors never reveal their age, especially in Hollywood.

He didn't tell me his age either and we played a guessing game the rest of the day. Eventually, I admitted I was in my early forties, and he fessed up to early thirties. Where exactly, neither of us said. He did say that he seemed to date older women, then quickly added, "Not so old that they're wrinkled and saggy."

He meant it as a joke, but I wanted to say, *If this is a date? Yeah, ya are.*

"Where are we going?" I asked, realizing I didn't know.

"Ikea. It's so far from Venice that I never seem to get there."

We walked through the huge showroom chatting and eventually to the area where the boxes of disassembled furniture were stored. We walked through aisles until we came to the hardware bins. He reached in, took out a screw, and declared, "I'm done."

"What do you mean, *you're done?* Who comes to Ikea for hardware? There are buses in the parking lot filled with people who spent hours to get here to buy furniture, bedding, and entire bathrooms and kitchens! All you need is one piece of hardware?"

"Yep. I have a screw loose."

"Apparently," I laughed. Then he laughed, and then I doubled over laughing harder.

When he dropped me off, even though we had spent hours together, it felt too soon to say goodbye. I still had all this fun energy inside me, so I sat down at my computer, and a new comic essay poured out. I loved the creativity he inspired and didn't care if we were dating or not. *Maybe he's just my muse.*

"What's the age difference this time?" Roxy asked when I told her about him.

"Somewhere between nine and twelve years."

"Yeah? Well, we're calling him Ashton, 'cause I've elevated you to Demi Moore status." I knew she was shaking her head in disapproval on the other end of the phone. I didn't care.

A few weeks later, he asked me out for a Saturday hike. He drove us to Griffith Park Conservatory in the morning, and we walked and talked. When we came to a place that was a bit rocky, he took my hand. I thought he wanted to hold hands until the rough terrain ended and he let go. At the highest point of the hike, he pointed to the street below and said, "There's our car."

Our car? Our? I wondered if that was a hybrid of being *we'd*.

We went to brunch, and after the waitress took our order, he asked me about my dating stories.

"There's no male-bashing. The worst thing I say about a guy is that he wanted to get married and have children."

"Why is that a bad thing?"

"Because I don't want to do all that again."

He took the info in without judgment, and I realized what a lovely job the mothers of his generation had done. They raised their sons to view women as equals. If we were dating, that would have been one of the perks.

As we sat waiting for our meal, he asked me to tell him a story. I have never been able to perform on request. At neither cocktail parties nor family dinners was I ever able to tell a proper story. People would interrupt, or worse, talk over me, silencing me mid-sentence. But suddenly I found myself telling Ashton the story of my first date with Eric. I even did the character voices. It all flowed, and I was entertaining. At brunch! I was so comfortable with him, I remembered every punch line and told it with performance-level polish.

"You have got some talent, girl. I'm going to enjoy watching good things happen for you."

You could fall for a guy like that, and I was. Even though the story was about meeting another man, it didn't seem to faze him. I knew right then that I would never have to hide anything about myself.

When the waitress put down the check, this time he picked it up and read it.

We're on a date!

"You owe twelve-fifty."

We're not on a date.

On our walk back to his car, we stopped at a store so I

could buy a new coffee mug. I found an oversized one I liked and walked toward the cashier. He stopped me. "You should get two, for the times I'll be over."

Who are you in my life? I didn't ask that out loud, but I did buy a second mug.

When he dropped me off there was no kiss, no "I'll see you soon." It was clear we were just friends, but I didn't care; whatever the relationship, I was enjoying myself.

The following Saturday, he asked me to go shopping with him. He wanted me to show him a shop I'd told him about in Venice Beach where I had bought a carry-on bag for twenty-five dollars.

Because he lived near the ocean, I picked him up in my Beetle bug. At six foot three, he barely folded himself inside.

"Is the store near Muscle Beach?" Muscle Beach is an outdoor weight training area where big muscled men lift weights. "I hope not."

"Yes. We'll be walking past it."

"Oh man, it's gross, those little speedos they wear, you see everything."

A response popped into my head, and in a split second, I wondered if I should censor myself. It's not something I would say to a man I was dating. But then again, were we dating? I still didn't know, so I decided to be myself.

"I like that it shows everything. You guys look at women and can see the size and shape of our breasts through our clothes. Why shouldn't we get a sneak peek at the goods?" I waited for his response. When he laughed, I continued, "Women should know the landscape of the area in advance. Just before sex—not an ideal time. Trust me. Size should not be a surprise."

After we bought the suitcase, we went to an Italian place on Washington Street for lunch. It was our third—date? Get-together? When the bill came, he grabbed it. "It's on me."

We are dating!

"But you can get the tip."

We're not dating.

We walked back to the car. It was winter and starting to get darker earlier. He suddenly stopped me and said, "Look at that sunset."

It was beautiful, the sun setting over the ocean through scattered clouds, shades of orange and red. But it wasn't the beauty of it that left me in awe. It was that he stopped to enjoy it. He was like a male version of my friend Victoria. We would be hysterically laughing one minute and witnessing a tiny miracle the next. I took it as a testament to where I was in my life, attracting amazing people of real quality. People who believed in me and were encouraging and saw my potential.

When I pulled up to his apartment complex, we both got out of the car. I opened the trunk; he took out the suitcase and then gave me a quick kiss on the lips. *Quick? What was that?* Was he nervous about kissing me? Or had we just progressed to being very close friends? *Which is it?!*

I'd had enough guessing. I needed to take control and find out what Ashton wanted from me. A few days later, I emailed him a suggestion that we get together for a drink. I figured alcohol would be the quickest quandary-quencher. Yes, I could have just asked him how he felt, but I needed him to make the first move, not because of Mother's rules, but so I could then feign an objection to the age difference.

He never answered my email. I took that as my answer. We were friends.

Six weeks later, he called late on a Saturday afternoon and asked if I wanted to have that drink. I knew if I went, I would be committing a significant dating faux pas: accepting a last-minute date. But you could meet a friend at the last minute. Besides, I had moved on. I had a date for breakfast in the morning. A date that I knew was a date because we had met on a *dating* website.

He picked me up, and we went to a restaurant and bar I liked in Toluca Lake. We sat in the bar area on one of the couches and ordered martinis. He told me all about Christmas with his family in Michigan and about a New Year's party in Chicago's

Union Station. Even though it was a singles' party, I'd never heard of it.

During the second round of martinis, I realized how silly I'd been. He was just a friend, a good friend. I had made a great, fun new friend, and our kind of connection was rare. With two martinis in me, I suggested we have dinner, my treat since he'd paid for the drinks.

He insisted we sit on the same side of the table, and when the waitress asked if we wanted a drink, we looked at each other, both of us knowing we were already tipsy.

"Split one?

He smiled. "Perfect."

We decided to split a salad and the salmon as well. It was just like being out with a girlfriend. Then he asked, "Do you think it's possible to be friends with someone you're attracted to?"

If he had an ulterior motive for asking, it completely went over my drunk-ass head. "Yes," I said, thinking about how Transition Guy had become one of my best friends. "I think it makes the relationship fun."

He smiled. Halfway through our dinner, I shared with my fun friend how confused I'd been over our friendship.

"How could you not know we were dating?"

I sat there in silence. I didn't know how to answer. I did, however, know how Roxy would answer: *"Cause you never picked up the tab, ya cheap fuck.*

"I was very attracted to you, but the fact that you don't want more kids held me back."

I couldn't believe it. His biological clock was ticking too? I couldn't catch a freakin' break! Well, that was then. This was now. Now we were not dating. Now we were friends. Good. Finally. Closure.

He dropped me off at my apartment, and I gave him the friendly quick kiss goodnight.

I was halfway out the door when he said, "I'd like to really kiss you."

I turned back to him. "Dude, you're back on the fence?"

Dude? Did I just say "dude"? I desperately needed to get out of the sandbox!

Instead, I let him kiss me. I hadn't been big into kissing since high school. Kissing never lived up to the hype. It was always uncomfortable. I never felt like I meshed with anyone. It always put me in my head, thinking, anticipating, and wondering: *Is my mouth open too much? Too little? Why does his tongue feel so fat? Why do I have so much saliva in my mouth?* Kissing was an awkward and necessary vehicle to get from where you were to where you wanted to be. I even felt that way with Transition Guy.

Kissing Ashton, however... Oh—my—God! It was awesome in the true sense of the word: awe-inspiring, amazing, spiritual, magical. I stopped to testify, "Wow."

And we kissed again. This time I went into my head, taking inventory as to what state I'd left my apartment in and what I had in the fridge for breakfast. Then I remembered I had a morning date. "Oh my God, I'm such a slut."

"It's no big deal, go on your date, we're just makin' out."

Making out? What are we, twelve? Then I saw the look in his eyes and realized he'd just said that to play it cool, but it was about to come out: the drunken declaration of his true feelings.

"You know we can't have a relationship because of the kid thing."

You're an out-of-work actor with three roommates; where you plan on putting these kids?! I didn't say that out loud, but it was right there on the tip of my tongue begging to be verbalized.

I did say, "Look, I'm significantly older than you, and I can't be with a man who has a problem with that. I like me too much." And I got out of his car.

The infatuation needed to end. Ashton was on the fence, and on the fence is a very unappealing place for a man to be with his feelings for a woman.

He emailed me a cute note the next day. He told me he'd had fun but made no plans to get together again. I was disappointed. Every instinct I had, as well as that vision of touching him on our first date, told me that we were meant to be. The way my cells came alive when I was near him, the way I never wanted our time together to end, and especially the magic in his kiss... But he was too young to know that sometimes "meant-to-be" doesn't mean meant-to-be forever.

Still, I liked him and, for the first time in a relationship, I liked who I was with him.

Wordless Farewell

A week after Ashton left me in the parking lot, I got a call from my brother: Dad. Cancer. Metastasized. Months.

I didn't know what to do. I knew I had to go home, but did that mean to get the next plane out or stay a few days to cancel my lease and put everything in storage? If I left the apartment intact, would I have the time to come back and pack it up later? If he was dying, how could I do that?

In that moment, I missed Steve. That's one thing marriage was good for. When something tragic hits out of the blue, you need a partner to help make decisions. I called Roxy. "Tell me what to do."

She didn't. She couldn't.

I talked to my brother's wife, who was at the hospital with my dad. She told me what to do: "Pack it up." Your family will always tell you what to do. What to do, what to wear, where to go.

My Dad took the phone from her. "I'm not going to die today, Judi."

"Promise?"

Hearing his voice was comforting. When I hung up the phone, I began to digest the news. My father had lung cancer that had gone undiagnosed until it spread to his brain, causing noticeable confusion. The cancer cell type was squamous and not treatable with chemotherapy. The doctors said he had six months to live. But that didn't make sense to me. If cancer would kill him, didn't that mean he had six months to die?

The Oakwood Apartments very generously let me out of my lease. I put what few things I had accumulated in LA into a storage unit and left my car in a friend's driveway—collateral—to make sure I came back.

I called Ashton to tell him I was going back to Chicago indefinitely. In my overactive imagination, the news would make him realize how much he cared for me, and he would rush over to see me one last time. I would tell him that everything I had was in storage, so I'd made a reservation at the Beverly Hills Hotel. He'd meet me there and we would make love all night.

Instead I heard, "Keep in touch." I slept alone on the floor of my empty studio apartment.

Things had begun to happen for me in LA. An internship I had taken through school with an A-list literary manager-producer turned into a job offer, and I had an appointment the following week with a writing agent who liked my work. Of course, I wanted to be with my father, but I cried for the dreams I had to put on hold—again—and for the life that still belonged to everyone else except me.

The first few weeks back in Chicago, my coping skills consisted of consuming a sleeve of Oreos nightly as my dad and I lay on our respective couches watching TV. His routine remained mostly the same in the beginning. In place of jogging, I drove him to the hospital every weekday morning at seven a.m. for radiation therapy. When we got home, he'd make himself breakfast. He didn't need a constant companion, so I would go to an exercise class to work off the Oreos. Later, I would go grocery shopping and make dinner while he watched the stock market report. On the days he felt like riding his bike, I would walk/jog next to him.

What changed was his diet. He had been on a strict no-cholesterol diet for twenty years, ever since his five-way bypass heart surgery. When the doctors said that chemotherapy wouldn't work and that his brain tumors were no longer responding to radiation, he went off his diet. He ate Swedish meatballs at Ann Sather's and discovered Krispy Kreme Doughnuts.

He even ate an entire box for dinner one night. Given that he was the most disciplined man I knew, it was fun to watch him say, "Fuck it."

He never lost his sense of humor and used a nasty fall to prove it. I knew he shouldn't have gone out alone that Sunday morning. He wasn't stable. I saw at breakfast how shaky he was, and as the morning went on, he was having trouble balancing. It was a side effect of the steroids; it meant he had taken too much. But he put on his coat and said, "I'm going to Osco to check my blood pressure."

"I don't think it's a good idea today, Dad."

"Oh, stop," he dismissed me as he zipped up his winter coat.

I was still in my pajamas. "Just let me just get dressed." I got up and started to leave the kitchen.

"I don't need you to walk me there, for God's sake."

"Just let me throw on jeans." He ignored me and opened the door. "Dad. Just wait one minute."

He snapped at me. "Don't treat me like an invalid!"

We stood there staring at each other—an impasse. I don't care how old you get: when your father yells at you, it's still frightening. It brings you right back to childhood. The little girl in me wanted to run away before I got hit for talking back. He left.

I yelled at the door he'd just slammed, "Fine, you stubborn ass, get hit by a bus. At least then my life will go back to normal."

Of course, I didn't want him to get hit by a bus, but part of me would have been relieved. I was afraid of watching him die. It's not always like it is on television or the movies where someone slips away peacefully. I feared the tumors in his brain would cause seizures or the ones in his lungs would cause him to choke to death when I was alone with him at night. At night everything is scarier.

After he left that morning, I took a shower and put myself together. I styled my hair and put on full makeup. Then I waited because I knew. I knew he would not be walking back into the house. I knew he'd fallen. When an hour passed, I called 311 and asked if an ambulance had picked up an elderly man, and what hospital they took him to.

I don't know which was worse: the guilt I felt seeing his bruised and battered face, or the realization in his eyes, admitting father didn't know best.

The next day when I took him to radiation therapy, the doctors and technicians glared at me as if I had abused him. With his sense of humor, that's exactly what he told people: "My daughter beat me."

"Dad!"

"What? It's funny."

"No. It's a thing. Do *not* tell people that."

He didn't get it, and I never took him back. That was the day the doctor told us that the radiation treatment wasn't working, so there was no need. Luckily, they didn't send a social worker to the house to make sure I wasn't abusing him.

He had one bad week before he died. It began with his arms swelling up. I didn't know at the time that his lungs were filling up with fluid. Sores began forming on his arms as the fluid tried to escape. I struggled to manage it with Band-Aids, but the next day it got so bad I had to cut his shirt off. Every once in a while, the scissors would hit the already compromised skin, and he would bleed. I hated the fact that I was hurting him, but I had to continue. When his shirt was off, we both looked down at the swelling and sores, and we knew. The battle had gotten bigger than both of us. We looked into each other's eyes.

An acting teacher once told me to never hold a look on stage for too long. "No one holds a stare unless they're going to sleep together," she said.

But my father and I did hold our look that day. That look said everything that hadn't been said: *I'm dying; goodbye; I've enjoyed this time together.*

I'm a writer; I use words. I'm a talker; usually, I talk too much. But that day it was all said with only our eyes—a wordless farewell.

Maybe that's how it is with parents and children. You look at your infant baby and communicate your love and caring through your eyes, almost telepathically. Perhaps when your parents are old, you get that connection back.

He died three months after diagnosis. The doctors were wrong. He didn't have six months to live; he had three months to die. My brother, Roxy, and I were by his side. Why was Roxy there? Because she woke up that morning and just knew she needed to be with me. Roxy was my rock.

Leaving LA to care for my father was a no-brainer because, as I had come to realize, I'm a caretaker. Even though the timing was bad and no one would have blamed me for staying in LA and hiring him a nurse, being there for someone in their final hours is a gift to both the caregiver and the care-givee. The Jews call it a mitzvah, a good deed of the highest form, because there is no way the recipient can reciprocate. I thought of it as witnessing the circle of life firsthand. It was an honor and a privilege.

The Puppy

We sat Shiva for my dad at my brother's home in the north suburbs. Eric, Transition Guy, came to the funeral and then back to the house. He took the entire day off work, and that touched me deeply. Roxy and I walked Eric to the door at the end of that long day.

Once outside the door, he turned back to us. "Hey, next Saturday I'm throwing a—no, sorry, it's too soon-"

I stopped him. "For what? A party?" Roxy and I looked at each other and smiled.

"Fuck yeah," she said.

"We can go," I added, and then continued in Mother's Yiddish accent to drive the point home, "A nice Jewish boy is throwing a party full of eligible men? You think my parents want I should stay home?"

We then got the details. Eric and a few single friends were throwing the party together. It was going to be the singles' event of the summer. I was moving to LA permanently in six weeks, "Plenty of time for me to have another almost-relationship."

At the party, Roxy met someone immediately. I was happy for her; it had been a long time since I'd seen her connect with anyone. He was well over six feet tall, almost a foot taller than she, and he smoked. They bonded during their many trips to the rooftop patio to have a cigarette.

I mingled alone, but since I knew a few people there, I felt comfortable. At one point, a man stopped me. "Judi? What are you doing here?" He was a friend of my younger brother.

"Hi, Eric and I are friends, you?"

"Same." Then he turned to the guy he had been talking to. "This is Judi, she's Rob's sister."

"I didn't know Rob had a little sister," the man with an irresistible smile said.

"He doesn't," I replied, and we spent the rest of the night talking. Roxy called him The Puppy because he had bushy, curly dark hair you just wanted to play with, big bright blue eyes, and followed me everywhere. He was not on any fence. He was clear. He wanted me.

We had a lot in common; he had lived in LA for two years, he was a lawyer in Chicago but had wanted to be an LA agent, and his father had also passed away recently. As the evening progressed, I knew he was going to ask me out, but instead of making a plan for the future he suggested, "Hey, wanna get outta here?"

Wow, leave with a guy? Can I do that? What the hell. I didn't know him, but my brother and Eric did.

"Sure."

I found Roxy and told her I was leaving. She and her guy were leaving too, and we rode the elevator down together. Once we were on the street, Roxy gave me a wink before we went our separate ways.

The Puppy got us a cab and took me to the Peninsula Hotel off Michigan Avenue for a drink. I ordered a glass of white wine but barely touched it. It was well into the early morning, no longer drinking hours for me. As I pretended to sip the wine, I asked, "What would my brother tell me about you?"

"Your brother will tell you that I'm the greatest guy in the world."

I smiled at his confidence. "Really?"

"You know his girlfriend, Amy?"

"Of course, they dated his last two years of college. We all loved Amy. We hoped they'd get married."

"He stole her from me."

"What?"

"Oh yeah, I brought her to a frat party when I was a pledge. Rob asked her out, and the rest is history."

"You didn't fight for her?"

"I was a pledge. Rob was two years older."

Of course he is, I thought to myself, because that made him five years younger instead of the three I assumed he was. I wondered if his interest in me was somehow related to the fact that he might want to get back at my brother, but since I was enjoying myself, I decided to wait and see how it played out.

When the bar closed, he escorted me home in a cab, even though the hotel was a few blocks from his apartment. It was one of those rare times when I was in the moment and felt comfortable and safe just being, not overthinking anything. We got to my dad's house, where I was still living, and I gave him a tour because he had told me his mother liked to buy properties and I needed to sell the family home as part of settling the estate.

I made some tea, and we sat on my couch talking. Later, The Puppy followed me into the kitchen and stood behind me as I boiled water for a second pot. He then turned me around and kissed me. It wasn't like kissing Ashton, but I thought we could work on it. And work on it we did.

We abandoned the tea and went back to the couch and kissed some more. The Puppy kicked his shoes off, and they fell to the floor. Then he lay on top of me, and I felt something.

"There's something very hard poking my hip."

"Sorry, it's my belt."

"I'm sorry it's your belt too." He didn't laugh as he took the belt off and tossed it aside. "It was a joke," I told him.

"Oh. Funny," He responded without a smile.

He obviously didn't get me, but that was okay. He was cute and snuggly, and that's all I needed him to be. "Come upstairs," I said as I got up from the couch. "I want to play a song for you."

We went to my bedroom because that's where my stereo and albums were. The music I had been collecting since childhood was my comfort zone and a way of communicating when my own words failed me. He sat on my bed as I picked the perfect song for us. I chose "Papa, Can You Hear Me" from the movie, *Yentl*. Since he lost his father too, I wanted to share the lyrics I found to be both relatable and inspirational.

When the song finished, he lay back against my pillow. "Come here."

I did. We stayed in our street clothes, kissed a little, and I let The Puppy sleep in my bed. He repeatedly said things like, "I can't believe how comfortable this feels," "We fit so well together," and "Where'd you come from?" He never tried to do more than kiss me, and I felt safe and protected with him in the house. I didn't even shut the bedroom door. From who would I need to hide?

In the morning, we started kissing and snuggling again. I liked that The Puppy didn't need to go out first thing in the morning. He kept saying he should leave, but he kept kissing me instead. The phone rang, and I answered it because the family home didn't have caller ID. It was my brother. The Puppy and I got a kick out of that.

I told Rob about meeting his fraternity brother at a party but left out the part about taking him home.

My brother replied, "Oh, he's the greatest guy! If he asks you out, you should go."

I smiled at The Puppy and repeated my brother's statement. "The greatest guy in the world, huh?" He flashed me his killer smile, and I told my brother what The Puppy had said about him. "He said you stole Amy from him."

"I did, at a frat party when he was a pledge." Everything The Puppy had told me was the truth.

When I hung up the phone, he started to kiss me again, then stopped abruptly. "Did you hear that?"

"Hear what?" I asked.

He shrugged and as he went in for another kiss. He stopped again, "That."

I listened but didn't hear anything. *Here comes the crazy,* I thought to myself. *Paranoid Puppy.*

But soon I heard it too. It was coming from the kitchen, sounds of rustling pots and closing cabinets—

"Could someone be making breakfast?" He asked.

I jumped out of bed in absolute fear and shut the bedroom door. "Oh my God, it's my son!" He was supposed to stop by later that day, but he must have decided to come early.

I panicked. In the four years since the divorce, my son had never met a guy I dated. Now he was going to witness a one-night stand?

I began pacing, pacing and panicking. "What am I going to do? What am I going to do? What am I going to do?" I repeated aloud as I paced and panicked. Different scenarios popped into my head; I could take the honest approach. After all, I had always been honest with my children. Then I remembered the look of disappointment on my son's face the night I came home late from being out with Edgar Winter. No, honesty was out.

"I'll just come down and meet him," The Puppy suggested.

"No!" I screamed softly. "I'm sorry. Please let me think." I hadn't meant to be harsh with The Puppy, but I was in panic mode.

I pleaded with The Puppy to stay, stay in the room, and as I opened the door to leave, it creaked loudly. "Shit," I exclaimed softly. I forgot; that's why we never shut it all the way.

I went down the stairs. When I got to the living room, I saw The Puppy's belt and shoes on the floor in front of the couch. *Shit.* I grabbed them and brought them back upstairs. When I opened the bedroom door, it creaked loudly again. *Shit!* As I opened the door, I saw The Puppy standing in the middle of the room tucking his shirt in his pants.

I closed the door and whisper-screamed, "What are you doing?"

"This is silly. He's a grown man. I'll just introduce myself."

"You so don't have kids. Please listen to me and don't come out." It was going from bad to worse. I didn't know this guy. I didn't know what to expect. "Please. Let me do this my way."

He finally agreed. I opened the bedroom door, and again

it creaked loudly. "Shit!" I said out loud and locked The Puppy in the bedroom.

I went back downstairs, and just as I walked into the kitchen, I saw The Puppy's cell phone on the counter. *Damn. The Puppy was shedding all over the house!* But it was too late to grab it and run back up because there was my twenty-two-year-old son cooking eggs.

"Hi, Mom."

"Hi, Baby."

"What brings you here so early?"

"Breakfast."

He had basketball practice in the city and was supposed to stop by on his way back to his father's house. I tried to act normal as I casually leaned on the counter to hide the cell phone and the fact that I was struggling to finagle it into my back pocket.

Once I had the cell phone safely in my pocket, I went to the kitchen table to sit with him while he ate in silence. My son, much like my father, loved silence. That morning, I was grateful for it.

"Whose cell phone was that?"

So much for silence.

"What? Oh, it's Roxy's. She slept over. We went to a party. It got late, so she slept over."

"You guys sleep in the same bed?" Busted. It was a four-bedroom home.

"Girls do that," I eked out contritely. I had always told my children the truth about everything, but this felt different. A boy, a man, thinks virtuously of his mother. Besides, what was I supposed to say? *Mommy has a man in her bed, but we didn't have sex.* It reminded me of the time Mother found a pack of cigarettes in my underwear drawer when I was thirteen. I told her I was holding them for a friend. Isn't that what my son would hear? *I just held him—for a friend.*

I sat with him for an hour, all the while praying The Puppy wouldn't get loose.

My son eventually left. I'm sure he knew I was lying. He

asked why Roxy and I were in the same bed. How did he know that nobody had slept in another room? Had he been upstairs? Did he see us in bed together? I couldn't allow myself to think about that. I was just grateful The Puppy hadn't come down and made a bigger mess for me to clean up.

The Puppy thought it was the funniest dating experience he'd ever had. He'd never been with a woman who had kids, let alone adult kids. I offered to drive him home, and just as we thought we'd made it to the car without being noticed by anyone else, we ran into my sister's very conservative husband. I introduced The Puppy as Rob's fraternity brother, but I don't think that explained why we were wearing Saturday night party attire at nine a.m. on a Sunday. I couldn't believe the way the morning had gone. I was so busted, and I didn't even have the sex!

The next night I met The Puppy in his neighborhood for dinner. I was in the middle of my second martini when he paid the bill and unfolded a small portion of the newspaper he'd taken out of his back pocket.

"Would you like to see a movie? I brought the listings."

I shook my head no.

"Did you have something in mind?"

I finished the last drops of liquid courage and told him exactly what I had in mind. "How 'bout we go back to your place?"

We did. Hey, half the members of my family thought I'd already had sex, *might as well just do it.*

He lived in a one-bedroom apartment on Michigan Avenue near the Wrigley Building. An upscale neighborhood, but his apartment was generic, cookie-cutter circa the 1970s, and in need of a woman's touch. Still, the location meant he had money.

"Where do you practice law?" I asked as I took in the view.

"I'm head counsel for *The Jerry Springer Show*."

If he had already handed me the vodka rocks he was making, I would have done a spit take. In a city that housed Springer and Oprah, I was definitely in Camp Oprah. The Springer show was extremely unsophisticated, regularly inciting fistfights between the guests.

"That's gotta keep you busy," I smiled, but I understood how he could work there. If I couldn't make a living as a comedy writer in Los Angeles, I still wanted to live and work in the industry. Working for Springer must have been his way of not completely leaving his dreams behind.

He played a Norah Jones CD as we sipped our drinks. There was no need for small talk. We both knew what I meant when I asked him to take me back to his place. "Would you like to dance?"

The old Judi would have been embarrassed, would have thought that dancing anywhere other than a proper dance floor was outright silly. But nonjudgmental Judi was happy to take the chance to connect with him. It would be the perfect transition to his bedroom. For the first time in four-plus years, I was finally going to have sex—sex that counted.

We stood in his bedroom kissing, and when we were undressed, I quickly got into bed and pulled up the covers. He smiled his irresistible smile and began kissing me.

That wasn't enough to keep me out of my head. My monkey mind was spinning. I couldn't let myself go. Part of the reason I didn't have sex with my high school boyfriends was that Mother was always in my head. Back then I felt her presence so strongly that I couldn't relax. I was afraid to do anything, afraid she'd see. My fear was so strong back then that I checked closets to make sure she wasn't hiding there. But I was a teenager back then. I chalked it up to guilt.

At The Puppy's apartment, I didn't feel Mother's presence in the room. Instead, I felt The Ex-Hole. I couldn't believe it. It was four years post-divorce, he had remarried, yet still he had a hold on me. I could hear in my head the comments he'd be making: "Who is this clown?" and "How can you let him touch you when you know you still belong to me?" and of course the arrogant "No one will ever please you the way I did." A small but real fear I did have.

Afterward, the only clue I had that we'd had sex was the

silly grin on The Puppy's face. I missed the whole thing. I was so distracted; I hadn't felt anything. *How did that happen?* I wondered; *Did I get bigger? Does that happen when you don't use it?*

I stayed the night, we snuggled, and I took my first walk of shame in the morning. Of course, my parents' neighbors were outside when I got home: busted again.

I went into the house, took a shower, and called Roxy. It was summer and I knew she'd be at her building's outdoor pool. "I'm bringing over lunch," I told her. I was excited to share my news.

When I got to the pool, I blurted it out. "I had sex!"

"It's about fucking time."

"On the first date too."

"Ah, my baby's growing up."

"What about you? With that guy you met."

Roxy got up to grab an ashtray and walked back bow-legged. "We did it last night."

"Why are you walking like that?" I asked as she carefully sat down on the wrought iron chair.

"He has the biggest dick I've ever seen."

"What?"

"Or felt," she continued with a smirk.

"Got it," I said to cut her off.

"I mean, we're talking porn star material here."

"Okay, I get it!" I began stabbing my salad with a plastic fork over and over but didn't take a bite.

"What's with you?" Roxy asked as she took a large bite out of the hot dog I'd brought her.

I lost it. I completely lost control and said what I was thinking. "I have never been jealous of anyone a day in my life. I don't care if someone is prettier than me, has more money, a better job. I don't have a jealous bone in my body. But right here, right now, with you telling me about your big dick date, I'm fucking jealous!"

"Seriously?"

"I've waited four years to have sex, and I didn't feel anything. It's not fair! That should have been my dick. You've had hundreds of dicks. I've had one dick my whole life and birthed two babies. I shouldn't have to downsize!" After I said it I laughed. It was silly. And not entirely true.

Roxy didn't laugh with me. "Hundreds of dicks?! Every man I sleep with is a potential relationship."

"I'm sorry, Rox. I was going for the joke, and I went too far."

She sat for a long time in silence, and I didn't know what she was thinking or what she was going to say. Finally, she spoke. "I did the math. I forgive you." We laughed.

The next time The Puppy and I had sex, we were at my house. He could sense that I was tense.

"Relax."

I couldn't. The Ex-Hole's presence was palpable. I could see him standing at the foot of the bed watching, judging, laughing. "You think it's gonna be better this time? Ha!"

"You need to let go," The Puppy said gently as his mouth kissed its way down my torso.

I wanted to. I wanted to let go in the worst way, not just because I missed the enjoyment of having sex, but to banish The Ex-Hole for good! And that angry thought gave me an idea. Since I couldn't cast out the image of The Ex-Hole, maybe I could use that to my advantage. So, as The Puppy did his best to pleasure me, I imagined that The Ex-Hole was being forced to watch and that seeing me with another man was excruciatingly painful for him. In my mind, The Ex-Hole was bound and gagged with toothpicks in his eyes to keep them open, just like in the movie, *A Clockwork Orange*. I found that very empowering. I even started acting out the part like a porn star to rub in the fact that another man was ravishing his wife. The angrier I tried to make The Ex-Hole, the more I was able to give in to what was happening to me until finally when The Puppy was finished, he was not the only one with a silly grin.

The Ex-Hole was exorcised.

The three-pack of condoms that had been with me over four years, back and forth across the country from coast to coast—twice—finally fulfilled their destiny. All three used in one night. Respect.

The Puppy kept asking me why him. Why, after four years, had I chosen him? I think there were several reasons, one being that there was something very familiar about him. I also liked that he was not ambivalent with his feelings for me the way the past several men had been. And my father had just died, and when both your parents are gone, it moves you up to next in line. Why was I saving myself?

Even though The Puppy knew I'd be moving back to LA, he still wooed me like a boyfriend, going far beyond the minimum requirements of a fling. One day he planned a "Chicago Tourist Day." We started at the café on Oak Street Beach, then went to the Art Institute, where I flitted around in a cute minidress and white Keds (my signature commercial "young mom" look). Then down the steps off Michigan Avenue to the Billy Goat Tavern. Walking with The Puppy, I turned my ankle on an uneven cement stair. It hurt, but we were close to the restaurant, so I powered through with his help.

After dinner, we took a cab to his place, had more sex, and I stayed overnight. He helped me into a taxi the next morning. Instead of going home, I went to Weiss Hospital Emergency Room. I had broken my fifth metatarsal, again; this had happened in the same way when I was in my twenties. I would be in a cast and crutches for the next six weeks.

I figured it was a good time to let The Puppy go, but when he showed up at my house with groceries, I realized that he was the only person in my life who understood I needed help. He totally stepped up, and we continued to see each other. He paid for cabs to take us a few blocks away when my arms got sore from crutching. He even found a place that rented out knee-wheelers, enabling me to ditch the crutches and scoot around the city, giving me back my freedom. He came to my nephew's birthday party with me and even met my children. I don't think they cared much for him.

"He's wearing a pink shirt," my son said with judging eyebrows.

"A wannabe with no staying potential," my daughter added.

The Puppy made me an instant part of his life. I saw him five times a week and spent the other two days with my kids. "The problem with you," he said one night as we were getting ready for bed, "is not that you have two kids, but that you see them on two different days." It was true, I spent alone time with each child, but what gave him the right to have an opinion? This wasn't a real relationship. He knew I was leaving for LA the following month.

The Puppy's office was at the NBC Tower, walking distance from his apartment. One morning while we were dressing, he called his assistant to ask her a quick question. Instead of asking the question straight-off, he made up a story.

"Where are you?!" he asked her with panic in his voice. "The meeting with the head of the network started fifteen minutes ago, and the presentation materials were not on my desk." I knew she had to be freaking out on the other end because The Puppy smiled and winked at me as he continued. "Your day off? Who approved that? No. No, it's on my calendar for next week." He went on like this for several minutes before he let her off the hook and asked his simple question.

When he hung up, I asked him why he did that to her.

"It's funny."

"That wasn't funny. That was mean."

"I played a joke on her. It was funny. People think I'm funny."

"I know funny. People think I'm funny."

He looked at me with a straight face. "You're not." Something in his delivery told me that was his honest opinion. I didn't ask for clarification; I didn't want to know the answer. Yet.

To ensure my return to California, even though I had graduated from Columbia, I signed up for the Semester in LA program again. I wanted an LA move do-over. This time I would be taking classes in television writing. I had secretly been writing half-hour comedies for the past ten years and knew that's what I wanted to do in LA: become a comedy writer for television.

In the meantime, The Puppy took me to a family function where I met his mother, brother, and sister-in-law. We went to a political dinner, the theater, and fancy restaurants. I enjoyed that kind of dating and didn't mind that it was all about him and his world. I knew in a few weeks I'd be back in LA, in my world.

A few weeks before I planned to leave, The Puppy invited me to a wedding in Indiana. "It's not so much about the wedding. I want to book a room at the hotel and have a special weekend with you." People who never been married are naturally curious, and in answering some of his questions one night, I revealed that The Ex-Hole was not a romantic guy. On our wedding night, he and his parents counted the money while I went to sleep.

"No romance?" The Puppy asked.

"None. On our honeymoon, he laid out in the sun all day, and at four p.m. he'd get up, announce he was going to take a nap, and leave me alone at the pool."

That night in the Indiana hotel, The Puppy booked the honeymoon suite. After the wedding, he locked himself in the bathroom for a long time—so long that I began to get irritated. When he opened the door, I saw the bubble bath he'd made for me with the candles and rose petals.

"For you," he said, kissed me and closed the door, leaving me alone to enjoy and relax. He knew there was no attractive way I could get undressed and maneuver into the tub from the knee wheeler, and I appreciated the privacy.

When I came back into the room, there was a tray of champagne and chocolate-covered strawberries on the king-size bed. "We are going to make love all night. I want you to have the honeymoon you deserve."

And I did. We had sex all night: seven orgasms for him, four for me.

The week before I was to leave for California, he said something I had been praying he would never say. I was sitting at the edge of his bed one morning putting on my socks when he said it. "I love you."

How did this happen? I was always clear that I was leaving Chicago, but had I ever explained to him that I wasn't looking for a relationship? No, I didn't. And now The Puppy thought he'd found a home. He didn't understand I was merely fostering.

I turned and looked into those Puppy eyes and couldn't hurt him. "I love you too," I said, and hoped he didn't notice my voice was several octaves higher than usual.

That night at dinner he was nervous, which made me nervous. "I have something to tell you."

"Okay." I waited, but he didn't say anything. "What?" I asked him.

"This is hard. Give me a minute."

My mind immediately flashed back to Indiana Boy's confession about genital herpes, and I panicked. I had already had sex with The Puppy, a lot of sex. "What? Tell me. Tell me cuz you're freaking me out!"

"I live with my mother."

Mother's Yiddish accent fell out of my mouth, "In the one bedroom?"

"No, she lives next door?"

"Oh."

"She bought two apartments to convert them into one, but when I moved back from LA she offered me one of the apartments temporarily."

That was several years ago, and he was still there. As a mother, my sympathy was with her.

I was relieved I hadn't been exposed to any STDs. Then I remembered all the lies he had to tell me to keep that secret. I didn't understand why.

"Are you going to break up with me now?" he asked.

"It's not a big deal. I don't know why you kept that a secret unless..." *Oh shit.* "Does her bedroom wall butt up to yours?"

He nodded, and I was humiliated. I had become very noisy during sex since I no longer had kids living with me. *No wonder he occasionally shushed me.* On some level, I must have known. I may have felt a mother's presence that first night, but it wasn't mine.

The next day he asked me to come to look at apartments with him. "I want to make sure you like a place before I buy it."

He saw a future for us as a couple in Chicago. I saw myself as single in LA. Yes, we had chemistry and a comfort level that's rare, but I still didn't want a relationship.

"You know I'm leaving for LA next week."

"I get it. I did the LA thing. I left my law practice, but LA is a hard city. You'll be back."

"I can't plan a backup life. That's making a plan to fail."

Realizing I didn't feel the same caused him to lash out. "You're in your forties, how the hell do you think you're going to make it in LA?!"

That's when I realized why he had felt so familiar. That statement, that tone, it was The Ex-Hole. While it hurt, part of me was glad he said it, it was the perfect set-up to let The Puppy go, "Look, this was fun, but I think it's time to end it."

"No, no." The Puppy begged, "I'm sorry, go to LA, see how you feel. Let's see what happens."

"I don't plan to—" I wanted to say that I didn't plan on returning to Chicago and he hated LA, so what was the point in waiting, but I'm sure he knew, and that's why he cut me off.

"Let's leave the door open," he suggested.

To avoid a scene, I agreed.

The next day the movers came and loaded up everything I owned into a small U-Haul. I planned to go back to the Oakwood Apartments until I found another place. Victoria flew in from New York, and together we drove across the country to get me set up in LA. Again. I couldn't let anyone, or anything, keep me from living my dream life.

Ashton: Part 2

As promised, Ashton kept in touch with me while I was in Chicago. His calls always seemed to come when I was contemplating staying permanently, those weak moments when I settled back into my Chicago persona of putting everyone before myself. Each phone call was a sweet reminder of my goals and dreams, and he promised not to let me forget how happy I had been in LA. I never got around to telling him I was seeing someone else. What was the point?

A few weeks after I settled into my new Oakwood apartment, this time on Riverside in Los Feliz, and had begun the routine of lectures and writing on the CBS Studio Lot, I called him.

"Hey, how about dinner Friday night? My treat. I want to thank you for being my personal Los Angel."

"I'd love to. Let's go near you because I want to see your new place."

"Great. Six too early?" It was too early for dinner, but I wanted as much time with him as I could get.

"Six is great. I'll see you then."

"Bah-bye."

"Judi!"

I had started to hang up. "Yes?"

"I'm really glad you're back."

Pause.

"Me too."

The plan was for him to come in to see my apartment first,

so I made guacamole and, not knowing what kind of wine he preferred, bought a bottle of both red *and* white. After showing him the one-bedroom apartment, I offered him a glass of wine.

"I was thinking we could go to the Brown Derby and have a martini," he said. "Your apartment is so close, and we really should check it out."

The Los Feliz Brown Derby was a famous Hollywood nightclub, and like its Brown Derby predecessors, it would not remain open too much longer. Ashton toasted my return in the dark bar with a warm, welcoming smile and eyes that zeroed in on me. *How had I forgotten how much I love his energy?* It had been six months since we'd seen each other, but we talked, joked, and laughed as if it had been just last week.

After our martini stop, we went to a nearby Mexican restaurant. We each ordered a margarita and finished them during chips and salsa. We then shared the cheese enchiladas and ordered more drinks. When the waitress asked if we wanted a third margarita, I was concerned that it might be too much alcohol for me, so I asked, "Split?"

He smiled, "Sure." Of course, we ended up splitting another one before I paid the bill. *So much for monitoring my liquor.*

When we got back to my place, I offered him a glass of wine. He opted for red. I poured one for myself and chose an album to play. Before I knew it, the red bottle was empty, as was half of the white. I had consumed far too much alcohol. I knew I couldn't drink like that, but I was always in the moment with him. As a result, I did what I felt in the moment, forgetting that in the previous moment I had already had too much to drink, and in a future moment I'd be in the bathroom, on my knees before the porcelain head.

"Oh my God! You have *Bye Bye Birdie!*" he exclaimed as he rifled through my record collection.

"Yes, I was in that play in college. Summer Dinner Theatre."

"No way, me too. High school."

He put it on, and we sang the songs we had once performed. We laughed and had a great time. Hanging out with him was the way I hung out with girlfriends. So when he asked me to sit next to him on the couch, I thought nothing of it, until he pulled my face to his and kissed me. And there it was again, the *wow* factor. Yes, we were drunk again and right back where we were six months ago, but there was no mistaking it. Kissing him was an out of this world experience.

I'd experienced a kiss like that once before, when I was seventeen. I was in the audience of a play my brother-in-law was in, and I was instantly smitten with one of the actors. The cast party was at my sister's apartment, and I went. My actor crush, Paul, and I talked well into the night. He was twenty. At that stage in my life, boys were always older than me. We left the party and went to a piano bar, and he sang one of the songs in my ear, *April in Paris*. It felt very grown-up and romantic. We kissed goodnight in my car. His kiss created an out-of-body experience that put me somewhere between earth and heaven, maybe even beyond. I think we kissed for hours, but perhaps it just felt that way, like time didn't exist. In which case we kissed for an eternity.

I told him I was seventeen, and I never saw him again. I did learn years later that he became a minister, and that made perfect sense: his kiss was a spiritual experience.

As wonderful as kissing Ashton was, I didn't want to make out for sport, so I stopped. "What does this mean? I thought we were friends."

"I want us to be more than friends."

Yeah, baby! "What about the kid thing? I mean, I could probably pop one more out." I couldn't believe I said that. That should have been my first clue into how drunk-off-my-ass I was because that statement was right up there with the other signals of drinking too much: craving a cigarette, slurring my words, and the newly discovered offering up a midlife baby.

"I want three." He was rigid and didn't get the sacrifice I would make for him. So at least we were clear. We would have a fling.

"Why now? Why not before?" I was curious. I had to know.

"Before, I was afraid of hurting you."

"Please, I'm like the guy in relationships!" I was specifically thinking of my relationship with The Puppy, but I was like that with my husband as well. And EW once called me a ball-buster.

Still, I didn't want to have a fling. I'd had a fling with The Puppy, and it didn't work because there was no emotional involvement. What Ashton and I had was something special. We genuinely cared for one another. With him, it would be more like an affair. That was it!

"We'll have an affair!"

"What's the difference?"

"An affair is more like a relationship, but certain circumstances, in our case the age difference, keeps it from being more. An affair is full of passion and love and lovemaking and emotionality."

"I like that. And we'll only date other people we think we can have a future with." I liked that suggestion because I still hoped to meet an age-appropriate, A-list Hollywood producer, specifically the cute one teaching my new class. He continued, "But you and me, we'll be sexually exclusive."

Tears came to my eyes. *Oh my God, he gets me.*

I called it our pre-sex treaty. It had all of the perks of a relationship with none of the trappings. Why hadn't I thought of this before?

"I'm thirty-two," he confessed.

"Forty-four. There's a twelve-year difference."

"Oh."

"Does that bother you?"

He thought about it. "Not right now. In the future it probably would, but not right now."

I loved his honesty, as much if not more than his kisses.

"When I was in Chicago, I was kinda seeing someone."

Was? I used the past tense. I made a mental note to call The Puppy in the morning and complete the breakup process.

"No big deal. Did you learn anything?"

"Yeah, I guess."

"Then that's the important thing."

Since Ashton was too drunk to drive home, he slept over that night. We stayed in our clothes. There was no animalistic rush like I had seen in movies. Kissing and holding each other was enough for the moment. Since the day we met, I had not been able to get him out of my mind. In his arms, his long embracing arms, and with his lengthy six-foot-three encompassing body wrapped around me, my head finally resting on that chest I had always wanted to touch, I was happy. We kissed most of the night and into the morning. Like bees to honey, neither one of us could get enough.

The only thing that bothered me was that I was about to go from sleeping with one guy in four years to sleeping with two in the one month. Was I turning into what Mother would call loose?

"Oy, I'm such a failure. My baby is a loose woman."

At least my numbers are low, Ma, under the radar for getting HPV.

The next few times he slept over, we never got out of our underwear. We took the time to really feel comfortable. By the third night, having consumed just the right amount of wine and with John Mayer confirming in the background what we'd already suspected, *your body is a wonderland*, we took it to the next level.

When I slid my hand into his pants, however, I didn't feel anything. I moved my hand from one side to the other, but I couldn't locate a penis. I couldn't believe it: he was six-foot-three. He wore a size thirteen shoe! *How could I not be finding a penis?* Then he gently took my hand, reached it back into his pants, and *down* his leg—and up popped the biggest penis I had ever seen. And I wish to this day that I had said *that* out loud, but the size wasn't the immediate shocker.

"It bends the wrong way!" I exclaimed.

"What? It doesn't bend the wrong way."

It did. Ashton's penis looked like Gonzo's nose, Gonzo the

Muppet from *Sesame Street*. Gonzo's nose was long and thick and curved downward at the end like Toucan Sam on the Froot Loops cereal box. I had learned since my divorce that penises came in different sizes—and also that there is no such word as peni—but I had no idea, NO IDEA, that they came in different shapes. Hence the regretful expletive, "it bends the wrong way!"

"How about we just try it?" he suggested with his coy, playful smile. And we did, but I must say that big isn't always better. Sometimes big is just painful, especially when the man's curve is in direct opposition of the woman's inner landscape. But Ashton was a gentle and caring lover, so I was never in danger of getting hurt, though traditional positions were definitely off the menu.

And so began our affair. We only saw each other once a week. Ashton worked the night shift at a special-effects studio, so we were limited to Saturday or Sunday, never both. Both would mean we were in a relationship, and there was that pre-sex treaty to uphold, a contract specially designed to keep us from falling in love—though he did throw in the occasional Tuesday night in those beginning months.

As a self-preservation tactic, when he was leaving, I always scanned my apartment to make sure he hadn't left anything behind. I didn't know how long our non-relationship relationship would last or how it would end. I didn't want physical reminders of what was lost or the pressure to return a belonging.

It was weird having sex with a friend at first. We'd go out to a movie or networking event, pal around, and then at the end of the evening, as soon as the door was closed in my apartment, he would kiss me, and I'd remember, *oh yeah, we do this now*. It was as if we had two completely different relationships because there was little or no affection when we were out in public but, alone in my apartment, that's all there was.

Our sex life was fun and explorative. I never had that with The Ex-Hole. And I always slept naked with Ashton, which I had never done before. He didn't want anything between us and neither did I.

I was happy with the arrangement. It didn't interfere with

my goals and my life. For the first time, I didn't need to give anything up for a relationship. I worked hard in class, made great contacts, and became a regular at the networking meeting and an active member at the Story Salon, where I told stories weekly. I finally had the relationship I'd wanted since my divorce. I didn't want to get married or be too serious, but I wanted my sex life back. I had to respect him, like him, laugh with him, and I wanted him to *get* me. He'd also have to be the kind of man I *could* settle down with, and of course, my kids had to like him too, on the off chance we stayed together.

And there it—he—was, live, and in my bed! It was all going great, even as we approached week six—the dreaded week six. No relationship post-divorce had lasted past week six, so I was concerned.

One day, The Puppy called. He said his cousin would be in town because he was thinking of moving to Los Angeles and asked if I would have dinner with him. I wasn't sure if he was trying to set me up with him or if I was being asked to be the LA greeting committee. When I first got to LA, many people had given me the names and numbers of friends to look up. One of those connections garnered me a talent agent for commercial work, so I agreed to meet The Puppy's cousin for whatever the purpose. After all, as per the contract, Ashton and I had decided we could date other people. Even though I didn't want to date other people, I felt it would help me maintain the friend-sex balance we had achieved.

We were to meet on Friday night at a Hollywood restaurant on top of the hill near the Magic Castle. I put on the flower print skirt with sandals and the silk tank my sister-in-law had given me years ago for that one date with the height and the glasses guy. As I was about to walk out the door, I realized I had forgotten to put on underwear. I laughed out loud, "Oops, the wrong date for that." I corrected the wardrobe malfunction and went to meet The Puppy's cousin.

At dinner, we talked about The Puppy, ate in awkward silence, and never saw each other again, not that I wanted to. I was happy with my arrangement with Ashton, but that date gave me a naughty idea for the following night.

It was week seven. Ashton picked me up for dinner, and I was feeling great. That week a producer had asked me to write a short screenplay, and I had just finished it. It was a comedy I was particularly pleased with, and I read it to him on our drive to the restaurant.

He laughed so hard I couldn't read the rest until he calmed down. "You're a very clever writer."

At the restaurant, we split an entree salad. Salads were all I ate with him, but not because I was watching my weight. I didn't want to be digesting anything heavy during the physical portion of the evening. We each had one glass of wine, and when he tried to order another, I stopped him, "I have a bottle chilling at home."

I had on the same skirt as the previous night but added a clinging white T-shirt and sexy slip-on open-toed sandals. "There's something you need to know," I told him when the check came. "I'm not wearing any panties." Then I got up and walked to the ladies room to let him digest the news. I loved how playful I was with him.

We made love all night. Yes, as corny as it may sound, Ashton and I always made love. We enjoyed each other: the climactic gratification of sex wasn't the priority, the connection was. That night he held me tighter and closer than ever before, and several times as he held me in his arms he kissed my forehead in the same spot that Mother had when I was a little girl. That kiss felt so loving; it brought tears to my eyes. It's funny, you don't realize when you're an adult plowing through your life, but most of us don't feel cherished anymore. But the pièce de résistance—the CD player that I always loaded with five CDs was playing Rod Stewart's *Song Book* recordings. While Ashton held me that night, Rod Stewart revealed my exact sentiments: *If this isn't love, it'll have to do until the real thing comes along.*

I didn't hear from him until Thursday, which was unusual. He always called within the next day or two to recap the highlights of the previous date.

Oh fuck. Why hasn't he called? Did I do something wrong?

When he called on Thursday, he made idle chitchat. Evidence he was backpedaling. "How about this drought? Is it raining ash by you?"

"I don't think I can do this anymore."

He sounded taken aback. "Why, what happened?"

"It's just starting to feel a little too casual for my taste."

"Are you wanting it to be more of a relationship?"

"I like what we've had; I just don't want to be taken—" *For granted?* I didn't know what I was saying, what I wanted from him. I was reacting to a feeling that wasn't fully formed.

Somehow, whatever it was that caused Ashton to pull back must have lessened in that conversation, because he called back that afternoon.

"Would you like to see a movie on Saturday? I'm thinking Culver City, so that we can meet up with my brother and his girlfriend."

"What movie?" If it was a scary movie, I could easily say no; I don't do scary movies.

"Mystic River."

Damn, good choice.

I didn't know what to do. On the one hand, I didn't want to go because of the age difference. Even though Ashton and I looked the same age, I was certain he must have told his brother I was an *older woman.* But on the other hand, he was bringing me into his life, as I had hinted.

I sucked it up and went. I was as polite and congenial as I could be while feeling like an outsider the entire time.

After that, he became very affectionate in public, and he called more often from work, just to talk.

Since he lived near the airport, I sometimes drove to his house and slept over the night before a flight. I would leave my car there, and he would drive me to the airport. We'd get in late, sleep, and leave early in the morning, so I rarely saw his roommates. One Saturday night he asked me to sleep at his place and then stay and watch football with him and his roommates on Sunday.

"We do this big brunch thing."

"Oh."

In LA, football begins at 10 a.m., so people watch with breakfast instead of with chili, as we did in the Midwest.

"I'm not sure how comfortable I'll—" His face looked so excited to have me over that I changed my mind. "Sure. Football. Brunch. Sounds like a new experience."

What could I do? We hadn't addressed the friends and family issue in the treaty. I had no legal out.

Sunday morning, I came downstairs for breakfast and watched as they made waffles and eggs. I didn't offer to help cook, because it looked like they had a routine.

"Can I set the table?"

"Sure," the only other woman answered, a twenty-eight-year-old in a strappy tank top without a bra. She was sweet and tried to include me in the conversation. "We were talking about *The Simpsons*; did you see that last episode?"

"No, I haven't seen *The Simpsons* since *The Tracey Ullman Show*."

"The what show?"

She was an adolescent when *The Tracey Ullman Show* aired, and I was married with children watching *Married with Children*. I pretty much stayed silent during breakfast and promised myself that I only needed to make it to halftime. I was uncomfortable hanging with Ashton's roomies like a college coed while in reality being the *mother* of a college coed.

The only other difficulty I had with our relationship was describing our relationship. "Are you seeing anybody?" *Kind of.* "What does that mean?" *Well, there's this guy, a friend really. We have sex, and we're exclusive, but we can date others.*

Finally, I just summed it up for Eric as "having sex with your best friend."

"It's called 'friends with benefits.'"

"That's a thing? I thought I invented it."

"Sorry, kid. But you know, these things have a shelf life."

My girlfriends got a more detailed answer. "Because our relationship has a shelf life, there are no expectations, no judgments. I don't look at his behavior and ask myself: *can I live with that?* It's all good. Also, I don't want to have any regrets when it's over like I should have given more, so I hold nothing back. *We* hold nothing back, and every time we make love, we make love as if it's the last time. Because it might be." They looked at me as if I had discovered the Holy Grail of relationships.

One morning I was swimming laps in the pool, which has always been a form of meditation for me. As I swam, I realized I was late. I hadn't had a period for a while. I counted backward and realized I was two weeks late. I had never been two weeks late except for the two times I was pregnant. For some reason, maybe because of the peaceful state I was in, I didn't panic. Instead, I imagined what a wonderful father Ashton would make and how great it would be to name the baby after my father: Henry for a boy and Henri for a girl.

I bought a pregnancy test: negative. But still, my period never came. A few weeks later I was visiting family in Chicago, and when I was out at a bar with Eric, I got my period. I had skipped an entire month. I shared the news with my friend. "It's the beginning of the end."

"End of what?"

"My sexuality. Menopause is looming."

He laughed, "You're a long way from that. You're still smokin' hot." And I remembered one of the reasons he was in my life: he always made me feel good about myself.

I didn't say anything to Ashton about my pregnancy scare because the follow-up conversation would have led to perimenopause, which would be a reminder of all those years we had between us.

At the four-month point, I thought about what Eric said about a shelf life and feared Ashton would soon end our relationship. Then again, we could go on indefinitely. Where would he meet someone? He worked five nights a week, spent one night with me, and was with his roommates on the seventh.

Right before Christmas, before he was to go home for two weeks, we had another amazing night. We saw *Something's Gotta Give*, the movie about a woman (a writer no less) who is divorced after a twenty-year marriage and has an affair with a younger man. We laughed nonstop. Diane Keaton's character also sleeps with two guys in the same month and writes about it! *Who would do such a thing?*

At dinner afterward, he stared at me across the table so lovingly. He barely even noticed the beautiful young waitress serving us. When she asked, "Can I get you guys dessert?" he took my hand in his and said, "I have all the dessert I need right here."

I was embarrassed, but I ate it up. His words were tastier than chocolate.

That night we made love. Four hours. It felt otherworldly, as if time didn't exist. We had a true spiritual connection. Sure, we would each climax occasionally, but it was a side effect more than a goal. We never stopped holding each other with the kind of intimacy that conveyed we were most definitely more than friends.

When we got up in the morning, he took my face in his hands. "You're so beautiful. You see it, don't you, when you look in a mirror?"

"I just see all the changes."

"Well, how great is that after the changes you're still so beautiful."

We made love again for another three hours. We simply could not stop kissing each other, and embracing each other, and one thing would lead to another... I couldn't get enough. We couldn't keep our hands or mouths off each other.

A lot of the time I monitored what I said to him. I'd think it through first before I spoke because I thought saying something too intimate would cause him to withdraw. But that morning I said something. It was out of my mouth before I even knew I was thinking it. We were in bed hugging—after, so I couldn't see his reaction when I said, "I love making love with you."

Oops, double love.

When I heard what I had said, I braced myself for the awkward silence and the inevitable pullback. But after the silence, I heard, "I think I'm getting hard again."

It didn't sound like a joke; it sounded like he had taken it in. I thought he'd retreat because hearing "I love..." would freak him out. He told me in his past relationships he'd withheld love from girlfriends, not letting them know how he felt. From this, I must have picked up on his fear of love, but after I said it, we did make love again. That morning when he left my apartment, I didn't shut the door. I watched him walk down the hall of my apartment complex as if I'd never see him again, and tears fell down my cheeks.

I stayed in LA and had a meeting with Mark Travis, the director who the head of the networking group had introduced to me. Mark Travis was a big name in the solo show world. He had directed *Time Flies When You're Alive* and *A Bronx Tale*. Mark agreed to come to the Story Salon that week to watch me tell a thirty-minute comedic piece about my dating life thus far. I called it, "Fornicationally Challenged."

"You really have something here," he said when I got off-stage, and agreed to direct my show.

"I don't have an ending yet," I confessed.

"That's okay. We'll get there."

We'll. He *we'd* me. But unlike the men of my past, Mark lived up to every promise he made.

During the holidays, Ashton started calling me every day from Michigan. Then twice a day. I believe the extra attention was in direct violation of the treaty, but I didn't complain. On New Year's Eve, he called me at eight p.m. from a friend's party in Chicago to make sure we got to speak to each other. He told me how much he wished he could spend New Year's with me. Then we talked again after midnight, and he told me how much he missed me and wanted me. Then he drunk dialed me at four a.m. with some sexy talk. I missed him too, and I was glad that our reunion was only a few days away.

I occupied myself by planning an evening together to do every fun and sexy thing we'd said on the phone. I booked a four-star Beverly Hills hotel room with a king-size bed and Egyptian cotton sheets at a huge discount, due to it being the post-holiday season. It had a two-person soaking tub, so I bought dozens of tea candles to put around it. I packed a bag with the CDs we listened to (John Mayer, Norah Jones), two bottles of Veuve Clicquot, and special balloons for him to make me balloon animals, remembering when I saw them in the store that he'd said he knew how. Besides, with him, the romance thing was goofy, sexy fun.

I planned to ask him to meet me at the hotel, saying that I had a seminar that day and would he meet me for a drink. I would wear the dress I'd worn to that charity event in Chicago but bought purple stiletto heels to wear instead of the boots and no jacket. I would then tease him at the bar, and just when he got really hot and bothered, I'd tell him we had a room upstairs.

Well, the day he was to come home he got snowed in and had to stay in Chicago with his friend. No problem. I rescheduled the hotel for the following night. But he couldn't get out then either. He finally came back on a Monday night and had to go straight to work, which worked out better because the next weekend we'd have more time. I rebooked the hotel for that Friday, and they honored the same discount from the week before. It was meant to be.

He called Monday night on his way to work, and then again Tuesday afternoon. He asked me what was new, and I rattled on for a while. Eventually, he said, "I have some *interesting* news."

"Really? What?" I just knew he was going to suggest a midweek rendezvous.

"When I got snowed in at Chicago—"

"Yee-ah?"

"I met someone."

My eyes immediately went to the bag I had packed for us with the sexy dress, shoes, CDs, candles, champagne, and those fucking balloons. Reminders of him were in my apartment. *Why had I broken my rule?*

"I'm sorry. What?"

"I met somebody, and I want to explore this, and I just felt I had to tell you, Judi."

Suddenly I was in the past: six years ago, when I learned my husband was cheating on me, and I fell to the floor.

There comes a moment when your past holds a mirror to your present. At that moment with Ashton, I could have gone off on him, but it wouldn't have been about him. It was Ex-Hole baggage, and I didn't want to carry it around anymore. Ashton was upfront and honest and acted within the guidelines of a contract I helped construct. If I blamed him, then that would mean I had learned nothing during the five years since my divorce.

I finally found my words. "Did you sleep with her?"

"No. Just kissed."

I was grateful we were on the phone, so he couldn't see the tears streaming down my cheeks. "Look, I'm glad you told me, but I can't be intimate with you anymore."

"I get it."

Pause.

"But it may not work out with her," he offered.

"Either way, we're done."

"I understand."

I couldn't be intimate with him anymore, just as I couldn't be intimate with The Ex-Hole after his affairs.

"We did promise to stay friends," he added, genuinely hopeful.

"Yes. We will. Just give me a few months." I had to get off the phone. The ugly cry was looming, and I didn't want him to hear the pain in my voice. I was the older one. I knew what I was getting into when I constructed the contract. I had to keep it together.

"Fair enough. Call me when you're ready."

"I will," I said and hung up knowing I would. Some people you do not throw away. He brought out the best in me. Why would I toss out the baby with the bathwater?

Did I feel hurt and betrayed that a week after leaving my bed he found himself attracted to a younger woman? Did I feel threatened, less beautiful, less desired, and less sexy? That he never really cared for me?

No. Because Ashton thinking he could love a woman he met on vacation and pull off a long-distance relationship on his small income was not about me. It was about him running away from the realness, the intimacy that we shared. It was about his not wanting to fall in love with me, or possibly transferring the love he wanted to express to me onto someone else. It was safer for him to think he could love her.

Strangely, that sex contract healed me of trust and betrayal issues. It allowed me to get close to somebody for the first time. So I had no regrets. I liked the woman I was with Ashton and the person I had become. I stopped being afraid to commit to someone and knew that I would be in a real relationship one day, because the past did not dictate the future. At any rate, the breakup did give me the ending to my solo show.

He's Got A Room

I was sad for a few months after the breakup with Ashton, but not crushed. His honesty spared me the destructive internal thoughts women say to themselves when a relationship is over. I didn't torture myself with: What did I do? "What went wrong? "He never loved me" and, the most damaging, "I'm not good enough." An honest breakup may be hard for a guy, but it's the kindest thing a real man can do.

Plus, I won the breakup. It didn't last a week with that other girl.

About six months later, I went to interview a photographer with three first names about getting new headshots. I'd seen his work and had been very impressed. We met at his home office. He was shorter than I, about five foot six. He had blue eyes, dirty blond shoulder-length hair, and a boyish face, yet he was clearly older. There was an instant attraction. As I thumbed through his portfolio of actor 8x10s, I came across a picture of a woman dressed in black bondage attire. When he saw me linger over it, a smile came to his face.

"That's what she asked for. I believe in giving my clients what they want." He leaned in. "What do *you* want?"

I felt a small stirring, but I kept it at bay. "A commercial shot, business, the usual. Plus something fun and playful for my one-woman show."

I could see the annoyed look in his eyes—*another one-person show*—but he politely asked, "What's it called?"

"Fornicationally Challenged."

He smiled an intriguingly coy, playful smile. I booked his next available appointment even though it would cost three times as much as a Chicago photographer.

On the day of the shoot, I used the attraction between us as motivation. I looked into the lens and thought things like, *You want me, don't you?* It was my first experience with a digital camera, so we saw the end results right away. They were the best pictures of me, EVER.

At the end of the shoot, I made an appointment with his assistant to pick up the proof sheet the following week.

A few days later, in Chicago at Thanksgiving, my sister-in-law asked, "Are you seeing anyone?"

"No, but I will be. A photographer I just met."

That Monday, I went back to his home studio, and we looked at the pictures. He circled his favorites, and as I handed him a check, he grabbed my wrist and held it.

"When are we having lunch?"

His mischievous smile was enticing, but I played it cool, as Mother taught me. "Probably shortly after you ask me."

"Tomorrow. Come by the house at eleven-thirty, and I'll drive us to Pasadena."

Pause. I stared at him. He raised an eyebrow expectantly.

"I still didn't hear you ask."

He gave me a smirk. "Would. You. Have. Lunch. With. Me?"

"Sure. Why don't I come by tomorrow at eleven-thirty?"

He smiled, shook his head, and gave me a look I recognized from other men I had known. It said, *Man, you're gonna be work.* I loved it.

I parked my car in his driveway, and we drove his Jeep to a parking garage.

"I keep a car here."

He parked his Jeep on the street, and we went into the structure. He took the tarp off a vintage Porsche Roadster. "This is my baby."

Although I love vintage cars and was glad for the mutual

interest, I didn't give him the satisfaction of saying anything. We got in, he took the top down, and my hair flew in every direction as we drove on the highway. I took out some clips from my purse and began pinning my hair down.

I was proud of myself for not asking him to put the top up, but when I finished, he said, "That's not a good look."

"I wasn't expecting my hair to be flapping in the wind."

He rolled up his window. "Roll up your window. It'll help."

It did, so I took the clips out. We had lunch at a quaint restaurant, and then we went into a coin shop, where he was taken into the back room and shown gold pieces and coins.

"I'm buying my nephew a coin." But he bought gold pieces for himself, too.

We left the store, and he opened the car door for me. As I got in, I asked, "Am I supposed to be impressed?"

"Are you?"

Wealth had never impressed me. My high school boyfriend came from money, and I'd always given him a hard time about it. I thought that I should be nicer as an adult. "A little bit."

We saw each other a few days later. He asked me over to watch a movie. "I don't live at my studio. I have one of the Disney Cottages."

"Oh." I pretended to know what that meant and took down the address.

"You have two houses?"

"Yes. The big one is where I work, plus my ex-girlfriend's son lives there."

"That's so nice."

"I felt bad. She took the breakup hard. She was addicted to me." Before I could process what that meant, he continued, "I like having a place just for me. Keep my life separate."

"I get that." The photographer with three first names was perfect for me. He had space for my kids and would willingly allow them to stay with us—in their own house.

I pulled up to the cutest little bungalow in Los Feliz. I found out there was a series of small cottages that Walt Disney had built in 1931 to house his animators.

We had drinks on the patio before he took me up to his bedroom. I stood in the doorway, and looked at him.

"What? It's where my TV is."

We each sat on a side of the bed with a huge space between us. When the movie was over, he invited me to sit in the window cubby with him. He fit perfectly; I was a little too tall for it. We kissed in there. I didn't expect to be swept away by the kiss, and I wasn't. I highly doubted anyone would ever kiss me again the way Ashton had.

After a bit, I got up to leave. "I gotta go."

"You sure?"

"Yes."

We had lunch again a few days later at The Grove, near where I lived. As we walked the mall, he stopped me. "Look, are we going to sleep together or what?"

It was only week two of my six-week protocol, but I didn't explain that to him. "Eventually," I said.

"Let's have dinner Saturday."

I knew what that meant, and I contemplated breaking my rule for him.

A follow-up phone call established wardrobe require-ments. "I'd like you to wear a dress, and stockings with a seam in the back. Real stockings with a garter belt. And shoes that look like they're from the '40s."

"I was planning on wearing a Diane von Furstenberg wrap dress and boots." Pause. I was stalling to collect my thoughts. "I'll see what I can come up with."

I didn't know what to do. No guy I'd dated had wardrobe requests other than, *Hey, could you wear that dress again?*

I went to Fredrick's on Hollywood Boulevard for ideas. I bought a pair of stockings with elastic bands to keep them in place and a black thong. *It'll have to do.*

He took me to the Beverly Hills Hotel, and we had dinner on the patio. He sat in the booth facing the restaurant, his arms spread across the top of the backrest as if waiting to be recognized because of that one film he was in in the '70s.

After dinner, he came up to my place and kissed me as soon as the door closed. "Where's the bedroom?" I pointed, and he took my hand and led me there with determination. "Get on the bed." I sat at the edge. "The middle of the bed." I started to take my shoes off. "Leave them on." I did as ordered.

He came to me on the bed and pulled me to my knees. He reached his hand under my dress and found I was wearing a thong and not the garter. "Tsk. Tsk. Tsk." He removed my underwear with flawless ease as he masterfully began to get me excited.

I started to unbutton his shirt, but he wouldn't let me. I wondered if he was flawed or had a small dick, but soon I stopped thinking altogether. His magic fingers were bringing me to a climax and then—he stopped. Just stopped.

"That's all for tonight." He kissed me on top of my head and left me there.

Guess who I called?

"He's got a room," Roxy stated with quiet certainty.

"A room?"

"Where he keeps sex equipment."

I remembered an episode of *Sex and the City* where Samantha goes home with a guy and when she comes out of the bathroom, she finds him in his closet, naked except for black leather straps around his wrists and neck. He was chained up and asking to be spanked.

"In the Disney Cottage?!"

"Yep."

"It was modeled after Snow White, for God's sake!" I stammered.

"She did live in a one-bedroom house with seven little dudes."

"Are you sure about him?"

Roxy was positive and listed the reasons: "The clothing requirements, he pleasured you and left you hanging. It's all about power and control. He's got a room. I'm just sayin'."

I thought long and hard. Roxy was right. All the evidence pointed to S&M. Part of me was intrigued. What could it hurt to experiment with something new? I had watched several episodes of *Real Sex* on HBO in the '90s. Some of it looked fun and titillating. But did I want to go there? What if I liked it and could never have regular sex again? Then I'd be the kinky one, out there alone, waiting for not only the right guy but the right guy with the right fetish.

I had plenty of time to think about it because it took him a week to call me. "Why haven't I heard from you?" I asked.

"What?"

"You didn't call me the next day."

"You didn't call me either."

"I'm not a casual girl."

"You know what? This is way too much work. I can't do this."

He hung up the phone, and I was glad the decision to either keep seeing him or break up was no longer in my hands.

The photographer with three first names revealed my boundary, and having boundaries is perfectly fine, especially because they were mine, not Mother's. I doubted Mother knew of such goings-on anyway. At any rate, Mother stopped haunting me. I guess she saw that I could take care of myself.

But still, I wondered: what was it that the ex-girlfriend found addicting?

Roxy

"**W**hy won't you just go away?!"
Never in a million years would I have thought or even entertained the notion that those words would come out of her mouth, but there they were: an exhausted declaration, a final termination of the relationship.

"Because it's me. Me! You know me."

I thought I had gotten through, but instead I heard, "Once again you have proven to be selfish and inconsiderate. I'm done."

I hung up the phone. I had to for self-preservation. My heart hurt, physically hurt, under the weight of those cruel words. I knew Roxy could cut a person to the quick with her tongue, but never me. I put the phone down and said under my breath, "I will always love you, Roxy." And I cried harder than I have over losing any man. Whatever her reasons, whatever she was going through, she had to go through it without me. I had to let her go.

It was Christmas day 2005, and I had chosen to stay in LA and not to go home, not after what happened over Thanksgiving. I walked around my LA neighborhood, crying, as I tried to figure out where it had all gone to shit.

Roxy and I met when we were fifteen. When I talked, she

listened, without interrupting, until I finished. She was the only person in my life to show me that consideration. We were, however, opposites. She was the crunchy granola girl that belonged in Colorado, whereas I was the fashionista that loved fast-paced city life, yet we were bound by a common childhood trauma that it would take us decades to unravel. Our mutual friends eventually stopped hanging out with Roxy because she was dealing with issues our teenage friends were inept to handle. I was happy to be there for her, but I wasn't brave enough to deal with my own trauma. Instead, I perfected the art of dissociation. In our senior year, my parents allowed Roxy to live with us so she could heal, no questions asked.

Both our mothers told us not to get too close, each warning about the dangers of trusting a woman, especially around your man. Roxy and I discussed it and decided we would keep our expectations low. Still, we trusted each other with our hearts and our secrets. That was more important to us.

We had fun. When we were together, crazy things happened. Senior year we met two guys from the rock band Foreigner, and they bought us drinks on Rush Street. Another time we knowingly dated the same guy, who thought he was playing us against each other. My favorite memory was what we did after reading a Jacqueline Susann novel that boasted of young starlets being given "vitamin shots" by a doctor on a film set. *Vitamin* was code for speed, so Roxy and I found a seedy doctor and asked him to give us vitamin shots. *Wink. Wink.* We thought it was a universal code. It wasn't. The only thing we experienced was florescent yellow urine.

Two years after high school graduation, I got married and started a family. Roxy and I maintained our best-friend status, but only spoke occasionally and saw each other a few times a year. She lived the life of a twenty-something city girl, walking distances from the bars on Division Street while I sat on PTA committees. Every once in a while, we'd see how the other half lived: I would do the bar scene with her and she'd come to one of my children's birthday parties.

Roxy and I were each other's memory. We each remembered things from our past that the other forgot. I knew I loved the album *4 Way Street* when I was a teenager, but given that I didn't own it, I didn't remember listening to it in my room. Roxy said I played it every time I went to her house. After we smoked pot, I'd lay on the floor with a speaker at each ear.

We filled in each other's blanks.

When I divorced at forty, we picked up where we left off in high school. Not only was Roxy a huge support for the pain and grieving I'd experienced over the loss of my family unit, she also became my partner in crime again. I dragged her with me to singles' parties. The real fun was not in meeting men; it was in our conversations. We came up with nicknames for the guys and invented funny scenarios. I started writing down our ideas, thinking that one day it would make a great television sitcom. Roxy and I found humor in any and every situation.

In the meantime, I had become part of a storytelling group that met and performed autobiographical material once a week. By the time I went to LA, I had most of the material needed to put together a one-person show about my dating follies. I hoped to catch the eye of a television executive and get hired as a comedy writer, and from there, sell the television pilot based on my escapades with Roxy.

As I put the finishing touches on my one-woman show in Los Angeles, Roxy and I talked multiple times a day. She was my muse. When I read her a joke and heard her laugh, I knew it was truly funny. She was one of the funniest women I knew, and she took comedy seriously. If Roxy laughed, the joke was audience-ready.

After Ashton and I broke up and my show had an ending, I workshopped the material in a class Mark Travis let me take in exchange for running his office. Roxy was a big support and flew out to see me perform the first rendition of the show at the Santa Monica Playhouse. I performed the show there for a packed ninety-nine-seat house. As the audience applauded at the end of the show, I pointed to Roxy, clapped in her direction, and took her onstage with me for the curtain call.

After that, I honed the script and performed the show at that theatre several more times. Roxy flew out and shared the spotlight with me through every version. I planned to open the show in Hollywood that winter, but first I wanted to trademark the title, *Fornicationally Challenged*. To do that, I needed to perform the show in another state. I chose Chicago, the Monday after Thanksgiving. I had a connection at one of the major theatres in town, and they let me rent the main stage for that one night.

The Edgar Winter guy helped me stage the show with the sound and lighting cues Mark and I had already worked out. We rehearsed that Sunday and on Monday I was ready. The house filled with almost everyone I knew; I was excited to show them all who I had become in LA: a funny and talented writer/comedian.

I may have been ready, but the Chicago audience was not. I received very little reaction, and hardly any laughs in the places that had always garnered roars. It was a painful seventy-five minutes to stand on stage and maintain performance-level energy while the audience sat in judgment. At the end of the show, I grabbed Roxy's hand, bowed, and we ran backstage to my dressing room.

"What the hell was that?" she asked as she plopped on the couch.

"I have no idea," I responded, grateful that she saw in the audience the same thing I had. "Was I that different than in LA?"

"No, it wasn't you. It's Chicago."

She was right. Chicago had a glass ceiling for me, as it always had. I couldn't be too pretty, too funny, too anything. Standing out was not acceptable. But in LA I could be everything I'd always dreamed I could be. In LA there were no limits.

"I don't belong here anymore." But I still had to go into the lobby and face the audience that was full of friends, family, and the friends and family of all my friends and family. Both Roxy and her mother had brought ten friends, and her brothers were there too. I got through the false praise of the people I knew, and Roxy and I went to the bar next door for our postproduction martini. We were joined by several of our close friends, while her older brother sat in a booth by himself. He would not say a word to me.

The next morning Roxy called me from work just before I was about to leave for the airport. "We have to talk."

"Okay," I responded and waited.

"Not now, but soon."

She was so serious, I had to know what was wrong. "Just tell me now."

"No, I can't talk now. Call me tonight."

I couldn't wait all day. "Just give me a preview."

I finally coerced a response from her. "I want credit in the show."

"Okay, whatever you want." There was anger in her voice, and it scared me. "In what way?"

She lost it. "You stole my words. You turned everything around. You made yourself look good at my expense."

"Wait, wait. What's changed? You loved the show."

"I told you I wasn't ready to talk yet. I'm at work. Call me tonight."

She hung up the phone, so I called my cousin. My cousin had been at the show, and her take was that Roxy's family and friends must have been mortified to see Roxy portrayed as man-crazy and foulmouthed.

"It's a writing device. I made the two women as different as I could; Roxy knew that. She loved the show."

"Until last night?" my cousin asked. "Until her mother and brothers saw it?"

I called Roxy that night when I got back to LA, but she didn't pick up the phone. The next day I got an angry email about how I had disrespected her and made it worse by making her talk about it while she was at work. She told me how selfish I was and how the last few years had been all about me.

She wasn't wrong, but relationships are never fifty-fifty.

They swing back and forth. Still, I had manipulated her the past few years, forcing her to live the "single" life she had given up. We tried to have phone conversations, but by the end of the calls, she was always angrier.

Before that, we had never fought. Ever. We had no history of making up after a fight, no shared or safe language to use with each other. I kept trying to get Roxy to see my side, which only escalated the issues. Finally, she threatened me with a lawsuit.

"The title, *Fornicationally Challenged*, is mine. If you use it, I'll sue you." And she hung up. I knew that was her older brother's influence. I also knew I had become one of the people that hurt her, and I hated myself for it. I was sorry. I wanted to make it up to her. I wanted, needed her to forgive me.

I wrote her an email explaining the writing process. That the show was mostly autobiographical; written from all the stories I had performed over eighteen months in Chicago. Because she never came to any of those performances, she didn't know the material. I explained that I used our friendship as a throughline but that I was still open to sharing credit, an offer that horrified my writing friends. That's when I got the call from her ending the relationship by saying that I once again had proven myself to be selfish and inconsiderate. Had I known better at the time, I might have just said "I'm sorry" instead of pushing her to see my point of view.

"All I can say is, you've lost another sister."

That was her final blow: a low blow. My sister and I had stopped talking three years ago, after our dad died, and there was no coming back from that salt-in-the-wound statement.

When I hung up, I placed a block on my phone and email. There was no way my heart could withstand another verbal assault. I gave myself time to grieve the loss, and when the holidays were over, I booked a Hollywood theatre and planned to open the show that February. The only thing I changed was her name. I should have done that in the first place; maybe then the fight could have been avoided. What I did not change was the title of my show. The trademark application was final. I had a certificate. I owned *Fornicationally Challenged*.

Friends tried to console me over the loss, telling me that it happened because of Roxy's issues and not mine, that Roxy was wrong. I found no comfort in being right. If given a choice between being right and being in a relationship, I preferred being in a relationship with Roxy. Besides, it takes two to fight. I played a role in the destruction of our friendship, and I would have to live with that regret.

Roxy certainly wasn't my only friend. I've been blessed to have several wonderful women that hold the "best friend" status in my life, but Roxy and I had shared over three decades together. Losing her was akin to losing a large part of what made me... me. Gone were my teenage years, my comedic counterpart, my secret-keeper, my sister, and, of course—the other half of my memory.

LA Richard

I chose The Hudson Theatres in Hollywood for the run of my show. I wanted audiences to associate me with the Comedy Central workshop located there. The theatre manager, Jake (a tall, dark, and handsome man that had me questioning why I had given up that type), showed me the three different theatres available at The Hudson. I settled on the forty-three-seat black box, the smallest and, I hoped, easiest space to fill.

I brought my director, Mark Travis, and a lighting designer through before I signed a lease. Every time I went to the theatre, the owner wasn't there; it was always Jake. I was glad. He smiled when he saw me and acted like he had all the time in the world to spend with me. I couldn't tell if he was interested in me, renting the space, or both.

He looked young. I didn't want to date another young guy, so I Googled him to get the intel. All I found with his name were the white pages for the Los Angeles area. There were three Jake Masons in the area, and their ages were twenty-two, thirty-one, and thirty-eight. I hoped he was thirty-eight. He didn't look thirty-eight, but I didn't look forty-six.

Every time I saw him at the theatre, I would ask a question trying to decipher which Jake Mason he was. "What music did you listen to in college?" I figured if he said Nirvana or Pearl Jam, he was thirty-eight. If it were boy bands, it would be a no-go for additional reasons.

"Jazz."

Shit.

Maybe I could figure it out by location according to those white pages. "Where do you live?"

"In Los Angeles." That meant any of the pockets between towns. One had a Los Angeles address if they lived between Venice Beach and Culver City or between Hollywood and West Hollywood.

I finally gave up my quest the day I was there signing the leasing agreement. After Jake explained the contract to me, he left me at a table to read it. A few minutes later, I looked up and saw him draped around the totally LA-ed out barista behind the coffee bar. She had black hair in pigtails with short bangs and wore a miniskirt, a white blouse, knee socks, and platform shoes. The way she dressed, and the overabundance of makeup applied, told me she was much older than she'd admit.

Suddenly I was interrupted by a young male barista with frenetic Jim Carrey energy.

"Hi, I'm Richard. Can I get you anything?"

"No. Thank you."

"I saw you looking at the bar. So I thought you wanted a coffee or something."

Busted. "Oh, I was just wondering who that girl was."

"Mia? She's Jake's lady friend. They've been together for years."

Lady friend? Who under the age of seventy-two says lady friend? As I took in the news that my crush had bad taste in women and was not available, he continued, "You have beautiful nails."

I started doing my own nails at fifteen, ever since my friend Susie told me I had nice hands. For the last ten years I had been giving myself French manicures weekly, and what I'd noticed since becoming single was that when a man commented on my hands, he was interested in me. I needed to shut this guy down.

"Look, I have to finish this paperwork for Jake," I told him, barely looking up.

"Oh, you're renting a theatre? Playwright, producer, or actor?"

The exuberant energy that came at me, though entertaining, bordered on the obnoxious, like a court jester.

"All the above." I kept my attention on the papers in front of me, hoping he would take the hint.

"Okay, I'll leave you to it." I watched as he walked away to join his friends behind the bar. He was a little guy, five foot eight in sneakers. He had long, dark blonde, kinky hair circa 1970s Peter Frampton, but he wore baggy pants around his hips like other men/boys his age. I laughed to myself, thinking of how Roxy would have had a field day with this one. *He's so young; even you wouldn't date him*—God, how I missed that woman.

I rehearsed my show on the stage for a week to get the lighting and sound cues locked down with Mark. After we opened the show, it became my entire life. I performed four nights a week, Thursday through Sunday. I never saw Mia or any other barista there again, only Richard. One night before a performance, I asked, "Can I get about an inch of coffee?"

"An inch? Never heard that before. You mean espresso?"

"God, no. I just need a little pick-me-up before the show."

"Gotcha," he said as he gave me two inches. "Let me give you a lid."

"No, thanks. I don't drink coffee from a sippy cup," I told him with a bit too much sass. "How much?"

"Please, for an inch of coffee?" Something in the way he shook his head told me he probably wouldn't have let me pay for anything I ordered.

After the show that night, I made it a point to say goodbye to him. It was just after nine p.m. and the two other shows' intermissions were over, so he had a lull. "Thanks again for the coffee."

"Hey, no thing," he responded.

I had no idea what that meant. Sometimes I would say "no big" in place of "no big deal," but *no thing?*

Shit, he's young.

"How's the show goin'?" he continued.

"Good. Fun. I love doing it."

"Hey, have dinner with me Tuesday night."

I hadn't dated anyone special in the two years since my affair with Ashton ended. I went to many events, but only to collect cards to generate a mailing list. Getting my show up and running had been my priority. Anytime a friend asked if I was seeing anyone, my response was that once my show opened, I would probably meet someone.

Still, when Richard asked me out to dinner, I laughed. Not him. I couldn't date him. He was way too young, but I shouldn't have laughed.

"I'm sorry, Richie, no," I called him Richie not just because his kid-like energy was exhausting, but to make it clear that this playground was for upperclassmen only.

"I prefer Richard."

"What?"

"My name is Richard, not Richie or Rich or even Dick. Richard."

Very grown-up. But then Richard turned to a young customer, and I heard "Boo-yah!" come out of his mouth.

Yeah, never gonna happen.

The following week, he asked me out again. And again, I said, "No."

"What's the big deal? It's just dinner."

"If you saw my show you'd understand. I can't date younger guys anymore."

The following Friday, Jake came backstage before the show and told me that there was no one in the audience and no reservations, so we canceled the performance. As I walked down Hudson Street to my car, I saw Richard talking to Jake.

"Hey, I came to see your show," he said as I approached.

"Sorry, time of death was called at seven fifty-one." He didn't smile.

"What are you going to do now?" he asked, clearly not giving up on his plan to see me that night.

"I'm going to drive around the neighborhood to distribute flyers and posters. I obviously need to advertise more."

"How 'bout I go with you?"

I thought before I said no, because it would be very helpful if he drove and I didn't have to repark constantly. "Okay, thanks. Can you drive?"

"Sure, no thing."

No, what?

His car was a small, green beater my college daughter would have called a POS: piece of shit. The doors were a different color than the rest of the car, and it had many dents. When he ignited the engine, it made a loud noise that turned into a steady rumble, and the rumbling sound spiked every time he accelerated. I fastened my seatbelt; something told me I was in for a bumpy night.

When I was finished distributing flyers, I asked him to take me back to my car.

"Let's get something to eat first."

Normally I found it difficult and awkward to say no to a man, but I had become quite accustomed to saying no to Richard. "No, Richard. I don't think that's a good idea."

"What's with the no? Ya gotta eat."

I went. It was just easier.

He took me to the Formosa Café on Santa Monica Boulevard. It's an old Hollywood hang from the Sinatra days: a dimly lit hideout with autographed pictures of celebrities on crushed velvet walls. Richard looked very out of place in the oversized red booth, and I resisted the temptation to look under the table to see if his feet reached the floor.

He proceeded to tell me all about himself. When he was young—young*er*—he was on the Junior Olympic team in tae kwon do. He'd lived in New York, San Francisco, Spain, and France. He was fluent in French, was learning Mandarin, had a master's degree, and had lived with four different women since college. I did the math.

"How could you have squeezed in four long-term relationships in that short of a time frame?"

"That I can tell you in one word: overlap." He said it with a smile, but I didn't think he was joking. I took him for another cheater.

This is so *not going to happen.*

Dinner was uncomfortable. Even ordering dinner was uncomfortable. There was nothing on the menu I could eat. There were no healthy vegetarian options. He ordered us a fried appetizer and a piece of chocolate cake to share. I hadn't had chocolate in years and didn't appreciate the temptation. Chocolate was a gateway food for me. One bite and I could be on the road to eating like crap, and for the first time in my life, I was happy with my weight and complexion.

"Would you like a glass of wine?"

Yes, please!

Before I could answer, he continued, "I don't drink, but please feel free."

"No, thank you," I said and wondered how I would make it through this ridiculous appetizer-dessert debacle sober.

He must have felt uneasy too, because his exuberant energy returned as he tried to be entertaining. He had been acting normal lately, so I'd forgotten about that side of his personality. He did all the talking the rest of the evening and I pretended to listen. I was grateful that I didn't have to contribute small talk. I just looked across the table at the man-child that wanted me so much and was pursuing me so fiercely. And I felt it, deep in my gut, a knowing that screamed, *No way!*

He drove me back to my car, and as I put my hand on the door handle to get out of the POS, I felt that familiar self-conscious feeling I usually have at the end of a date.

"We should do this again."

I knew it. "Are you thinking this was a date?"

He shrugged. "There was food. We ate. I paid. It was our first date."

"How old are you?"

"Age doesn't matter," he said in a grown-up voice.

Wow, that means he's super young. "Sure, *Opie.* Age doesn't matter. Just the same, how old are you?"

"It's just a number." It took a while, but he finally told me. "Thirty."

I laughed, hard. I was in the middle of a theatrical run where I talked about dating younger men that were *older* than he! "I'm sorry," I said when I finally got ahold of myself. "It's just that you're only five years older than my son."

He didn't find any of it funny, and I felt bad about laughing in his face. Still, he looked younger than me. No one I've ever dated actually *looked* younger than me. I had to draw the line somewhere.

As the weeks passed, I continued to see him at the theatre. He continued to ask me out, and I continued to say no. "I have to say," I told him one night, "it takes an enormous amount of confidence to repeatedly ask a woman out knowing the answer will be no. Where does confidence like that come from? Cause you could teach a class."

He didn't reply. He just smiled sheepishly.

I always needed to unwind after a performance, so we talked in that quiet hour he had between shows. I began to notice his energy calming down again. His behavior became more real. His opinions on life were interesting, and I grew to like him as a theatre friend: a person who becomes a huge part of your life for a short period of time.

I learned that his parents divorced when he was young—er, and his grandfather was his prominent male influence, which explained why he had the language of an old man, saying *horse-shit* instead of bullshit and *lady friend* in place of girlfriend. He was also grumpy: people easily annoyed him, especially the children he told me about that played near his yard. I started calling him Morty because on the inside, he was really an old Jewish man. When he started complaining, this is what I heard: "Oy, kids today, I never vant to have "em." It was too bad. Since I didn't want more kids, he might have been a good match for me.

He always made sure I left the theatre before he got

slammed with customers because he insisted on walking me to my car. I wasn't sure if he was being a gentleman or wanted the hug he gave me when we reached my Beetle. I let him hug me. *What the hell.* I heard somewhere people needed at least eight hugs a day. At least I was getting one.

The next time he asked me out, I teased him instead of saying no. "I'm going into West Hollywood tomorrow to pass out flyers and posters for my show. Come with me and wear a tank top. Something tells me boys love you."

That's when I saw his arms for the first time and wondered how I could have missed them the past few months. He had big muscular arms that were barely contained by the short sleeves of his T-shirt. Guns. When he caught me looking, I felt blood rush to my cheeks. I left without the walk to my car.

The following week he didn't ask me to dinner. "Have lunch with me."

I finally agreed, thinking it would shut him up, but then he got sick and had to cancel. I didn't see him at the theatre for weeks. I knew he must have been really ill, but secretly, I was relieved to be off the hook.

Eventually, he claimed the rain check. We met on a weekday at a new restaurant across from the Farmer's Market on Fairfax. The restaurant hadn't officially opened. We were the trial customers. We both had iced teas, which the waitstaff kept refilling. I soon learned that since he had no experience with alcohol or drugs, caffeine got him high, in a fun, slightly drunk way. Our conversation was excited and amusing and eventually turned to sex. He revealed he always used condoms, got tested after every relationship ended, and finally that he hadn't had sex in several years.

"Me too!"

"I'm just not attracted to women my age. They're immature. They want to go to clubs, meet their friends at bars. I don't drink, so I end up having to take care of them. It's not fun."

"Easy there, Morty."

He smiled. He liked my nickname for him. He told me he

had lost his virginity at fifteen.

I had no interest in dating him so, I was honest. "I lost mine at fourteen."

"In your show, you say your husband was your first."

"He was actually my second. I did it one time with my high school boyfriend."

"You got me beat. As it turned out, I sucked at it."

I laughed. "Really?"

"Oh yeah, but the girl was experienced and taught me. A lot." I hoped he'd spare me the details. It had become a side effect of my show: people thought they could talk to me about sex. To that point, he then asked, "What's the best sex you ever had?"

It didn't feel like an inappropriate question. It was fun to think about it. Since I initially thought The Ex-Hole and I had great sex until I met Ashton, I came up with the perfect answer. "I think the best sex is the sex you're currently having."

He thought about it and agreed.

After lunch, he walked me to my car. I had heels on, so I was three inches taller than him. When I opened my car door, I said goodbye and quickly got in before he could even think about kissing me. I'd had a great time with him at lunch, and it felt like there could be something sparking, but he was still too young. I wanted our relationship to remain platonic.

When I got home, Mark called with great news: the *LA Times* was coming to review the show that Saturday night. "You'll need to fill the house." I knew that wouldn't be a problem considering the friends I had made and the networking group. "And call the theatre, see if we can rehearse in the space tonight."

Richard was the first person I called to tell the good news. He was very excited for me. When Mark and I rehearsed that night, I was still on a high from the iced teas and conversation, and I kept getting distracted. In the middle of talking about how young Ashton was, my thoughts went to Richard and how much younger he *actually* was.

Mark stopped me. "I've never seen you this way. You're unfocused."

"You're right."

"Is there something wrong? Are you nervous about the *Times* coming?"

"No, nothing like that."

"The show has New York potential."

I loved hearing that. "I know what it is, Mark. I know what's wrong with me. Don't worry. I'll shut it down. Saturday will be great," I promised him.

When rehearsal was over, Richard was waiting for me in the café. I wanted to tell him that I couldn't date him, but there were too many people around. He followed me back to my apartment. I parked in my designated spot, but it took him a while to find a space on the street. When he came to the door, he was cute, saying he wasn't coming in but just wanted his after-date kiss.

"No. I can't kiss you. I have to keep my head in the game."

"Excuse me?"

"I was preoccupied in tonight's rehearsal. I can't stand on stage and talk about other men if there's a man in my life pulling my focus."

"I'm a man in your life, pulling your focus?" he asked, smiling.

He started to come in, so I ran and stood behind the 1940s chair I took from my parents' home. "You can't kiss me. I'm serious."

He immediately retreated to the doorway, where the door was still open. Once again, I admired the way women after Mother's generation were raising their sons.

"Okay, I'll wait until after your show."

"Fine," I said to get him out of there.

"We'll have dinner after your show closes."

I agreed. I felt like the Miller's daughter promising Rumpelstiltskin my firstborn child to get what I wanted at the moment.

My show was supposed to close in a few weeks, but after the *LA Times* gave me a good review, I extended the run another month, and then another month after that, which meant I didn't have to fulfill my end of the bargain with Rumpel Richard.

One day, my computer crashed. Dead. No backup. My show was gone, the plays I had written were gone, screenplays—gone, short stories—gone. Everything I had ever written disappeared. I hired a computer guy to retrieve my work, but all he was able to do was put random files on disks.

"So-called 'computer experts' don't always know what they're doing. They just have to know more than you," Richard told me. "I could help you, and you wouldn't have to pay anyone."

"Thanks, but I couldn't ask you to do that."

"Vhat asked? I offered," I heard Morty reply.

Richard came to my rescue. We spent weeks together in my apartment going through the files on the disks and downloading them onto my new Mac. He usually came before dinnertime so I would prepare a meal for us.

"No one has ever cooked for me," he said the first time I put a plate in front of him.

"Your mother didn't make dinner?"

"No, I cooked. I took care of everything in the house, including raising my little brother." He took a big bite, and we were done talking about him. "I can tell you're a great mother."

I thought he was using a line on me, so I called him out. "How can you tell that?"

"Because you're making sure I'm fed, you're kind, and because you're only now starting to live your own life after your children have grown."

Wow.

"I still feel guilty about being in LA," I confided. "That's why I pushed so hard to open my show. If it doesn't get me a writing job, I need to go home."

"Have you ever produced a show before?"

"Never, not even a PTA talk."

"I've produced many shows. I'm impressed with all you've done."

"I'm lucky; every next step revealed itself to me. I met

the director when I needed one, heard about the Santa Monica Playhouse when I needed to test it in front of an audience. The connections mostly came through my networking group. Their support has been a godsend."

He had finally stopped asking me out, so I was able to relax and enjoy his company. Sometimes I'd be working on something else in the apartment, and he'd roll over to me on the task chair. It was the cutest thing, him rolling across the room. It made me smile.

When he finished with my computer, all my files had been retrieved, organized, and backed up on an external hard drive. He then taught me how to back up my work and sync my Blackberry. It turns out he was a techie. He'd been a part of the whole dot-com industry in the '90s.

"You're not a barista?"

"Jake owns the café. I know him from college. As a favor, I sometimes work Saturday nights."

"But you're there every night I am."

"I trade shifts with people to make that happen. I like seeing you." There was no crazy energy in his manner, only sincerity and vulnerability.

I had been searching for true love for the past six years, and in front of me was a man who was crazy about me. He was smart and helpful and sweet. Why did he have to be sixteen years younger? And not to mention—broke.

I wanted to properly repay him for all the work he'd done for me, but I also knew that giving him money would be insulting. He had once revealed a love for opera so, I bought him two tickets to the LA Opera's current production of *The Marriage of Figaro.*

"These are for you, as a thank-you for saving all my work."

"That's terrific! When are we going?" he asked with the proper amount of excitement as he opened the small envelope.

I corrected him. "They're for you, to take someone else."

"Who else would I take?"

"A girl, a friend, it doesn't matter."

"I choose you."

"I can't date you."

"You bought the tickets."

I didn't know how to answer, so I agreed to go. It was just easier. At that time the opera was weeks away, but it ended up being two nights after my show finally closed and the day after my promised dinner date with him.

On that dinner date, he took me to a local vegetarian place in Hollywood. I ordered a salad while he tried to order a plain salad with hummus. His order baffled the waitress. "Hummus isn't a dressing," she told him.

"I know, but I'm going to use it as a dressing."

"The hummus plate comes with pita bread and vegetables. Not lettuce."

"I don't want the pita bread or the vegetables or the stuff you put on a salad." I had a flashback to a movie my sister took me to in the '60s called *Five Easy Pieces*. In it, Jack Nicholson tries to order toast by ordering a chicken sandwich on toast and telling the waitress to hold the chicken—between her legs.

Richard eventually communicated what he wanted, and the waitress left the table. He rolled his eyes. "How hard was that?"

"She's probably new," I defended.

"It's not rocket science. I just wish people would do their jobs."

He was so different from easygoing Ashton.

Back at my place, I played some early Zeppelin and Emerson, Lake & Palmer, albums I thought he'd enjoy. He sat on the couch, I on the floor near my stereo. Then he came over to me and stated with quiet confidence, "Stand up. I'm going to kiss you."

I stood. The kiss? Not great: way too much tongue for a first kiss, too much to think about and, like him, too busy.

"You don't like my kiss?" he asked, so I told him why.

He took my hand and led me to my bedroom. "Show me. We can practice."

We did. We practiced and talked well into the night. He somehow manipulated my shirt off, but I refused to give up anything else. "What's the big deal?" he asked. "It'd be like wearing a bikini."

"That has to be the worst, and I mean *the worst,* line ever. And I gotta say, I expected better from that educated mouth."

Around three a.m., I told him it was time for him to go.

"What?" He was genuinely surprised. "No one has ever asked me to leave."

"Well, I am."

"You're not serious."

"I am serious," I said as I put my shirt back on. "I'll see you tomorrow."

"Wha—?" He was still dazed as I led him to the door.

"The opera. Pick me up at seven?"

The following night he wore a suit—with Converse sneakers. I wore my new Diane von Furstenberg brown cashmere wrap dress with high-heeled boots. Once again, I was taller than him, and we drove to downtown LA in the POS.

Shortly after the second act began, I felt Richard's touch on my hand. Electricity shot through my veins. I looked over at him. He was looking at me. We sat there holding hands and staring into each other's eyes, and suddenly, I had a vision of him unwrapping the Furstenberg. *Shit.* What a difference a day made. I certainly hadn't felt this way the night before.

Oh, what the hell, one more young guy, I thought to myself. After all, he was in his thirties. Yes, I managed to convince myself that being thirty meant he was technically in his thirties. It wasn't like he was twenty-nine; now, twenty-nine would have been too young!

Back in my bedroom, he took off his shirt, revealing a body that did not belong to a kid. It was exactly like the musculature figures drawn on anatomy charts. Every muscle on his body was clearly defined and protruding through his skin: strong, broad shoulders, bulging biceps, and not six- but eight-pack abs.

Down to only his boxers, he dove into bed and started

tossing me around. I didn't know if we were making love or per-forming a Cirque du Soleil routine. I knew his energy and agility would either be the greatest sex I ever had or break me in two. But I was ready to find out. When he removed his boxers, I finally understood the reason for his *enormous* amount of confidence.

"Wow," I said, stopping him when I caught sight of his penis. It too, was a beautifully chiseled work of art: long, pink, and perfectly shaped. Yet I found the thickness and length wor-risome. "I'm afraid there's 'no room at the Inn.'"

He smiled with the confidence of a man who knew how to handle himself. We did not leave my apartment for two days.

"I want us to be exclusive," he said the next morning en-thusiastically when I awoke.

Exclusive. Was that Richard's way of asking me to go steady? As I looked at his smiling face, I realized that his level of commitment was exactly what had been missing with Ashton. As nice as it felt, I knew it was just for a little while. I agreed, knowing we were just having fun.

That second night we made love for hours but expended enough energy to rival three intense workouts. At one point he got up to go to the bathroom, but by the time he reached the foot of the bed, his legs gave way, and he passed out on the floor. I crawled to the edge of the bed to see if he was okay but passed out there myself. He woke hours later and then woke me.

"How did I end up on the floor?"

"You passed out on your way to the bathroom."

"And you left me there?"

"I tried to help but passed out in the process."

He laughed and scooped me up and we snuggled back in the bed. Then he laughed.

"What?" I asked, smiling back at him.

"I still have to go to the bathroom." As he got up, he added, "Get dressed, we need sustenance."

He took me to Le Pain Quotidien on Melrose. He ordered himself a croissant and me a yogurt in perfect French. Then we went back to my place and made love until it was time to replenish again.

That night we talked as we snuggled. "There's a painting in a museum back home that's a favorite of mine. I never knew why until I saw you for the first time." I sensed a story coming, and I listened with my head resting on his bare, chiseled chest as he spoke. "It's a beautiful swirling mass of majestic colors of two equally-sized figures that are interconnected. After I met you, I realized that the figures were souls, twin souls, and in this crazy universe of you living your life and me living mine, we finally found each other here in LA. How wild is that? It's crazy. All the pieces that had to fall into place for us to finally find each other."

"Yeah, well, you were late," I said, trying to keep things light.

"What?"

"Okay, so maybe we were up there, souls in heaven, and it's time to come to earth to find each other. I jump first, but you, being you, start talking to some angel for *way* too long, and you ended up following me too late—sixteen years too late!"

He laughed and hugged me. "Yeah, sorry, 'bout that."

When he finally left my apartment after that two-day stint, I picked up my cell phone to give Roxy the details. Tears welled up when I remembered we were no longer friends. It made me feel better to imagine our conversation.

"How was the sex?" It would have been her first question.

"I'd rate it E."

"E?"

"Every. Time."

She'd take a minute and laugh when its meaning sunk in, then she'd say, *"I fucking hate you."*

How I missed that woman.

A few months into my "exclusive" relationship with Richard, I felt a shift. He started to look at me differently.

"I really care for you, Judala."

He'd started calling me Judala, like Mother. And he said it with such increasing sincerity that it was obvious what was happening. Especially when he put his hand on my heart, looked into my eyes to make sure I was listening: "I really care for you, Judala."

I love you was coming. I knew it. What was I going say back? I didn't want to hurt him. I planned to reply with something funny, so he'd get the message that our relationship could not go there, that we had no future together.

He said it one night, right after the most incredible orgasm of my life. Because of his size, he put me in new and different positions, which reached my G-spot. Throughout the years I'd heard tell of such a spot in the vagina but thought it was an urban myth.

That night, he looked at me afterward. "I love you, my Judala."

I looked into his eyes and tried to think of something funny to say in response. "I—I—" Simultaneously, the realization hit as it fell out of my mouth, "I love you too, Morty."

Shit.

Instantly, we were a couple. Richard came over every night after working at the café or a tech job. I stopped going to the networking meetings and the storytelling group, thinking that as the newness wore off, I'd go back. He wanted us to spend as much time together as possible.

I took him to a party, and that frenetic side of his personality was suddenly back, the hopped-up, in-your-face, no-one-else-can-get-a-word-in-edgewise persona. I saw people actually cringe, and at one point, I pulled him aside and asked him to put that guy away. "People love that guy," he said earnestly. I had to go into another room; I couldn't watch. My friends remained my friends, but we were never invited out again as a couple with them.

He asked me to give up my Sunday morning coffee and workouts with a childhood friend. "Sunday is our day."

How could I argue with that? It was the one day of the week that we had entirely to ourselves. Sometimes we would walk three miles to have breakfast at Jinky's on Sunset; sometimes it was a movie and Indian food for dinner. I felt we were spending too much time together, and I eventually told him I needed to go back to my group meetings several nights a week. In response, he asked, "Did you ever know that you would be loved this much?"

Wow, so this is what love is, I thought to myself, feeling as if I were finally in a healthy relationship.

Four months later, I got a letter from the New York Fringe Festival inviting me to do my show in Manhattan that August. I asked him to come with me.

He took the invitation as more than just coming as my boyfriend. "Judala, I have some ideas for your show." At his request, I made him producer for a two percent cut if we sold the script.

He immediately got to work. He took new pictures of me, rebranded the show, made flyers and posters, and told me to rewrite the ending. He said it wasn't relatable to the younger crowd. I listened to him even though the script changes never felt right.

He took over everything: the media, the marketing, even finding a New York publicist along with lighting and tech people. He also made me a website and wanted me to blog after every performance.

He knew how to do everything. I didn't have to do anything other than act in the show. It was awesome. What a partner! Once again, he used his superpowers and made my life easier. After spending a lifetime taking care of everyone and everything, I secretly loved it.

I also secretly didn't like living with him in New York. He was moody, high maintenance, and always made us late. New York, being the hot angry beast it was in August, heightened those annoyances with the sweat that poured profusely from my face.

I introduced him to my dearest friends, Victoria and Michael. We met them for dinner, and to my relief, he didn't bring out his gregarious alter-ego. He was himself, but overly affectionate with me. Over-the-top affectionate, kissing my cheek, saying things like, "This is my girl" in the middle of conversations as if trying to prove to them how much he loved me. I found it embarrassing. On the subway ride back to our lower east side sublet I had rented for us, he told me how well he could zero in on a person's weakness.

"Prove it," I said, not believing him. "Tell me about Victoria." Victoria was the most spiritual and loving person I knew. Not a flaw could I find even with the most powerful magnifying glass.

"She thinks she's not good enough," Richard said. He'd nailed it. How many times had Victoria called me while in rehearsal, crying that she didn't feel talented enough?

"Okay," I continued, "What's Michael's weakness?"

"Victoria," he said, and he was right. Michael loved Victoria. She was his whole world.

"Okay, I'm impressed." And I truly was. He was by far the smartest person I'd ever met. He was an autodidact and an avid reader of manuals, references books, and trade publications. From then on, I trusted him with every major decision.

The last time Mark Travis came to New York with a one-person show, De Niro's production company bought the rights for a million dollars, and it became a big motion picture: *A Bronx Tale.* Unfortunately, our best efforts weren't enough to garner New York interest in my show. It was August, and most people in the industry leave the city in August. For whatever reason, I, once again, closed the show with no plans for it and had once again spent a big chunk of the inheritance money my dad left me on the dream.

When we got back to Los Angeles, I received news that a teleplay I had entered in a competition, after making it to the final round, did not win. One of the judges happened to be a member of my networking group and told me that my script was the front-runner and would have won if John Ritter hadn't just passed away. John Ritter's television show, *8 Simple Rules to Date My Daughter,* stayed on the air, introducing his father as a new character. Because my teleplay was about a grown woman with two college-age children moving back in with her elderly father, the consensus was that it was too similar. So my show didn't win, the pilot would not go into production, therefore it was not considered for the fall television line-up.

"We could do it. Film a promo, upload it to the Internet, and create a stir," Richard suggested, so we got to work hiring a small film crew and casting it. I used more of the money my father had left me.

"We should cast Victoria."

"As the friend? It's too small a role to fly her in for, and we look too similar."

"As the lead."

"I wrote that role for myself."

"You have to make a decision. Do you want to be a writer or an actor?"

Both. But I didn't say that. I let Richard make that decision.

Soon after we finished filming, he convinced me to move in with him, using the same tactic he had used to persuade me to go on a date with him. He simply wore me down.

"You'd be saving money," "I'd feel better about your safety," "Your landlord can get more money for your apartment, they want you out," "Walking distance to Trader Joe's."

Even though we had only been together for six months, I agreed. However, the downward progression of my life was not lost on me: a five-bedroom home with a husband and two kids, to a three-bedroom condo for myself and two kids, to a one-bedroom apartment for me and zero kids, to a studio for myself and Richard.

As we packed up my apartment, he convinced me to sell most of my furniture.

"You don't seem to have a cohesive style." It hurt my feelings. I knew how to decorate, but what I had in my apartment was an eclectic collection of the few things I had left of my life. Still, it was tasteful and clean. He tried a new approach: "Maybe it's time to let go of the past and start over."

That statement I could wrap my head around as I gave

away the coffee table I loved, sold the bedroom set I bought after I moved out of the marital home, and gave away the chandelier I purchased in New Mexico. I did keep my parents' chair, my stereo, and my album collection. He knew I'd never part with any of those things. He helped me go through all my books ("It's time for others to enjoy them") and my clothes, too ("So outdated"). *Goodbye, black sequined Carmen Marc Volvo dress* ("When would you ever wear that?").

When we were getting ready to paint his apartment, I found a skateboard in the kitchen pantry next to his snowboards. *Oh, my God, I'm moving in with a skater boy.* He came in and read the look on my face. "That's not—I'm getting rid of that. It's old." With that, he took the skateboard out of the apartment. I never saw it again.

We sectioned off a bed area with sheer curtains, leaving us with a small living room space and a workstation for me, complete with a little Ikea desk. His office was the alcove outside the bathroom, and every time I had to go, I had to pay a toll.

"Sit on my lap."

"Morty, I'm too old for that."

"Judala, sit on my lap." I would, and then he'd hug and kiss me. "Did you ever know you would be loved this much?" It was not a rhetorical question. "Did you ever know you would be loved this much?" he'd repeat.

I found the whole thing silly, "Morty, I—"

He'd cut me off, "Judala, did you ever know—?"

"No. I never thought I would be loved this much," I'd finally answer to end the silliness.

"I love you more than anything in the entire universe," he added, and then I was allowed to go to the bathroom. If he were still at his desk when I came out, we'd do it all again, every time I passed his desk.

Many times, my issues came up. "Morty, I'm forty-seven. When you're my age, I'll be sixty-three."

"And tomorrow I could get hit by a bus. What's your point? Judala, my skin is fair, my hair is thinning. Give it five years; I'll be wrinkled and bald."

"Oh, Morty, you promise?"

Truthfully, I liked the idea of his aging. I was okay with the age difference in LA. LA was chock-full of strange-looking couples; we fit right in. But if we were going to have a future together, and it looked as if we were, I needed him to age.

Richard and I spent all day every day together, but it worked for us. He'd get up at seven a.m. to go for his run, and I would start cooking steel-cut oatmeal. By the time he was home and showered, breakfast was ready. We spent hours editing the footage from the promo we shot, but eventually he lost interest, and never uploaded it to YouTube.

Because he was a much better cook, I would start dinner, and he'd put in the finishing touches when he came home at night. He continued to do IT jobs and was looking for a new career.

Our new Sunday ritual was to ride bikes to the farmer's market. I had given up riding when I left Chicago, and he brought me back to it by fixing up my old bike and buying himself one off craigslist. We didn't make love all night anymore but had settled into more of a typical three days per week routine. Some nights while I knit in bed, he would read aloud. I was truly happy and more than loved: I felt treasured.

One night he turned to me matter-of-factly. "Let's get married."

"Married?" I panicked for many different reasons: he hadn't met my kids, he had no money, and he was so much younger. Besides, he'd said he never wanted to get married. It was one of the things we'd bonded over: no marriage, no kids, no pets, and no plants. "I thought you never wanted to get married."

"I didn't until I met you. Let's fly to Vegas, and just do it."

Quick! Insert joke here. "What is this, a Nike commercial?" He didn't laugh. His eyes were so hopeful; I knew I needed to choose my words carefully. "Richard, I'm a mom. I can't just run off like that. I need you to meet my children."

"But you're not saying no."

"I'm saying someday."

Through his power of observation, he knew why I was hesitant. "We'll get married in the backyard of the house I buy for us."

I smiled because he knew I needed him to make something of himself first. "Sounds perfect."

While Richard began researching a career in finance, I set about writing the screenplay version of my show. A producer had approached Mark and asked him if there was a screenplay. I made two attempts to write it, but both times I came to a halt around page seventy.

"Agh!" I screamed at my computer after my last attempt.

"What's wrong?"

"I can't write the third act. It all goes to shit."

"Do you have an outline?" I gave him a dirty look. "Do you want me to read it?"

"I would love that."

He read it. "You've strayed from the original story. Use your solo show script as your outline and get rid of all the new extraneous characters you invented."

"Will you help me?"

He thought carefully before he answered. "If you make me an equal partner when it sells."

Because we planned to spend the rest of our lives together, half would belong to him by LA law anyway. "Sure."

We worked great together. Richard's strengths were in outlines and structure, mine in story and dialogue. Occasionally he would say, "We need a joke here." I would write one. Inevitably he'd say, "You can do better." After first cursing him out, in the end, I would write a funnier joke. It was so great to have the same partner for both my work and love life. I was living the Hollywood dream.

The holidays came, and we shared an intimate Thanksgiving for two, followed by a movie. Long before I met him, I booked a trip to Australia and New Zealand with my daughter. I'd be gone over Christmas and New Year's. There too, Richard added to my life by finding obscure and exciting tours for us to take while there. At the end of the trip, our plane flew to Los Angeles, where my daughter briefly met Richard at the airport before connecting to a Chicago flight. She was mildly impressed when she saw him standing in baggage claim with my favorite flowers.

On the way home from the airport, Richard had news he was so excited to share he could barely contain himself. "I wanted to wait a few days, but I can't. I talked to your friend Victoria while you were gone because I think we should move to New York."

It was completely out of left field. Who moves from LA to New York? It's the other way around. My brain, struggling to make sense of his statement, quickly found a correlation between his looking for finance jobs and New York being a financial epicenter. "For a financial career?"

"To resume my voiceover career. That's why I called Victoria." Victoria had a lot of success in the commercial world, both on and off camera.

"I didn't know you were still interested in that," I said, hating how that sounded. As an actor, I should have been more supportive, but as an older woman, I did not want to live the life of a starving artist. I knew he'd left a promising voice-over career in New York to try to break into animation in Los Angeles, but instead, his livelihood came to a screeching halt.

"Ultimately I want to go back to what I'm good at it. I know I can make a living for us there."

Shit.

I loved him, but I didn't want to go back to New York. Our relationship barely survived it the first time. Besides, I loved LA. I'd found myself in LA. It's where things were happening for me. I was home.

"You should go; stay with Victoria and Michael. We'll be a bicoastal couple."

"I won't go without you," he said, and we tabled the discussion. After all, I had just gotten off a thirteen-hour flight. We tried to enjoy our reunion, but we both felt a bit disappointed in each other.

The next morning, I reiterated my feelings. "I'm serious. You go to New York, and we'll figure it all out later." Secretly, I was hoping he would go alone. I was anxious to get back to my networking and storytelling groups to figure out the next steps toward my own goals.

"I can't do that."

"Why?"

"Now that I've have found you, I can't let you go. I can't live without you."

I can't live without you. The full weight of Richard's feelings hit me, and it didn't feel healthy. I had entered a relationship with a man far too young, and I had to tread lightly. But still, I didn't want to leave LA. I struggled with internal questions: *If he stayed, could I live with the fact that I crushed his dreams? Would his staying tear us apart eventually?*

Because he rarely took no for an answer, he didn't give up. I'm sure he knew from our short history together that he could eventually get what he wanted. This time he used a more complicated and strategic campaign. "Nothing is happening for you here, career-wise."

Blindsided.

"You can get an agent in New York, Victoria's agent, go back to doing commercials."

Hmmm.

"You could do your show there. It's the theatre capital!"

Maybe that would be good for me.

"New York is a lot closer to Chicago. You can see your kids more often."

My kids, I do miss my kids.

I succumbed. When the person you love, your hero, says he can make a living for you both in New York, you're supposed to go. Right? He had spent so much time and effort trying to get my writing career started. What kind of person would I be if I didn't reciprocate? Didn't I owe him the same? Or was Rumpelstiltskin returning to collect his due? Had I gotten comfortable and forgotten, I had made a deal to give up something I loved?

No. Richard loved me so much. He said he couldn't live without me. I let him fall in love with me. I made that bed: now I had to lie in it.

Several weeks later, when reality set in that we were actually moving, I had a panic attack and finally told him my feelings: "I don't want to start over again." I started to cry.

He hugged me. I felt safe confiding in him, but he didn't ask me to expand, and I didn't explain what it meant. I didn't want to start over like I was twenty, with no money, and having to work a day job. More importantly, I didn't tell him that leaving LA meant giving up my dreams.

On the other hand, I was in love for the first time in my life; I grew up on Fairy Tales and wrote romantic comedies. I wanted to believe we were walking into the sunset to live happily ever after. Although, the sun doesn't set in the east.

NY Dick

I didn't think it was possible to downsize any more than I already had, but Richard felt the best way to move across the country was to get rid of as much as possible. Several LA friends offered to hold things they thought I might eventually regret giving up.

"I'll take your mother's china; just know it's here if you ever want it back," Patricia offered.

I gave my daughter serving pieces that belonged to her grandmothers but refused to part with my art collection. He compromised by taking the paintings out of their frames, knowing how expensive it would be to reframe. I also took my stereo, albums, and the chair my parents bought in 1944. We sold my television, my new Tempur-Pedic bed, his coffee table, his piece of shit car, and my precious little Beetle Bug.

"No one needs a car in New York."

"What if I just left it upstate with Victoria and Michael?"

"I'm not driving across the country with you."

I wanted to tell him I didn't need him to drive across the country with me. Instead, I found a new owner for my car. Then, because most of the things left were mine, I paid a moving company to ship our belongings, and we each bought a one-way ticket to New York.

Victoria and Michael were illegally subletting their furnished Upper West Side apartment. The plan was for us to stay in their home for a month until their current city tenant moved out.

In the middle of the commotion, Richard felt we should take a trip to Paris. I once mentioned that my friend, Laura, had been taken there for her birthday. He must have thought that I was hinting, that it was how people my age celebrated, or maybe it was a distraction tactic. He found a reasonable all-inclusive package I knew he couldn't afford. When we became a couple, he confided that he was thirty thousand dollars in debt.

"I paid off my previous girlfriend's loans," he said, but it didn't bother me. I was chill about those kinds of things because I had a six-digit bank account.

Still, I didn't want to go to Paris, not with a man who couldn't afford it, not in the middle of all the turmoil moving across the country created, and certainly not when it was still cold there. But he had booked it as a surprise before he told me about it.

When his travel agent called because something went wrong with the reservation, he had the option to rebook or get a full refund. I finally spoke up. "Get your money back."

"Why?"

I put on my big girl shoes. "I don't want to go."

That hurt his feelings. "I wanna do something nice for you. Why won't you let me take you to Paris?"

I looked into those sad eyes and sucked it up. He rebooked the trip, and two days after we flew to New York, we left for Paris. I had been waiting my entire life to go to Paris anyway, to walk the Champs-Élysées, to drink coffee in a café, and to write in a journal like so many American authors. I knew I would love Paris.

I hated Paris. It was cold and wet and gray. I didn't have to fly seven hours and suffer jet lag to experience that; I could have just gone back to Chicago. I didn't have a warm coat, supportive shoes, or the right traveling companion. Richard made me walk too much, mostly due to his high-maintenance mealtime requirements and so-called allergy to cigarette smoke. We would walk for miles to find a restaurant that met with his approval after first walking for miles sightseeing. One restaurant would have a good menu but too many smokers, and on and on we walked and walked. Every day. Every meal. In the museums, I made sure we saw each exhibit. He said we didn't have to see it all, but I wanted to prove I could keep up.

I couldn't keep up. The daily pounding on the cement floors in my cute, flat shoes destroyed my feet. Richard would rub them out at the end of each day, but the bones hurt. Still, the walking never stopped. It was our first trip. We did not know how to travel together.

Back in the U.S., in Victoria and Michael's home, I walked —limped—around in a daze.

"What's wrong?" Michael asked one day.

I heard myself answer: "I have nothing. No home, no car, no furniture, no stuff, no job, no agent, no plan." He didn't answer. What could he say?

Victoria introduced us to her agent, and he agreed to represent Richard and me. After a month, we moved into the apartment on Amsterdam Avenue, and a week later, I couldn't walk.

I saw Victoria's foot doctor, who said I had a stress fracture in the fifth metatarsal on my left foot—yet again. He put me in a cast. It wasn't a walking cast, so I had to use crutches. When the cast came off six weeks later, my foot wasn't healed, and the other foot was strained from bearing the brunt of my weight. He recast me. The recasting went on for almost a year. I didn't usually worry about outcomes, so I did what I did best, dissociated.

Not being able to walk in a walking town sucked. I couldn't do my show because I couldn't stand. I had to stop auditioning because I couldn't walk. And I stopped writing because I lost my sense of humor. Nothing was funny. Nothing motivated me. I watched back-to-back episodes of *Law and Order* and *Charmed*. *Charmed* was too much for Richard's educated palate.

"Write something," he begged as if it were that easy. But given that he'd sold his computer in LA to get money for the move, he had commandeered mine and used it all day, every day. *When do I have time to write?* I didn't ask that out loud.

Richard did the grocery shopping, the cleaning, the laundry, and the cooking. He was the perfect partner. I relied on him. What's more, I trusted him. I had never trusted anyone before. He was my security, my safety net. I was no longer afraid of getting sick or developing Alzheimer's disease, like Mother. I finally understood the movie *The Notebook* because my Morty would do that for me. He would move into a nursing home to be with me. He loved me that much.

"I know you hate it here, Judala, so as soon as I make enough money, I will buy us a home in LA, and we'll go back." *Buy a home* was still code for getting married.

At that point, I wanted to get married. I felt being married would alleviate the difficulty I still had with our age difference. That somehow the commitment of marriage would stop the imagined, and maybe real, looks and sneers.

"How long do you think that'll take?"

He couldn't answer. He didn't know. I was still paying most of the rent. He was nowhere near ready to leave New York, but through Victoria's contacts, his IT business and voice-over career were off to a good start. His future looked promising.

Richard and I had a Skype conversation with Mark about the script we wrote. Mark had joined forces with the producer that wanted to turn *Fornicationally Challenged* into a film. He gave us feedback on the screenplay with rewrite suggestions. He also revealed they had secured financial backing from a well-known Hollywood producer. It was enough money to make their first five films. Ours was second on their agenda. Finally, I had something to be excited about and creative work to do on my computer. For some reason, Richard wasn't as thrilled.

"I don't have time to write."

"You'll need to make the time. You're in this for fifty percent," I reminded him.

"You're right. I will." But he put it off as long as he could, and when we did sit down to write, it was no longer fun. He was easily distracted. I assumed he felt that writing a romantic comedy was beneath his intellectual capability. Occasionally I wrote alone, but when he read the pages later, he'd tell me it was no good.

"Then write with me!"

I feared that his doing everything for us was taking its toll. Yes, I was assuming, but when your partner stops confiding in you, you struggle to connect the dots. I threw money at the presumed problem by hiring weekly laundry pickup and a grocery delivery services, hoping that would lessen his load.

As our first year in New York ended, I found a new doctor, a recommendation from a woman who'd had a similar problem and was now walking perfectly. When the new doctor looked at my X-rays and MRI, he told me I had been misdiagnosed. There was no break. I had had a subluxation of the cuboid bone. The ligaments in my foot had become lax and could no longer hold the bone in place; it had shifted. He then explained a procedure he was confident would repair the damage. The very same that cured my friend.

I called Richard from the doctor's office to tell him the good news. "I never broke my foot. The doctor is going to push the bone back in place, then shoot sugar water into my ligaments."

"What?!"

"It's called prolotherapy. He's going to aggravate the ligaments. Make them do their job. You always say, 'I wish people would do their job,'" I laughed.

"You sound high."

"The doctor gave me Vicodin. I'm getting like fourteen shots in my foot."

"Who is this guy? Don't do anything until I research him."

The doctor had come back into the room, and even though I usually let Richard make the decisions, I knew I was doing the right thing. "I'm doing this. It'll be fine. I'll take a cab home."

When I got home, Richard was worried, but it came across as anger. "Doctors can just as easily fuck you up. How could you have let someone do a procedure on you without researching it first?"

"Because it felt right."

"That's so hippy-dippy. This is your health on the line. Your ability to ever walk again!" He calmed himself down. "Look, I know it's been hard on you but—"

"But nothing! If I listened to my instincts in the first place, I never would have gone to fucking Paris and fucked up my bones from walking so *fucking* much."

"So, it's my fault?"

"Yes!" I said, and realized immediately I had gone too far. I should have said, *You don't take no for an answer. You don't trust my feelings. You only go with what makes intellectual sense, and while that has a place, it doesn't have a place in every decision.* But I didn't say that since I was less than articulate around him.

He went to the computer, and I went into the bedroom and shut the door. As was his custom, he came in and sat beside me. For some reason, I could never apologize to him, but he always came around.

"I love you more than anything in the entire universe," he said as I stared at my book. Then he put his hand on mine and asked, "You know that, don't you?"

I nodded.

"You know I want you to walk again. I want to be out there, walking the streets of New York with my baby on my arm."

I looked into his eyes, and with my reading glasses still on, I saw clearly. *Wow, you're young.* I had forgotten how young he looked since my eyesight began failing me outside the reading realm.

He mistook my silent distraction for anger. "I will fight anyone for you, even you. Do I have to fight you for you?"

He was so patient, so loving, and so strong. I knew he was strong enough to fight a mugger on the street and intelligent enough to question any doctor on my behalf. I had a real partner.

"I love you," I finally said, "And I'm sorry." Instead of saying why I was sorry, I added, "You're my hero."

He smiled. "That's a lot of pressure."

"You can handle it."

I went back to the doctor every six weeks for shots and went to physical therapy three times a week. Within months, I was able to walk.

However, I still didn't have much of a life for myself in New York. I would wake up, do my foot exercises, go to the health club, watch TV, do my foot exercises, have dinner with Richard, and watch a show he picked out for us.

Dissociation turned into depression. Richard tried to fix me. "Why don't you write a children's book?" he asked, as if it were that easy.

"Why?"

"Cuz I know a children's book editor."

Just when I thought things couldn't get any worse, the hot flashes began. There was a burning that radiated heat out of my back and chest randomly and often, as if I had a furnace in my core. I became overly emotional, crying over commercials, and even more depressed. Occasionally I lashed out.

"Shut up. Shut up. Just shut the fuck up!" I yelled at Richard one day on 103rd Street. It wasn't entirely out of nowhere. Richard tended to talk so much and for so long that it had become increasingly difficult to get a word in edgewise. Still, other than the *fucking bones* rant when I was on Vicodin, I'd never spoken to him that way before. I wouldn't. The Ex-Hole and I used to fight dirty; we had no filter and said very mean things to each other in anger. I swore I'd never do that again. Richard was kindhearted. If I interrupted when he was in a foul mood, he'd still answer me kindly.

In his never-ending quest to fix me, Richard suggested I go back to school to study nutrition. "Most of the books you read are about nutrition. You should get the proper credentials and write a nutrition book."

"I think I want to take the stories from my solo show and turn them into a book."

"Why? That's over. *Fornicationally Challenged* didn't get you anywhere." When he realized he'd hurt me, he softened. "You're smart. You'll write something else, something better.

You don't want to be a one-trick pony. Do you?"

I gave up the idea of writing that book (this book) even though I felt it was unfinished business. It was easy to believe Richard was right. I was almost fifty and hadn't achieved success in any of my artistic endeavors. His suggestion about studying nutrition wasn't without merit. Maybe it was time to put that all behind me and stop trusting that voice in my head that told me talent would win out in the long run.

I looked into classes, and the most economical bang for my buck was to attend City University of New York (CUNY) to become a registered dietician. I started classes immediately in the Bronx, an easy commute from the Upper West Side.

Shortly after that, we lost our illegal sublet. We had to move out of our rent-controlled city apartment, and finding an affordable apartment in Manhattan proved impossible.

"We could go to Queens, it's reasonable there," Richard suggested.

"Oh, hells, no!" I said.

He looked harder for apartments. He found something he thought would work: a five-story walk-up on the East Side in desperate need of repair. I knew Richard could make it livable, but I was afraid of the stairs. If I were ever in a cast again, it would be challenging to crutch up and down five flights. As the deadline grew closer and we still hadn't found an apartment, we were forced to move back in with Victoria and Michael. We sold their apartment furniture for them on craigslist, including the television. I told Richard to add my stereo and albums to the lot.

"No, you love your albums."

"I'm not packing it all up again." My stereo had broken in the move across the country; Richard kept saying he'd get it fixed but never did.

"No, you'll regret it one day and then blame me," he tried to reason.

I never played music anymore. Richard hated my taste in music, which I never understood because I loved everything from the Carpenters to Snoop Dogg.

"Just sell it all."

He did.

This time Victoria and Michael's home did not feel like a welcoming sanctuary. It was awkward; I didn't feel we were wanted. They were dealing with private issues: work stress, putting down their sick dog, and actively trying to adopt a baby. The last thing they needed was an audience. When an apartment broker found a place in Queens, I thought it a better option than to risk the friendship of such wonderful people.

The apartment was by far the nicest place we had seen, a large one bedroom with a huge foyer that had room for both our desks. Richard loved it. The broker said we had to pay first and last month's rent, a security deposit, and the apartment broker fee, for a total of six thousand dollars.

"First, last, and security are normal, but a broker fee? Renters don't pay that," I said when we got back on the Metro-North train.

"They do in New York," Richard said, and then added, "They want proof we can pay the monthly rent. You'll need to show them a bank statement, but I'll block out the account number, don't worry."

Don't worry? He didn't address the elephant on the train: he didn't have any of the money needed to get the place, which meant it was on me. As we rode home, it ate at me. It was a large sum to take out of the bank, and my foot issues had recently claimed another big chunk. I had needed more physical therapy than insurance covered. When we got back to the house and went to our room, my concerns fell out of my mouth: "I'm hemorrhaging money here. My father didn't leave this money for you. He left it for my future."

The look on his face was the same as if I had just shot him in the stomach for no apparent reason: surprise mixed with betrayal and, for the first time, anger. "This, this right here, is why I never, *never* ask anyone for anything!" he whisper-screamed, but it was loud enough that I knew Victoria heard from the kitchen downstairs.

I wasn't proud of myself and hoped he'd forgive me. "Richard, I just—"

He got ahold of himself and said, "I can't right now." He turned away from me. He'd never done that before. I left the room and went down to the kitchen. Victoria looked at me with a raised eyebrow to let me know she heard, but I couldn't tell if the sympathetic look was for me or for Richard.

I knew that couples sometimes said mean things to each other in the heat of stress, so I was sure he'd get over it eventually.

We moved into the apartment in Queens the following week. I told Richard that since I paid everything up front, he should pay rent. He took catering jobs on the weekends to make extra money. Victoria and Michael hooked him up with the same catering company they'd worked for when they were first starting out. He liked catering and became friendly with a fellow bartender. I was glad he had a friend, but when he asked me to meet him one night, I declined.

"Pete asked to meet us for dinner tonight," Richard told me one night.

"You go alone, have some bro time."

"I want him to meet you."

"Another time," I said but didn't mean it. I didn't want to meet his new friends. I knew I'd be embarrassed about the age difference. He went out, and I stayed home—alone—no TV or stereo to keep me company in Queens.

I hated Queens. It felt like a punishment: I'd been banished from Manhattan. I was not happy with the neighborhood, the commute, the limited number of stores, and the isolation. It was an ugly suburb surrounded by five-story tenement apartment buildings as far as the eye could see. At that time, it was oppressive, nothing at all what it is today.

I knew I was miserable, but didn't realize I'd been taking it out on Richard. I didn't see that I was complaining, was short with him, and snapped at him regularly until the night he yelled at me about my behavior.

"You act like you don't want to be in this relationship anymore. If that's the case, just tell me. But treating me badly and making me feel insignificant is just plain mean." It was the second time he'd yelled at me in our eighteen-month relationship. I sat there, listening to all his points, which went on for a while. He was right: I had been mistreating him. Before I could say anything, he added, "Fuck you."

When it was finally my turn to speak, I made a joke. "Well, you sure told me." He didn't laugh or even smile. He just stared at me. "Look, you have every right to be mad, but 'fuck you'? We don't talk like that to each other," I added, and I went to the bathroom to wash up.

While in the bathroom, I processed what he had said. I asked myself, *Do you want to be in this relationship?*

My answer was yes. Yes, I did. I loved Richard. I needed to make a go of this life with him. Right or wrong, I'd agreed to the move to New York, but never put the proper action behind it. I promised myself I would make it a point to adapt to my surroundings and be kinder to him. I never actually told him about my revelation, my internal thoughts. I planned to let my actions speak for themselves.

Meanwhile, I still missed Roxy. She was about to turn fifty without me. "I think I should call her," I told Richard in late October.

"For her or for you?" he asked.

I was confused. "For her birthday."

"She doesn't want to be your friend anymore. Calling her will make you feel better, but you'll only be upsetting her on *her* birthday."

I listened to him and didn't call her. Six months into our relationship, Richard told me that I should be over the fight with Roxy. If I wasn't, I needed professional help. I never confided in him about her again. I didn't tell him that I still cried over the loss from time to time. I Googled her. She had a Facebook page that revealed she now lived in Colorado. She was right where she belonged.

One night while I was on the makeshift stationary bike in the bedroom, Richard popped in and asked if we could make love. "After my workout," I told him.

He came back several times to see if I was ready, so I got in the shower to clean myself up first. From the shower, after turning the water off, I heard him on the phone with Lisa, a girl he knew from catering. I knew he'd been spending a lot of time with her. Her computer had broken down, so he helped recovered her files, went shopping with her to buy a Mac, and had been downloading files and programs into the new computer in her apartment over the course of several evenings. She baked for him in return. Sound familiar?

I came out of the shower and stood in the hall with only a towel draped around my body. He'd gone from wanting to make love to not acknowledging my presence. He made no attempt to get off the phone. I stood there, watching him smiling as he listened to her voice on the other line, smiling with his lips *and* eyes.

Holy fuck.

I got dressed and went into the kitchen to make myself a tuna sandwich. He was extremely allergic to fish; it was a passive-aggressive way of saying *fuck you*. Besides, we had stopped having meals together. He was too busy. Even when he was home at dinnertime, he felt we should make our own meals. It was easier than trying to find something we both liked.

When he got off the phone, he came to the kitchen doorway. "What are you doing?"

"Who were you talking to?"

"A client," he answered. He may have also considered her a client, but he hadn't used his IT voice on the phone. He laughed and talked excitedly, the way he used to do with me.

He spent the rest of the night on his new computer. I tried to study. We didn't make love.

When it was time for bed, I couldn't sleep, not next to a man who could be cheating on me. I went to sleep on the couch. In the middle of the night, he woke up, found me, and asked what was wrong.

"Are you overlapping me?"

He laughed until he realized I was serious. He told me they were just friends and went into far too much detail. "If you don't want me to be friends with her, I won't be."

I didn't want to seem distrustful. "No, that's not necessary."

One night, he finally took me to dinner at our favorite place in Manhattan but spent the entire time texting. I assumed he was texting a client who had an emergency. As we walked to the subway after dinner, I asked him who he'd been texting. When he said, Lisa, I lost it. I pointed to the ring he bought me for Christmas, the silver band that only fit the ring finger on my left hand. Instead of saying that his actions were hurtful or demand an explanation, my hormonal rage screamed, "This ring means nothing!" I took it off and threw it at him.

From there, it was an easy descent into reading her emails on his computer when he wasn't home. They were planning a party for a mutual friend; innocent enough, but they also had plans to meet beforehand. I read it in her email to him.

When Richard came home that night, he asked if I read his emails.

"No," I lied.

He asked again. "No? Are you sure?"

"Yep."

"Did you use my computer at all?"

"Nope."

"Well, I have emails marked as read, and they should be new." Back then, I didn't know about changing an email status to "mark as unread." He caught me in a lie *and* a cover-up. I was unrecognizable, even to myself.

He was disappointed in me and changed his password. I apologized for lying to him. "Maybe if I met Lisa and your new friends it would be easier for me. Take me to the party with you. I'm ready to meet your friends."

"It's too late. You can't just come to a birthday party when you don't know anyone."

"Yes, I can. I'm your girlfriend. I can go anywhere you go."

"No. I'm not taking you."

He left me alone in the apartment and went out to meet his new friends.

I'd never had a roommate before, but it felt like I had one now. We didn't eat together, sleep together, or spend time together. He no longer requested I sit on his lap or asked "if I ever knew that I would be loved this much?" I even missed the days when his affection embarrassed me.

I didn't tell anyone there were problems. Richard didn't like me to speak about him to my friends and family. I wasn't even allowed to answer the question, "How's Richard?"

One night we went out to dinner in Manhattan with the one catering friend I did know. She was one of Victoria's friends. I had known her for years. She and Richard talked about the people from work, and when Lisa's name came up, he revealed he'd just had dinner with her. It was the night he said he was out with Pete.

I took it in and waited until we were alone on the street outside the restaurant.

"You had dinner with Lisa behind my back?"

"What?"

"You told Missy you had dinner with Lisa. You told me you had dinner with Pete."

"I had dinner with Pete. Lisa was there too."

"So, you lied."

"I didn't lie. I didn't want another fight with you."

"What is going on with you and her?!"

"I am not having this conversation on the street. People are looking at us." He walked toward the subway with all the arrogance of a man who expected his woman to follow. I walked behind him like a petulant child, down the subway steps, and stood behind him on the platform while he looked off into the tunnel, waiting for a train to appear—his back to me the whole time. It was a horrible feeling, being treated like that by a man who supposedly loved me and couldn't live without me. His back told me, "I can't even look at you."

How the hell did we get here? Here, underneath the dirty city in a rat-infested cavern with moldy water pooling at my feet from the rusting pipes within the crumbling cement above. I missed the palm tree-lined streets, the sunshine, and the Hollywood Hills in California.

I left the subway unnoticed. I walked around the city and eventually sat on a bench in front of the Plaza Hotel. He called my cell phone many times, but I ignored it. I couldn't talk to him, not without knowing what I wanted.

But I did know what I wanted: I wanted out. Even though Richard had told me so many times that it would kill him if I left. I finally answered one of his calls and told him I was on my way home.

When I got home, I took a small suitcase out of the hall closet, went into the bedroom, and shut the door. But I couldn't pack. Where was I going? Upstate, to Victoria and Michael's? Chicago? Los Angeles? What about school? What about the comment Richard made that he didn't believe in getting back together after a breakup? *Am I ready to make that final decision right here, right now?*

I didn't pack the bag. I went into the bathroom and washed up for bed.

He was waiting for me in the bedroom when I came out. I spoke calmly. "What does it say about our relationship that you don't take me with you when you go out?"

"What does it say about you that you think I'm having an affair, and you're still here?"

It was the most hurtful thing he ever said to me. *Because I made a commitment to you. Because you said you loved me more than anything in the entire universe. Because you promised you would never overlap me. And I believed you. I still believe all of it.* But I didn't say it out loud. I couldn't be that vulnerable. Instead, I just stared at him.

What else did I have to lose? In 2008, forty percent of what remained of my money! The stock market crashed due to the real estate bubble bursting, and the backers pulled out of the producer's five-film project. The screenplay I wrote would not become a film.

"I'm getting too old to play me in the movie anyway," I told friends, to keep up the appearance that I was okay. In reality, I lost the last hope I'd had of ever fulfilling my dreams.

Richard took a Sunday off and suggested we go to brunch on the East side. I was so excited. Maybe things were turning around for us. It was about time.

He seemed distant and introspective while we ate, and I wondered if he was judging the amount of cheese in my omelet.

"Let's take a walk in Central Park," I suggested as we left the restaurant.

"You can't walk," he snapped.

It hurt my feelings. Yes, I had plantar fasciitis, but I wasn't an invalid. "I can manage."

"Fine," he replied, and we sat on a park bench a few feet from the park entrance. Still, it was nice to be out, even if he was quiet.

"You should buy a condo in Chicago," he suggested when he finally spoke.

"What?"

"You always wanted to. The market took a nosedive. I think it would be a good investment."

When we first met, I'd mentioned that I wanted to have a condo in Chicago and a house in LA.

"I'm enrolled in school here," I reasoned.

"You could transfer to UIC."

He's given this some thought. "Why?"

"UIC has a much better program than a city college."

Are you breaking up with me? I wondered but didn't ask. Not because I was afraid of the answer, because I knew I wouldn't get the truth.

We sat quietly for a moment. Then Richard said softly, "I just think if you intend to buy a condo, now is the time. Prices will never be this low."

"I will," I said. "When the time is right."

He persisted, "I'm just saying, the housing market has dropped. You might want to take advantage of that now."

I barely saw him after that. He either came home late at night or when home, worked at his computer into the early morning. He was crabby and exhausted, too exhausted to talk and too exhausted to make it into the bedroom. He slept on the couch.

"Can we make love tonight?" I asked from time to time. I was sure if we got that connection back, he would remember how much we loved each other.

"That would be nice," he'd answer, but proceeded to work at the computer until I fell asleep.

Through all of this, we still had snuggle time. Almost daily, Richard would announce, "Snuggle time!"

We would then undress to our underwear, get in the bed, and snuggle. Getting undressed was not a sexual thing. Richard didn't allow us to sit on the bed with clothes we'd worn on the subway. While he spooned me in our bed, he'd call me his *snuggle bunny, cuddle creature,* or *soft skin baby.* It was the only place I still felt loved and the reason I felt that when his stress lessened, he would become himself again.

The last straw came one Saturday. Shortly after he left for an all-day catering job, Victoria called to invite us to their home for the weekend.

"I can come for the day, but Richard just left for a catering gig."

"At the mansion? We can pick him up tonight from the cater house; just pack stuff for him."

I called Richard to ask if he wanted to sleep at their house, but he never picked up the phone. All day. That was unusual. I wasn't sure about deciding for him, but Victoria's excitement was so contagious that I agreed to take the next train upstate with a bag packed for Richard and me.

After all, Richard loved spending time with Victoria and

Michael. When the four of us were together, Richard dominated the conversion, asking her questions about the voice-over world and sharing with her the details of how his career was going. On the one hand, it annoyed Michael and myself to be left out, but on the other, I learned about Richard's life. He had long stopped sharing anything he did with me. I didn't know when he had an audition, when he booked a job, how he felt about the job, or how much money he was making. He was supposed to be my partner, but shared more with Victoria in a few minutes than he'd shared with me since the move to New York.

That afternoon while Victoria and I planted her vegetable garden, I finally confided that I thought he was cheating.

"What?" She was shocked. "No, not Richard. He loves you." She was reacting from the memory of how overly affectionate he used to be—*used to* being the operative phrase. We had stopped getting together with them as a couple because Michael didn't like feeling left out.

That night, Victoria and I got all gussied up. It was so much fun to share a bathroom and play in each other's makeup. That's one of the things I loved about Victoria, our ability to go from nature girls planting in the garden to hot mamas out on the town. Mostly it felt great to laugh and play. It had been a long time since I had smiled. It felt foreign on my face.

My cell phone rang. It was Richard telling me he'd heard the message I left about taking all his toiletries and that we were picking him up. He was angry. He didn't want to stay at their home.

"Why?"

"I have work to do tomorrow! Jesus, Judi! What were you thinking?! What gave you the right—"

"Fine, fine, we don't have to stay," I conceded. "We'll pick you up, and I'll take the train back with you."

"No, don't go there! Do you hear me? Under no circumstances are you to show up to the catering house!"

"Okay, I'll take a train home tonight."

He hung up on me; the man who used to insist on walking

me to my car after my show in LA was now fine with my taking a train into the city and then the subway back to Queens after midnight.

When I hung up the phone and went to tell Victoria, she stopped me. "I heard." And I could tell by the look on her face that she now believed what I'd said about him. He must have been out with another woman.

I forced myself to have fun that night, dancing with Victoria and drinking with Michael. I got drunk, very drunk, as a *fuck you* to Richard. Richard didn't drink, and although he danced, he never danced with me. I was on a mission to have fun even if I had to pay for it when I got home. At the end of the evening, Victoria and Michael drove me back to Queens.

"You're cheating on me," Richard said before I could even shut the door.

"With Victoria and Michael? Explain how." I laughed.

"You have scratches on your neck. Who were you with?" He was serious.

I looked in a mirror. I did have scratches, but I was drunk and dancing. I had no idea how they got there, and he wouldn't let it go. "My ex-girlfriend came home with scratches, and she was cheating," he added, showing a vulnerability that I knew was difficult for him.

"Well, I'm not cheating on you," I said. "Are you cheating on me?"

He questioned my question. "Why do you think I'm cheating on you?"

"Because you don't share your life with me anymore. All I know is what I piece together from your behavior."

"I am working so hard for us. I'm under a lot of pressure, and your constant nagging doesn't help."

"So tell me you're stressed. Share your thoughts with me."

"I'm protecting you."

It was a ridiculous and outdated concept from someone so young, but I knew I wouldn't be able to make him understand, in much the same way that I couldn't make him realize that telling white lies was still lying. We dropped the conversion and went to sleep. I never got the chance to ask how he got home before me from the catering house.

I did apply to UIC and was accepted. Soon my daughter graduated from college and moved back to Chicago, and my son called to reconcile with me. He and I had stopped talking after he told me that the age difference in my relationship repulsed him. With both my kids in Chicago, it was an easy decision. I would go home. I imagined if Richard and I were in different states and had to make plans to see each other, we would spend quality time together. In the meantime, I could be spending more time with my kids. Win-win! I honestly felt that was exactly what our relationship needed.

"I think I'll start looking at places in Chicago, but UIC is a lot more money than CUNY."

"Don't worry about the money," he said, which I took to mean he was going to help out financially.

My decision perked him up, and he was happy to help in any way he could. Within the course of a few months, I had flown to Chicago, found a place, made an offer, gotten accepted for a mortgage, and set a moving date.

"It's right across the lake; there's a great jogging path for you," I told him when I got back to New York.

He didn't reply.

"When do you think you'll visit me?"

Mr. Talks-too-much had no answer.

"Are we breaking up?"

"How could you ask me that? How could you think that? That hurts me." But he never answered the question. Our arguments were one-sided, like a parent lecturing a child. Long rants on how I was wrong, and he was right, always ending with me apologizing to him. Yes, I had become very adept at apologizing. It ended his tirades.

His actions spoke for him. He still slept on the couch every night.

"Why aren't you sleeping in the bed?"

"I'm considerate. I work late, and I don't want to wake you up."

I just wanted him to tell me the truth. Then we could have lovingly separated from each other. I never understood why people want to spare others from the truth. The truth doesn't hurt as much as deceit. I could deal with any truth. *You're too old for me. I fell out of love. There's someone else.* Truth is tangible. It's understandable. It's what I needed. Hell, it's what I deserved.

"This feels like a divorce," I said as we divided our belongings.

I truly felt if we could have been honest with each other, everything would have been fine. Honest Richard would say, "Yes, it does feel like a breakup."

Honest Judi would ask, "And why do you think that is?"

HR: "Because we need to break up."

HJ: "I agree."

HR: "I love you."

HJ: "And I love you, more than I have ever loved anyone else."

HR: "I'll probably never love anyone as much as I do you."

HJ: "But we don't work."

HR: "No, that's obvious."

And Honest Judi and Honest Richard would share a melancholy laugh.

And then we could have devised a proper plan to get me back on track. Was that an unrealistic expectation? No. So why did I get lies and cover-ups? Maybe it was the consequence of being the only adult in the relationship.

Instead, when I said, "This feels like a divorce," Richard screamed, "Stop saying that!"

Reaching my limit, I met his anger. "Just fucking man up already. If we're breaking up, tell me!"

"Man up? That's how you talk to me?" he seethed back at me. Once again in my life, I felt silenced by hostility. Then I was privy to another thirty-minute lecture on how hard he was working, for *us!* He used his intelligence as a weapon against me, turning my words back at me, spinning my reality.

"When people show you who they are, believe them," Maya Angelou famously said, but which was the real Richard? The one he presented those first few years we were together, or the one I had been living with for the past eighteen months? I didn't know, so I did nothing. I took a wait-and-see approach.

On June fourteenth, a friend called to tell me that Roxy's mother had died on the golf course. She had been run over by her partner. I tried to call Roxy, but the cell number I still had memorized no longer worked. The funeral was in Chicago the next day, so I asked my brother to get her phone number for me. She called that night while Richard was out.

"Oh my God, Roxy, Roxy sweetie, I'm so sorry about your mother."

"When I heard she was dead my first thought was, 'How am I going to do this without my JuJu?'"

I booked the six a.m. flight out for the next day. When Richard came home that night, he was less than thrilled that I was back together with Roxy. "You're dropping everything? Just like that? Why?"

"Because it's Roxy."

"But she hurt you. How can you forgive her so easily?"

Uh, I forgive you daily.

"Because it's Roxy."

"But I planned to take Sunday off to be with you. How can you leave me with nothing to do?"

I did not feel sorry for his one day alone in the apartment. I had tons of those days *and* nights. I didn't even have a TV to watch in Queens; Richard didn't believe in them. He did have a projector for movies, but I wasn't allowed to use it. It was linked to his computer and I didn't have his password. He had never forgiven me for reading his emails. He never forgave an infraction.

In Chicago the next day, I walked into the Shiva house and spotted Roxy immediately. Her back was to me. I came up from behind and put my arms around her shoulders. Her hands touched my arms, and she exhaled as she sank into my embrace. Without turning around, she said, "You're here."

"I'm here," I repeated, and then we hugged.

The following night we shared a pitcher of margaritas at our favorite Mexican restaurant—the one where we dislike the food but love the tequila. She placed a pack of cigarettes on the table. "Yes, I'm still smoking."

"Not judging." But I was disappointed she'd never quit.

"Let's not talk about what happened yet," she suggested, and I agreed. It wasn't the time or place.

"I did the show in New York."

"I know, I read about it. I live in Colorado now."

"I know. I Googled you." And we laughed at ourselves. "Nice to know our teenage stalking skills have progressed with the times," I added to the one person in the world who knew what incident I was referring to because she shared my past, my memories.

We spent the rest of the night talking, laughing, and filling each other in on the past three and a half years. I told her about Richard, but not that things were bad between us; she didn't even make a joke about the age difference.

"How's the sex?"

"It has an E rating."

"E?"

"Every. Time."

"I fucking hate you."

Just as I had imagined. "I missed you."

"I missed you more."

"Probably." And we laughed.

Two months later, I moved back to Chicago. One week later, Richard called. "We have to talk."

I don't know why I'm always happy to hear those words. I guess it's because I genuinely believe the other person wants to talk. I had been trying to get him to open up for over a year.

"Great," I said and snuggled into the couch he had picked out online for me.

"I'm sorry, I love you, but I have to let you go."

What? No. No. His rule; don't threaten a breakup. Those words are final. Oh my God, he's breaking up with me. Who breaks up without talking things out first?

I don't remember if he kept talking because pain began to creep into my heart along with the question, *how will I survive?* I had completely given myself over to him. I trusted him with every decision. I had stopped making choices for myself, had believed his words of love and loyalty and forever. I remembered the pain of my lost teenage love: how that breakup came without warning, and the pain I hid from everyone, how much I wanted to die back then. I had never wanted to love again, to trust. I married a man I didn't trust, but meeting Richard changed that. I felt like I was in a cloud that was getting darker and colder. I couldn't scream; thin walls. Knees buckled; I was on the floor. When had I stood up? *Did you ever know you would be loved this much?* Gone. Love—gone, sex—gone, partner—gone, best friend—gone. Impossible. Heart hurts, shattered. Shattered dreams, shattered future. Strong arms—gone, hugs—gone, snuggling—gone. Fool. I trusted. Old fool. *I love you more than anything in the entire universe.* Memories painful. Open window, seventeenth floor, over in seconds.

I finally found my voice as my pride jumped out the window. "Don't do this. Don't do this. Please. Don't do this, Richard." He was silent. I used his words that had worked on me: "Do I have to fight you for you?"

Nothing would dissuade him. His mind was made up. I knew from experience that when your younger man breaks up with you, you have to walk away with dignity, but I couldn't.

Then he said, "I've never been friends with an ex, but I'd really like us to try."

His words snapped me out of pain and into anger. *In the past two years, you were no friend of mine!* But that's not what came out of my mouth. I still couldn't fight with him. I still didn't want to hurt him. I hung up the phone. The anger I felt was a great motivator and a lifesaving emotion.

The commitment I made to Richard in LA to spend the rest of my life with him created invisible bars, keeping me jailed to the New York Dick. But then he spent so much time away that the door to my cage opened; there was plenty of time to pack and make an escape. Still, I never left.

I didn't write either. I couldn't. Inspiration had always come from events that happened in my life, and nothing was happening in my life. But wasn't that my fault? Like Ariel in *The Little Mermaid,* had I not willingly given up my voice for a man?

I learned the hard way that just because a man is kinder and more thoughtful than your Ex, it doesn't mean he's "the one." It's okay to break up, because if you're staying in a relationship for someone else, no one will be happy.

I spent twenty years of my life waiting for The Ex-Hole to revert to the sweet, caring man that courted me in college. He never did. That guy didn't exist. I wasted time and sacrificed my own ambitions waiting.

How the fuck did I let that happen, again?!

How, in heaven's name, had I become a bit player in the Judi Show?

Six years post-divorce, I had grown, discovered who I was and what I wanted, trusted my instincts, and was living the life I'd always known I was meant to live—until I met Richard. How had an innocent fling, what was supposed to be my last dalliance with a younger man, thrown me into a backward and downward spiral?

That I can answer in one word—Pliable.

Right after I got married, Mother pressured me to have a baby. I did. Shortly after he was born, she asked, "When's the next one coming?"

"Did you pester my sister like this?" I asked.

"You're more pliable," Mother said.

Pliable. Pliable. Pliable.

That word vibrated its truth in my brain like waves in a television sitcom dream sequence. I was pliable. I'd always gone along to get along.

By the time I met Richard, my heart was open and I was ready to trust and fall in love, and that left me vulnerable. I'd never dealt with the core reasons why I was pliable, and Richard zeroed in on the weakness, my willingness to put myself last on the list, and he manipulated me into a relationship. He also manipulated me into moving in with him, giving up my dreams and possessions, and into moving across the country, away from the only place I'd ever truly belonged. A place where I had finally felt safe and happy, west, where the sun sets.

Jaded

"**Y**a gotta admire the patience, planning, and sheer endurance it took to spend eighteen months orchestrating you out of his life so that it looked like you left him," Roxy observed.

"Fuck him and the white horse he fell off!"

I didn't recognize the person I had become in New York, and I certainly didn't like her. How could I have expected Richard to fall back in love with me when *I* didn't even like me? Gone was the woman who wrote and produced and came alive in Los Angeles, the funny girl who made her own rules and lived her dreams.

Of course, after word spread about the breakup, friends told me how they really felt.

"I didn't like you with him," Susie confessed. "I feel like I finally got my friend back."

"It was painful to watch you disappear," added Patricia.

So there I was, back in Chicago, living in a studio apartment I would not have bought if I knew it was going to be my full-time residence. I didn't want to be in Chicago full-time anyway. *Fuck him!*

I was also in school, studying biology and chemistry to become a registered dietician. I had two more years and would incur over thirty thousand in student loans. I had never wanted to switch careers in the first place. *Fuck him!!*

Even though I didn't like to quit anything, I quit school

and started looking for a job. This time around post-breakup, I had a college education and had racked up plenty of office experience. How hard could it be to find a job?

As it turned out, in 2009, it was very difficult. Jobs were hard to come by. I applied for everything I saw on craigslist: administrative assistant, receptionist, cashier, barista, even waitress—but no one hired me.

Being broke this time around was worse. After the divorce, I had child support and some commercial residual money coming in so I could jockey around paying the bills. This time I had zero income. All the money my father had left me was gone—the last of it used as a down payment on my condo because I needed at least one tangible thing to show for the money.

I started living off credit cards. When I met Richard, he was thirty thousand in debt, and I had 360 thousand in the bank. Now he was living in New York, debt-free and getting ready to buy a house, while I had no money plus eight thousand owed in school loans because he told me not to worry about the UIC cost. How the hell had we swapped lives? *FUCK HIM!*

I knew I was angry. I knew I was heartbroken. But I didn't realize I was jaded until I visited Susie after her recent move to La Crosse, Wisconsin. She'd been after me to visit for a while, but I was hesitant to take a road trip. I feared the radio, more precisely; country music with lyrics asking questions that plagued my broken heart. "Do I ever cross your mind?" and "How am I supposed to live without you?"

I reconciled with the radio and made it to Wisconsin on my last twenty dollars. After a lovely dinner in their home, Susie asked if I would be willing to watch the second *Twilight* movie. It had just arrived, and she was dying to see it.

"Sure," I responded.

"Are you into them? Have you read the books?"

I confessed I hadn't.

"But this is the second movie, and you haven't seen the first."

"It's okay, put it in," I insisted, because really, teen love aside, who doesn't like a vampire movie?

She put the DVD of *The Twilight Saga: New Moon* into the player, and we watched it. The movie is about a young vampire who falls madly, hopelessly in love with a mortal teenager. However, they can't consummate their relationship without him losing control of his vampire urge to kill her. As a writer, I thought it was a pretty cool premise.

Then he broke up with her, said he was leaving town and didn't want her to come, that she didn't belong in his world. The final blow: "You're just not good for me." She was devastated. She spent months in her room, staring out her bedroom window. Then they reunited, and he said he lied, the only reason he left was to protect her. "I swear, I'll never fail you again. I'm so sorry."

"Pause it!" I demanded, unable to control myself.

Susie's husband paused the DVD player.

"This makes me so angry," I continued. "These movies are so popular with the young girls, and here they are perpetuating the myth that men don't mean what they say. And that's bull crap! When a guy breaks up with you, it's over. He doesn't come back and recant. Young girls need to know that early."

Susie laughed at me.

"Why are you laughing? All those romantic comedies, boy meets girl, they hate each other, then fall in love and live happily ever after? No! Those differences they hate will rear their heads and become the reasons for the divorce later."

She laughed harder. "My husband loves those movies."

I looked at him. He had been politely staying out of the conversation. "You do?" I asked.

He shrugged, still staring at the frozen TV screen.

"He watches them endlessly. He watches them more than I do," Susie continued.

"Why?"

"I like them."

"But they're not real! Men do not make grandstand plays to get the girl back. It doesn't happen!"

Still he sat there, not wanting to engage his crazy houseguest in a heated debate. Suddenly I realized, looking at him sitting next to the woman he loved: that wasn't a fairy tale for him.

He had been in his mid-fifties and resigned to living alone when he met and married my friend, his perfect soul mate. They were truly living happily ever after. They were one of those couples that seemed to have it all figured out.

There was nothing wrong with him. It was me. I was jaded. And I'm sure it looked as ugly as it felt. I had been broken up with more times than I cared to admit, but until that point in my life, I had never felt jaded about love.

"I'm sorry. Un-pause it. Please," I requested softly.

"I can watch it tomorrow," Susie graciously replied.

"I have to see how it ends."

I needed a happy ending.

Mr. Age Appropriate

I was at a party in the back room of a bar on Wells Street in Old Town. Being single left me without a home base, so I stood at the bar, acting like I was waiting for someone, just as I had done at singles' parties. A twenty-eight-year-old started to chat me up.

"Hi, I hear you just moved back from New York."

"Yes," I answered. "That's right."

"I lived there for a bit myself. I miss it."

"Not me." I wasn't sure if I meant New York or Richard.

"There must have been something you liked about New York." He moved closer to talk into my ear over the loud music. I felt his hand on the small of my back as he whispered, "Tell me a favorite New York day." He pulled back and stared into my eyes.

I looked at the kid. "I'm sorry. I have to go."

It was an engagement party for my daughter. The guy was one of the groomsmen. Was he hitting on the MOB—Mother of the Bride? I found my children, said goodbye, and left, totally blaming Richard for putting me out there and not being by my side. Was I wearing a sign that said, "I date younger men"—Did everyone in Chicago know my dating history? Of course, they did. I fucking wrote and performed a show about it and even brought it to Chicago.

What was I thinking?

I came home and cried. I didn't belong in Chicago anymore. Everyone at the party I had once known to be single, divorced, or widowed was coupled up. Everyone had moved on in life except me. I needed a man, an age-appropriate man. I could not be single, not in Chicago, not with my daughter getting married.

Richard had been my home the last four years, but he never fit in with my family. This time around, I would find a mate who did. And this time I would get married. Never again would I be in a relationship that could end in a phone call. The next time around if someone wanted out, it would cost him. No way was I going to be alone and broke a third time. Security. I finally understood what Mother meant when she said, "Judala, it's just as easy to fall for a rich man as it is to fall for a poor one."

I'm with you, Mother!

Yes, I wanted to be in love, but I planned on falling head-first.

"For the love of God, please don't take me to any more singles' parties!" Roxy pleaded.

"No problem. I am not leaving this up to chance."

I went online and chose a dating site. I checked the boxes that said he could be divorced and widowed. I said no to separated and no to single. I felt both revealed commitment issues. He would also have to be age appropriate. I had never liked being with a younger man. It did not make me feel young; it made me feel old and embarrassed.

I knew a man my age would likely have children, but I wanted them grown and out of the house; no teenage drama—and no pets! I liked my freedom and a clean house. Hey, my own kids were grown and gone. Why on earth would I want to do that again?

Money! He would have to have money. That had never been on my list before, but it sure as shit was on it now. No more paying for dinners, no more splitting the bill. I needed to make better choices—and no more actors! I needed stability.

He'd have to be in good physical shape. I never thought I liked muscles, but as it turned out, I did. A sense of humor we both shared would be great. I wanted him to be cultured, neat, know how to cook, and most importantly be someone my children would like and respect because my goal was to meet the love of the second half of my life and dance with him at my daughter's wedding the following spring.

I was concerned with how I would attract a man with my hormones at half-mast. My mood swings had stabilized, and the hot flashes were few and far between. Although it was a welcome change, it also meant that full-on menopause was setting up camp in my ovaries. Those pheromones that attracted men to me in my forties were disappearing. I had no time to waste. I had to rally the troops for one last mission. I'd learned in biology that after menopause, estrogen is manufactured in adipose tissue, the fat cells. How was a skinny girl supposed to make new sex hormones?

My life had become a parody of my favorite children's book, *Are You My Mother?*, where the little lost bird looks everywhere for his mother.

"Are you my hormones?" she said to the computer.

"No," said the computer.

"Don't worry so much about *your* hormones," Roxy told me. "Dr. Oz says that a forty-year-old man has a twenty-five percent chance of having erectile dysfunction and it increases by ten percent every decade after."

"So, *negative* thirty-five percent is the new penis?"

"Shit, we're old."

I realized that finding a new man with my diminishing hormones could prove to be ideal. No more going to networking meetings and letting mere attraction take over. *Who's that guy? Are we dating? If it's not clear, it's not good! Look at the kindness in his eyes.* No! Where had hormones gotten me? I had moved across the country, had given up my dreams, and completely lost myself. Hormones. Fuck. You. Up. Any teenage boy with a pockmarked, pimpled face who can't control his hard-on will tell you: hormones suck. And any girl whose breasts are either too big or too small will agree.

Hormones, I don't need you anymore! Thank you for the mem-

ories, but you led me down a path I couldn't control. Good riddance!

After I got my picture and profile up on the dating site, I went to bed. The next morning, I had thirty-five emails, three flirts, and two e-cards I didn't know how to open.

Deciphering profiles was easy. I applied the same tactic I took when looking for real estate, where *cozy* was small, *character* required renovation, and *motivated*—just plain desperate. For example: *love my job* was code for works too much; *has young kids* meant I'd be last on his list; *hate my ex*—he fights dirty; *my ex and I get along great*—he wants her back.

I was saving time, the guys were saving money, and I felt pretty smart without those hormones.

My first Internet date was with a man in his late fifties. He asked me to meet him at a chic restaurant in Chicago's River North area. He was of slight build, had grey hair, and was several inches shorter than his profile disclosed. As much as I aspired to date older men, I knew it would take some getting used to. My last boyfriend was thirty-three. Age-appropriate men would be fifty-three to sixty-three. That would be like going to bed with Justin Timberlake and waking up with Larry King.

The waitstaff was very attentive, probably because they didn't have much to do; after all, we were having dinner at 5:30 p.m. I ordered a martini while he opted for a glass of red wine. The martinis were twenty dollars each. I felt bad, so I planned to order a small salad to balance the cost.

Our conversation consisted of the usual questions: *how many kids do you have, what do you do, how long have you been divorced?* His answers failed on every level. He was older than I, but his kids were still in high school. He was looking to change jobs so he couldn't offer security, and he wasn't even divorced. It had been fifteen months since they filed the papers.

"As soon as I filed, we were divorced within months."

"It's complicated: we're both lawyers." His answers alone were enough to write him off, but then he asked a question. "What previous relationship stands out most in your life?"

I answered without hesitation. "That would have to be

Ashton, an actor I met in LA. We weren't together long, but it was the most connected, the most loving relationship I've ever had. I was my best self with him."

"What happened?"

"We knew from the start it wouldn't last. He wanted marriage and kids and I didn't."

"You wouldn't marry him?"

"Well, there was an age difference. He was twelve years younger."

"You're a cougar!" he exclaimed, as if he'd heard about that particular type of beast but had never actually seen one up close.

I stared at him with silent loathing as the waitress interrupted. "Is everything okay here?"

"On second thought, I'll have another martini, the lobster for dinner, and feel free to stroll that dessert cart around."

Wow, if that's how he felt about twelve years, I could only imagine what he'd say about Richard. I had heard the word "cougar" before, but it did not apply to me.

"Have I offended you?" he asked, but I didn't hear an apology.

"I am not a cougar. Dating younger men does not automatically make you a cougar."

"Okay."

"According to Webster's Urban Dictionary, a cougar is an older woman who frequents clubs in order to score with younger men."

"You've done your research."

I finished my drink and took my meal home in a takeaway bag so I could eat it in peace in front of the television with a real man, Lennie Briscoe. Needless to say, I never saw him again, and he was smart enough not to call.

The second Internet date was with a man one year older than me. He was a cute, tall motivational speaker and world traveler. We met for a bike ride in Lincoln Park but quickly locked up the bikes so we could walk and have a proper conversation. Although I enjoyed his energy, his youthfulness, his smile, and his looks, I didn't like that he traveled often. "I make enough money to travel, and when it runs out, I come home, make more, and do it again."

There would be no security with him either. He also said he had an extensive collection of artifacts. I sneezed just thinking about the dust.

That night I came home to the perfect profile: an age appropriate, fifty-two-year-old grown-up. He was six foot two, divorced, and had two grown boys who lived out of state. His income answer box ticked at the highest amount, he owned a hospital supply business, had no pets, and loved to travel. He wrote, "I'm as comfortable in Dominick's as I am in Home Depot. I can rewire a home, make gourmet meals, and I dance like Fred Astaire. Well, maybe not Fred, more like Barney." The well-crafted joke impressed me. He was born and raised in Indiana, so I assumed he had Midwest values, and he currently lived in Elmhurst.

"Where the fuck is Elmhurst?" I asked Roxy.

"I think it's in Iowa," my fellow city friend replied. "He's what you call 'good on paper.'"

In a follow-up email, he told me his name and that Elmhurst was in DuPage County, a suburb west of Chicago. "I'd like to take you to dinner. Pick a place in your neighborhood."

I loved that he didn't ask me to audition for the date with coffee or a drink and asking me to pick a restaurant in my neighborhood showed that he was unassuming, respectful, and mindful of the fact that I was meeting a stranger. I returned in kind by emailing back the names of three different restaurants so he could choose. He settled on an Italian restaurant a mile from my house.

I didn't drive my car because re-parking in my neighborhood at night was impossible. "Rox, it's a little too far to walk, but if I ride my bike, I'll get helmet hair."

"I love that you still believe a man can see above breast level."

I got to the restaurant a few minutes early. I planned to fix my hair before he got there, but as I was outside the restaurant, bent over my bike, running a chain through the spokes, I heard a man's voice ask, "Judi?"

I looked up. He was as tall as his profile boasted, and thin too. He wore a suit and had short, neat gray hair. His whole demeanor screamed grown-up, and the cut of his suit boasted his success. I had on black-and-white gingham capri pants with a V-neck T-shirt, which, still bent over my bike chain, revealed far too much cleavage. I stood up straight. "Yes."

"May I help you with that?" Mr. Age Appropriate offered.

"No, I got it. But thank you." I turned my back to him before I bent over again. He was early, too. I had been so used to Richard being late that I'd forgotten it wasn't the norm.

It was a Tuesday night, so we were seated at a table right away. After I ordered a glass of red wine, he declined and told me he didn't drink.

Another one.

"I never liked the taste."

"No one does at first." I didn't add that most people drank for the feeling it gave them. Sitting across from a suited gentleman felt very grown-up. "That's a beautiful suit."

"Thank you. I have dozens. More, maybe; I seem to have filled every closet in my house."

"That's a lot of suits."

"I love suits." He looked down for a minute, pausing, and then back up at me. "Growing up, we were dirt poor. I had one pair of pants and two shirts in high school."

He didn't have to continue. I understood. Mother grew up in the Depression and had to go without, so as a doctor's wife, she shopped as if her next breath depended on it.

As we continued to talk, he confirmed he didn't want pets and loved cooking and going to museums. He was everything his profile stated. It was refreshing.

"I'm learning to speak French," he told me.

"Are you taking a college class?"

"I have a private tutor."

I was impressed, "A private French tutor?"

"I have a ten-day trip planned to Paris and the south of France in the fall."

"Nice. Have you ever been?"

"No. You?"

"Yes, but I didn't see Paris the way I had hoped I would. And I've never been to the south of France."

Until you take me.

I could tell he was gentle and kind, the kind of kind you can't fake.

"I was turned out of the house at eighteen. I got a job and put myself through school at the University of Indiana annex. Junior year, my boss offered to pay for the remainder of school."

"To keep you working there?"

"No. Just out of kindness. The catch was that one day, I do the same for someone else."

"And you did."

"Several kids, including my two sons and two stepsons."

"You've been married twice?"

"Yes. I believe I put that in my profile."

Damn my poor retention skills.

"Is that a deal-breaker?"

I thought about it. "No. Hell, if I had married Richard when he asked, I'd be divorced a second time too."

"Richard?"

"My recent ex." *Very recent.*

"Is that over? I don't want to pursue this if you're not available."

I smiled. "It's over."

I loved his honesty. He had a small-town mentality, yet he was cultured. He loved going to art galleries, so I knew he and my daughter would have something in common. He was every-thing I was looking for in a man, the embodiment of what being in your fifties was supposed to look like: able to relax and enjoy life, travel, and do the things one had to put off when they were younger.

I enjoyed his company. We liked the same music, had the same points of historical reference, and both remembered listening to The Beatles before they broke up. Age-appropriate dating was cool, and I found it comforting to know that at no point in the evening, under no circumstance, was the man going to say "Boo-yah!"

I'm going to marry you.

When the waiter put the check down, I remembered Transition Guy, telling me it was important for a woman to reach for her wallet and offer to split the bill. As I turned to get my purse, I stopped myself, turned back and said, "Yeah, I'm not even going to pretend to try." He didn't laugh or ask what I meant. I think he was still distracted by cleavage.

After dinner, he walked me to my bike. "I'd like to see you again."

"That would be lovely," I answered, as if starring in a 1950s film.

It was ten months post-breakup. I was fifty-one and being with Mr. Age Appropriate made me feel younger, prettier, and sexier than I ever had when I was with Richard. Younger men and older women work due to simple biology: you match sexually and hormonally, until the older woman in question has no more sex hormones.

The next morning, I went to my computer to send Mr. Age Appropriate a thank-you email. To my surprise, there was already one from him in my inbox, along with a request for a second date. He wanted to meet at the Art Institute in the late afternoon. I had plans to meet Susie and her husband for dinner because they were in town, so I called Susie and asked if she would mind my bringing a date to dinner.

"It's weird—unless you think it's going to turn into a relationship."

"I'm going to marry him."

"Wow. Okay, I'd love to meet him."

It was hard to manage the museum with the plantar fasciitis, but he was very supportive and happy to sit on the benches with me when I needed to rest. I enjoyed not feeling the need to keep up with him, as I had with Richard.

We met my friends for dinner at the Park Grill in Millennium Park. They loved him. They were just his type: small-town folk of little or no dramas. Dinners with these friends and Richard had felt tense, since Susie's husband was twenty-seven years older than Richard.

I felt comfortable with Mr. Age Appropriate, so I let him drive me home after dinner and walk me up to my apartment. I invited him in, and we sat at opposite ends of the couch. It was very awkward. He sat there not saying much with his hands folded on his lap, his demeanor matching my mid-century décor. I wasn't sure if he wanted to kiss me, but the thought of kissing him did nothing for me. I had never missed my albums more. They were a tension-releasing device, perfect for first dates. Without them, I was in a muted limbo.

Finally, I told him it was time to retrieve his car from my doorman, and when he left, he gave me a simple kiss goodnight. I didn't feel anything from the kiss except dampness on my cheek and wondered from where that had come.

"Maybe you don't like him that way," Roxy offered.

"Yeah, well, how can I know for sure with my hormones disappearing?"

"Are you my hormones?" she said to the desk.

"I am not your hormones. I am a desk," said the desk.

He asked me out for lunch that Sunday. Before I could tell him I was meeting Roxy in the suburbs because she was in town, he said he wanted to take me to lunch in that very same suburb. *Fate.* I asked him to pick me up from the Botanic Gardens, which he did.

At lunch, I told him that I had a job interview the following Tuesday.

"I didn't know you were out of work," he said, and I wondered why he hadn't been able to decipher that information from my profile: *free spirit, looking for new opportunities.*

"Yes," I said, "been looking for a job over a year now. Is that a deal-breaker?"

He smiled.

We went for a walk after lunch. He held my hand, and still, I felt nothing except a sweaty palm. Richard's hands never felt sweaty, but at least I was walking with someone.

I went to my job interview at an architecture firm on Tuesday morning, and they offered me the administrative position by the end of that day. It was my brother's birthday, so I was at his house when I got the call. My sister-in-law gave me six dresses from her closet. "On loan, until you can go shopping." I was grateful for her generosity.

I started work the following day. I got up at six-thirty a.m., showered, dressed, took an hour bus ride in the rush-hour traffic, and worked from eight-thirty a.m. to five-thirty p.m. When Mr. Age Appropriate picked me up that night for a celebratory dinner, I almost fell asleep in my profiterole. I actually had to put my head on the table during dinner. I was happy to have a job, to cease living off credit cards, but I missed the schedule of a working actor: sleep until you wake up, work out, go to an audition, and meet a friend for lunch.

When he dropped me off at my apartment, he gave me a quick kiss on the lips, and I left his car with a wet cheek. *What the hell is that?*

I saw Mr. Age Appropriate several days during the week after work and we had a standing date for Saturday night. It was all very adult. We went to nice restaurants and saw plays. I loved that kind of dating, and we enjoyed each other's company, but there were no butterflies in my stomach. Sometimes I felt like an observer, as if I were watching a movie I had seen before. Every time he said something sweet, I wasn't hearing it for the first time. His words, his sentiments, and the succession of the statements were exactly what Richard had said to me four years earlier. Both men followed the same script:

1. Where did you come from?
2. How come no one has snatched you up?

3. You're so beautiful.
4. I enjoy being with you.
5. You'd be so easy to fall for.
6. How could anyone have let you go?
7. I really care about you.
                    Eventually, we would hit:
8. I love you.
9. I would never overlap you. (Though Mr. Age Appropriate would use the word "cheat.")
10. I want to spend the rest of my life with you.

Yadda, yadda, yadda...

After yet another failed relationship, how do you hear all this for the first time? How do you not compare? How do you stay in the present? And, most importantly, how do you believe any of it?

I wanted to believe. We were making plans for the future, but I kept thinking about how when I'd made plans with Richard, none of them came to fruition. They just hung over our heads and bound me to a relationship that was long over. How could I have faith? How would I trust again?

A month into dating Mr. Age Appropriate, there was a shower for my daughter not too far from his home in Elmhurst. "If you spent the night at my place, it would be an easy commute in the morning," he suggested.

I knew what that meant. He was ready to take the relationship to the next level: the sex level. Part of me wanted to. In the past, sex usually solidified my relationships; something about the release of oxytocin that causes women to fall in love after sex. It would be just the push I needed to override my lack of hormones. However, part of me was scared to have sex with a new man. It had been a year since I'd been intimate with anyone and several months since I stopped having a period. I wasn't sure if my parts still worked.

"Roxy, can you still have orgasms?"

"Yes," she reassured, "but it takes a village."

Oy.

Lying in bed with Mr. Age Appropriate that night wondering if we were going to have sex was even more excruciatingly awkward than sitting in silence on the couch, wondering if he was going to kiss me. Since neither of us had verbalized a sexual intention, I don't think he knew how to proceed. We just lay there in his bed in our pajamas. Every once in a while, he'd kiss me, and just as it became passionate, he would stop and pull away. *What the...?* It was very frustrating. Was he waiting for me to initiate?

Finally, out of sheer frustration, I asked, "Are we going to have sex?"

That's all it took. He started to kiss me again, only this time with purpose. The kiss progressed to touching, groping, and fondling body parts, and for the first time in years I had missionary position sex! I wasn't sure if it was because that was his style or because he wasn't extra-large, like my last two partners.

In the morning, I woke up happy; neither of us had plumbing issues! But then he wanted to do it again, and I was turned on by the Keurig in the kitchen.

"So, no passion?" Roxy asked.

"What's so great about passion? It's not sustainable. And then you spend the rest of your relationship saying, 'Remember when we couldn't keep our hands off each other?' Sexual attraction is great, but it doesn't withstand the test of time."

"But still, beginnings are the best part."

"Not to me. I love the comfort in really knowing someone."

"Boring."

"Isn't this what passion turns into in your fifties? So what if we went straight to an old married couple? I like it. I think he's the one."

"The *one*? You had the *one*; you married him, had children with him. Then you had the *one* in New York. At this point, you just need *another* one."

I liked being with Mr. Age Appropriate. I liked being part of a couple again. He met my children, and they liked him, accepted him.

"He won't give you any drama. You can tell that about him," my thirty-year-old son observed.

My twenty-seven-year-old daughter gave her stamp of approval: "I like how he treats you."

One night we went to an outdoor restaurant with his French tutor and her boyfriend. It was all very romantic; we even danced to live music. I had five glasses of champagne in me and planned to give him oral sex that night. Having been accustomed to Richard's perfect penis, it was alarming to find myself face-to-face with a Gollum doppelgänger. For those unfamiliar with the film, *The Lord of the Rings* —long, straggly, gray hairs protruding from the bald head.

No wonder most women only give head on their partner's birthday.

The next morning, I asked if he would start trimming the hedge.

"What? Who does that?" He was shocked.

Every man I've ever been with.

"A lot of men do it these days."

"Well, not me," he stated. "It's just weird."

Fine. Don't. See where that gets you.

I didn't understand why a man who wanted a woman to put her face in his crotch wouldn't want to make it a nice place to visit.

We took turns sleeping at each other's places. Our sex life averaged about once a week, and I was fine with that, although less would have been okay too. One morning we awoke in my apartment on a weekday, and he heard me sigh as I looked in my closet. "I have nothing to wear!"

"Women always say that. I bet I could help you pick out an outfit."

"I would love that." I moved out of the way. "Good luck."

He quickly picked out the only business dress I had. "Here ya go."

"Wore that yesterday."

He then chose my black pants.

"Wore those the day before."

"So, wear them with a different blouse." He searched through my closet. "Where are your blouses?"

"Don't have any."

"I only see jeans."

"Exactly."

"You genuinely have nothing to wear to work. We need to go shopping."

"I can't afford a shopping trip yet."

"Let me take you."

"What? No. I couldn't let you do that."

"I want to."

"Thank you. No."

"You're saying no to the universe," Victoria exclaimed when I told her about his offer. "You need clothes. He offered clothes. Why can't you just say, 'Thank you for the clothes'?"

The next time he offered, I took him to Fox's, an off-price designer clothing store. I got several dresses, slacks, blouses, and sweaters. The total was under two hundred fifty dollars. When he saw the receipt, he turned to me and smiled. "I spend more than this on a tie."

I went in for a thank-you kiss, and that's when I saw it: a drip hanging from his nose. The reason for my damp cheek after a kiss—snot from his nose!

I pulled back and took a tissue from the counter. "Your nose is running," I told him as I handed him the tissue.

"Perpetually," he said as he wiped.

"It must be allergies, ever try taking an antihistamine?" I said, hoping I'd solved my wet cheek problem.

"No. I won't do that."

Fine. Don't. See where that gets you.

After that, shopping became our thing. He loved to shop. The Nordstrom salespeople in the men's department were on a first-name basis with him. He told me he couldn't dress his first wife because she wouldn't get out of her sweatpants. She was a small-town girl and thought he was acting too ritzy with all his fancy clothes. His second wife was a businesswoman, but since she was short, clothes always needed to be altered. It wasn't fun to take her shopping. But I was sample size. I could buy a complete outfit and wear it out of the store, so he loved dressing me. I needed clothes and he wanted to buy them for me; it felt like a good match.

Our life together seemed to revolve around the mall: shopping, dinner, and movies. It lacked excitement, but it was secure —though his kiss kept me on my toes. Every time he came in for a kiss, I was cautious not to let his nose touch my cheek, which was challenging because he had a very, very long nose. His kiss never really got me excited in the first place, and the constant drip that clung to the tip of his nose was like aversion therapy.

He did ask me to meet him in Paris. I said yes, and of course, there was a shopping trip before we went. As we stood in line at Nordstrom Rack to buy me a lined raincoat (the coat I initially told Richard I should take to Paris), he spotted a T-shirt. "We should get that for you," he said, and when I saw the words on it, I was *very* offended.

Sugar Daddy.

"Is that what you think? You're my Sugar Daddy?"

"It's funny."

"No. It's not." I wanted to throw the coat in his face and walk out of the store. Fuck him! We were at the outlet store; I never let him pay full price for me. But I couldn't leave since we were out in suburban Oak Brook. I had recently sold my car, so walking out on him in a store over thirty miles away from the city seemed futile. Uber wasn't a thing yet. I sucked it up and let him buy the coat. We argued in the parking lot, and although he finally apologized, I never felt like he understood why I was hurt.

"'Sugar Daddy' may be what he wants to be," Roxy concluded.

"Well, it has negative connotations to me."

He went to Paris, and I joined him during his last week

there. He had a car pick me up at the airport, and he was waiting for me at the hotel with flowers, French champagne, presents, and the perpetual snot hanging from the end of his nose. It was early morning and I needed coffee, but I had sex with him first. After all, isn't that what you do for your Sugar Daddy?

Being in Paris with him was more civilized than it had been with Richard. Mr. Age Appropriate was happy to linger over coffee in the mornings and sit with me at cafés during lunch, and we took taxis when I needed to get off my feet.

The south of France was my favorite. He rented a small Italian sports car for the day and drove us to Monte Carlo in the convertible. He wore an Armani suit. I wore a Parisian sundress with oversized sunglasses and a scarf around my head, circa 1960s Audrey Hepburn, against the convertible wind. He loved my dressing the part of a rich man's girlfriend as we lived out his fantasy:

We drove up to the casino, gave the car to the valet, entered arm in arm, took a lap around, and went to the roulette table, where he put one hundred euros on black. When he won, we walked out. He was a simple man with simple fantasies. We then went to the gift shop and bought my kids souvenirs. Affording souvenirs was *my* fantasy.

He came with me to family dinners and events for the upcoming wedding, even paid the tab for the extended family when we met for dinner. I finally felt like a contributing member of my family, instead of the one that worried people. I loved that he towered over The Ex-Hole and had to look down at him. He took my children to dinner and wanted to plan a family vacation for both families in Tuscany.

I thought the relationship was perfect. I could be "Mom" again. We could have a home with a big dining room for family dinners and extra bedrooms for future grandchildren. I felt it would make up for abandoning my children for LA. I still felt guilty about that. Back then, I was confident I would sell a television series or a screenplay and come home victorious, and that would have rendered my LA time worthwhile. Instead, I came home broke and broken. Being with Mr. Age Appropriate was what I thought I needed to repair my family.

On one shopping trip, at Bed Bath & Beyond to buy a shower gift, I wandered from him down the magnifying mirror aisle and stumbled upon a lighted makeup mirror that had 10X magnification. I was used to 4X, which I had in my bathroom. When I looked at myself with 10X magnification, I screamed.

He came to my side because I never overreact. I had screamed only one other time in my life. I was a child, sitting in the front seat of my father's car. At the wheel, my father didn't see a little boy step off the curb and was about to hit him. I couldn't formulate words. I just screamed in fright, and my father reacted by slamming on the brakes. It saved the boy. What I saw in that mirror in the aisle of Bed Bath & Beyond horrified me so much that words failed me again—and I screamed.

"What's wrong? What happened?" He asked. He was genuinely concerned, but I couldn't tell him. As open as I was about ailments and hormonal imbalances, I couldn't tell him I had seen black hairs growing from my upper lip. Some secrets must be kept.

"I saw a spider," I lied.

"Fucking menopause. What's next? Incontinence?" I asked Roxy.

"No, bladder leakage. Be careful when you laugh or sneeze," she replied, and I didn't laugh. Some things are just not funny.

Still, I had to psych myself up to have sex with him once a week. Once he pressed the right buttons, I was good to go, but if given a choice between sex and an episode of *Breaking Bad*, I chose the Meth makers.

In my defense, full-blown menopause had set in, squashing my sex drive. But I'd heard that eventually the drive comes back. Mr. Age Appropriate was a good man, a good catch, and good on paper. I just needed to wait out the return of my sexual desire.

Instead, it got worse. Sex became increasingly painful, and

occasionally there was blood on the sheets. Since I still taped *The Dr. Oz Show*, I learned why. In a segment that was probably called "The Aging Vagina," Dr. Oz had three different scenarios arranged on the stage to demonstrate. There were three different mini trampolines set up. He threw a rubber ball at the first, and it bounced right back as if the circle was thick and malleable. That represented a young vagina. That same ball thrown at another circle bounced back slower as if it had hit a brick wall. That represented a middle-aged vagina. In the third example, the traumatizing example, he tossed the same ball at the last circle, and not only did the ball *not* bounce back, it cut right through the circle like it was paper.

He then turned to the camera, so it felt like he was talking to me, "That's a menopause vagina. The walls are thin and brittle."

"Hence the term 'dried-up old woman,'" Roxy said, trying to be funny. I still wasn't laughing. The loss of hormones had claimed my vagina. *My vagina!* It wasn't enough that my sex drive was nonexistent, my hair and eyelashes were falling out, and I was growing a mustache? Now my vagina was compromised?!

Menopause: the thief that keeps on robbing.

I knew baby boomers wouldn't stand for that, so I went to the gynecologist to see what she recommended. I was prescribed an estrogen cream to be applied internally. She guaranteed it would thicken up the walls of my va-jay-jay and it did.

I shared the news with Roxy. "We can rebuild it," I told her. "We have the technology."

"Bionic. I love it. The six-million-dollar vagina."

One night, Mr. Age Appropriate and I were spooning in bed. "Tell me," he said softly in my ear. "Tell me about the writing and acting. It all sounded so interesting in your profile, but you never talk about it."

"Yeah, I don't really do that anymore. I need an income. Office work doesn't pay as much as TV commercials, but it's steady, and I have benefits."

"That doesn't sound like an artist's life."

"Security is not overrated."

"I Googled you, read the reviews. They were very good."

"I look at those too sometimes. I honestly don't know who she was, where she came from, or how to get her back." I could feel tears running down my cheeks and was glad he couldn't see them.

"If you had the opportunity to act and write, would you?"

"It just doesn't appeal to me anymore."

"That kind of passion never leaves you," he said softly.

"Yes, it does. It leaves. It goes away with no warning. And one day you find yourself alone, staring at a blank computer screen, and there's nothing, nothing inside you that wants to come out. Nothing is funny. It's just gone."

"Maybe that's why I'm in your life," he said.

I knew what he meant.

"I make a good living. If you lived with me, you wouldn't have to work. You could focus on writing and acting."

"I won't live with anyone again," I told him. "Not unless I'm married."

"I'd marry you." He said softly, "I love you."

I didn't respond.

"Do you love him?" Roxy asked when I told her.

"No. But I have no hormones. So, maybe I am in love, and I just don't know it yet."

"Are you my hormones?" she said to the light.

"How can I be your hormones? I am a light," said the light.

We started looking at houses in the city. He felt he could get more for his money in the suburbs. He liked Elmhurst because of its proximity to so many highways, and offered to renovate his home to accommodate me.

"You're on the road half the week. I think the one who's left behind should love where they live." I thought I stated my case against the suburbs well.

"Yes, but I know me, and the extra forty-five minutes of drive time will frustrate me." He had a point, but there was no way I was moving to a place I didn't want to live. Not for a third time. In the end, we tabled the plan to live together.

We went to Palm Springs over Valentine's Day. The desert air was good for him, dried up his nose. I planned to tell him that I loved him, but never got drunk enough.

I prayed my hormones would rally for the last time and push me over the edge. I wanted to love him. He was kind, and it was nice to have a partner, someone to pick me up at the airport, drive me to work when I was late, and take me to the doctor when I was sick. It was great, not being alone. And he never complained. He was patient and kind, and when he got a little angry with me, '50s sitcom Dad emerged: "Dear" "Yes, dear" "If you would just let me finish, dear." He was perfect for me, and with the right amount of Zyrtec... Who knows.

In the spring, my daughter got married. I wore a beautiful dress Mr. Age Appropriate bought me. It was a gorgeous gown I couldn't afford on my own, yet I didn't have him sit in for any of the pre-wedding pictures.

That fall, we planned a trip to New York. Victoria and Michael had adopted a baby, and her first birthday was coming up. "What if we run into your ex-boyfriend?" Mr. Age Appropriate asked.

"I'd be embarrassed."

"Why?"

"Then you'd see how young he was."

"But that's a reflection of how attractive you are."

God, how I wanted to love him.

We spent Friday and Saturday strolling around Manhattan and saw several Broadway shows. I loved how he trusted the way I got tickets, by showing up at the theatre and putting my name on a list. On Sunday, we took the Metro-North to the birthday party. By late afternoon, he said he wanted to leave, but I didn't. Victoria was my dearest friend. I'd planned to wait out the departure of the other guests and stay until after they put their daughter to sleep, but he said he'd had enough. Making me leave Victoria meant he didn't really know me and what was important to me.

That night, after consuming several glasses of wine with dinner, I agreed to sex, but in the morning, he woke me up to do it again. I thought the act from the night before bought me at least another week. Instead, he went running in Central Park, and I packed my suitcase.

Several weeks later, he confronted the issue. "Judi, I love you, but there's no passion. This relationship feels like a friendship, and I want more."

He wasn't wrong.

"We haven't made love in weeks," he continued.

"Really? Weeks? I'm sorry."

"Maybe you're just not a passionate person."

A montage played in my head, an X-rated assortment of passion and positions starting in my twenties with The Ex-Hole and ending in my forties with Richard, where I literally passed out from sheer exhaustion. I *was* a passionate person. Just not with him. But I couldn't say that. I didn't want to hurt his feelings.

"I'm sorry. It's not you. It's me."

We agreed that we didn't work as a couple. I had given it a fighting chance, eighteen months, but it was time to let him go because he was right. We all deserve passion in our relationships. I missed it. I missed the heightened sense of excitement I had with Ashton. I missed the marathon sessions with Richard.

I remembered a conversation I once had with Richard and wondered if I'd jinxed myself:

"What are you staring at?"Richard asked.

"I want to memorize your body. You've ruined me for other men. After you, the best I can hope for is companion guy, someone with the same taste in food and movies."

"So you think you set that in motion?" Roxy asked.

"No, I think Mr. Age Appropriate was like you said: good on paper."

"Yeah, but paper doesn't always translate to real life."

"He was a good transition guy."

"Helped you get over *Dick*."

"He preferred Richard."

"Then he shouldn't have been a Dick. You should've broken up with Mr. A. A. earlier."

"Much earlier, like after the first few months."

"And you know why you didn't?"

"Yes." I wasn't proud of the fact, but I knew. I wanted a man to take care of me. But no amount of monetary gain could replace real love or self-respect. Wherever I was in life—broke, alone, unfulfilled. I needed to rescue myself before I could ever hope to have a happily ever-after with someone else.

At least I knew where my hormones were: at Walgreens, one prescription away.

WTF?!

I was warned. I knew the odds. I had kept the information at the forefront of my mind for so long: "If you've been with more than three people, you have a one hundred percent chance of getting it."

I practiced safe sex. I should have been safe. Right? Ha!

I got the call a few weeks after a routine gynecological exam. "You need to come in for a colposcopy."

"What's that?"

"A biopsy of your cervix. Your pap smear tested positive for human papillomavirus," the nurse explained in a matter-of-fact tone.

What the fuck?

"HPV?!"

Had I been with more than three people? Try six. Boss Man *did* count, as did a guy that I failed to mention in the book, but I always used condoms—until Mr. Age Appropriate. I figured since I'd hit menopause and he'd had a vasectomy, we were safe.

"That reasoning is exactly why our age group ranks highest in STDs," Roxy said.

"Go, Boomers!"

I was pissed off! I called him. It had been several years since he and I had spoken, but since the break-up was amicable, I'd kept his contact info in my phone. I told him he gave me HPV.

"How do you know it's me?"

Fuck you.

"It could just as easily be Richard."

"Richard and I never had unprotected sex."

He got off the phone quickly but called back a few days later. "I just got tested. I don't have it."

"You're a carrier. You carried it to me." I didn't want to argue with him. Winning an argument wasn't going to cure me. "Look, I just told you so you'd be careful and not infect any more women."

"You have genital warts?"

"No, *thank God*; precancer cells on my cervix."

That shut him up. Neither of us knew that HPV could cause cervical cancer. There was nothing more to say to each other. I couldn't be mad at him. I knew the risks of unprotected sex, but over time, I guess I got lazy. Was this my punishment for staying in a relationship for all the wrong reasons?

I stopped dating. It wasn't like I turned anyone down; I just closed my account on the dating site. After all, dating could lead to intimacy and intimacy could lead to sex and sex would definitely lead to the STD conversation, and then I would have to admit that I had HPV. It was easier not to date.

After two more years of semiannual checkups and painful yearly cervical biopsies, I finally broached the subject with my doctor.

"So if I ever meet someone, I need to tell them I have an STD. Right?"

"No. Everyone has it. It's absolutely not necessary." She saw the relief on my face. "You don't have to worry about getting cervical cancer as long as you continue to come in for your regular appointments."

I felt more relief over the news that I didn't have to talk about HPV, but it was a nonissue. I still wasn't dating.

A Journey Of Self-Discovery

When I began my search for a non-relationship relationship, I never dreamed it would become a journey of self-discovery.

The raging hormones of my forties coupled with pheromones that entered a room before I did—attracted the opposite sex. In my fifties, however, men no longer noticed me. I became wallpaper, background noise. It was a complete one-eighty-degree turn. Occasionally, once a year (if that), someone offered to fix me up, but I never got asked for a second date. And I was glad. It saved me the trouble of saying no.

A woman came up to me after a performance of *Fornicationally Challenged.*

"I dated younger men after my divorce too," she shared.

"It's in the divorced woman's handbook," I answered, still playing the part of the comedian. "It's mandatory."

"I heard it's because your dating mind is the age you were when you got married and stopped dating."

It gave me pause. If that were the case, I had been emotionally dating as a twenty-year-old, choosing cute, young men. Agh!

During my original twenties, I remember telling Roxy, "When I lose my sex life, just shoot me."

But after the breakup with Mr. Age Appropriate, months

went by without sex, and then the months turned into years, and the years turned into three years. Then four. Five. Six and counting, but it was no big deal.

The break from relationships helped me find my writing voice again. That's the beauty in menopause: when you actually give men a pause, we, as women, become more productive, more creative.

Finishing this book was a defining moment in my life, not just because I finally saw the project through to fruition, but because I was honoring the most important relationship of all: the one I have with myself. I finally got back on my path.

Everyone has a path they're meant to follow, and you can't get off track. Oh sure, you can certainly take a wrong turn—like getting lost in Queens, NY—but you'll always find your way back. You can't stray from your destiny.

I knew I was in a healthy headspace because I no longer heard Mother's voice in my head. On the other hand, I'm sure my celibate lifestyle enabled her to rest in peace.

"Judala, mein kin, not so easy to be a floozy when you're an alter kaker, is it?"

Alter kaker means old shit in Yiddish. At sixty, that's what I felt like, and maybe it was time to embrace it: to go mall-walking with "the girls," eat dinner at four-thirty p.m., and complain about, well, everything.

BUT
    THEN
        SOMETHING
            HAPPENED

I got a random voice-mail message from The Puppy. He said we both indirectly worked for the same company and would I like to meet and catch up. I called him back the following night and agreed to meet him for drinks at a quiet bar in the Gold Coast.

I arrived early, fixed my face and hair in the ladies room, ordered a glass of red wine, and sat at the bar. I wondered what he'd look like after sixteen years, and—would he think I'd aged well? Mostly I pondered what he really wanted from this meet-up. I heard Gwen Stefani's voice in my head, singing her opinion, *I ain't no hollaback girl.*

It's just too old friends catching up, I decided.

Then he walked in, hugged me, and settled into the stool next to mine.

"You look great." He said with that same killer smile.

He was wearing a black suit with a white shirt, and no tie. Classic. He looked older; his dark bushy hair now tamed and spectacled gray, a cross between JFK and Matthew Broderick. He was about twenty pounds heavier, but when I looked into his eyes, I saw the irresistible puppy that I just had to bring home sixteen years ago.

"So do you," I said and meant it.

We talked about family, our jobs, and about my book.

"You have a chapter," I told him.

"Really? I'd love to read it." Which told me we would see each other again.

"Sure." I said, already thinking about how I would soften his chapter to make it more palatable for him.

He sat back in the stool and looked at me, really taking me in, then revealed, "You broke my heart, you know."

"I'm sorry. I thought it was clear we were having a fling."

"I know, but—come on." His blue eyes searched mine for recognition, asking if I remembered the intimacy we shared. He pulled out all the stops when we were dating. And that romantic night we spent in the honeymoon suite in Indiana...

And just like that, something inside me stirred. Something I hadn't felt in years, a tingling, a—desire? Was it? Yes, it was. Attraction. *Sexual* attraction. I wanted him—in that way. I wanted sex!

In an instant I felt younger, sassier, and dare I say it—sexy.

He put me in a cab an hour later, asking if he could take me to dinner next week.

"Sure, that would be nice."

And he kissed me goodnight. It wasn't that great of a kiss,

but I looked forward to working on it.

I called Roxy as soon as I got home.

"I'm ba-ack."

"From where-air?" she answered, mimicking my sing-song rhythm.

"From hormonal hiatus! I saw The Puppy tonight. I felt things."

"What puppy?"

"Not a real dog, remember, sixteen years ago, I dated—

"The Puppy! Yes. How did he look?"

"Older, like the rest of us, but still cute."

"Did you sleep with him?"

"Roxy, we just met for drinks... But that's my plan... Wait, I can't sleep with a guy on the first date. But is it a first date if you've already slept together? Is he thinking that's all I want from him—again? Or would we have a real relationship this time? Could he actually be '"the one'" after all these years?"

"Oh my God, Judes, I'm too old to go through this with you again."

"Condoms! I need condoms! Yes, I know I can't get pregnant, but that HPV thing is a Bitch."

"Please tell me you can buy them yourself this time."

I thought about it and a happy acknowledgement of how much I'd matured washed over me. "Yes, I'm totally comfortable buying condoms—just not in my neighborhood."

When we hung up the phone, I made a bikini-wax appointment in anticipation of our next encounter. What can I say? Hormones made me do it. Welcome back, old friends.

ACKNOWLEDGEMENTS

Before the book, before the show, there were stories. I wish to thank **Darryl Warren** and all those associated with Story-Tellers back in 1999 who held space for me to find my voice. And my friend, **Stephanie Rogers**, whose encouragement back then gave me the confidence to take the stage.

From 2003, when the material became a show, I wish to acknowledge **Beverly Mickins** of Story Salon for featuring me, **Marc and Elaine Zicree** for advice at every stage, and **Mark Travis**, Director extraordinaire.

When I gave up on writing, **Jill Howe** and **Rachel Smith** brought me back to a story community, Friends with Words. I remain eternally grateful. Thank you all for your unconditional and valued support. And **Jill Howe**, my story editor, you gave me structure and purpose.

My dearly departed soul mate, **Marge Royce**, who not only championed *Fornicationally Challenged* in life, she then encouraged me from the great beyond to write the book. I miss you.

Thank you to all who volunteered to read and give notes: **Patricia Overly, Lindsey Monroe Bougher, Ellen Barish,** and **Anne E. Beall, PhD.** You make me better. And **Anne,** thank you for motivating me to finally publish.

Debbie Zoub, my sister, my friend, my memory, and partner in comedic follies, your wit and humor inspired me then, now, and always. Your friendship is the throughline of my life.

I also wish to thank my editor, **Diane Telgen** for her contribution to this book. She is a stickler for correct punctuation, grammar and adherence to the Chicago Manual of Style. Her attention to detail is reflected everywhere in this book.

Most of all, I wish to acknowledge my children: **Justin Brandwein** and **Sarin Lerner**. Teaching you that you could be anything you wanted forced me to live by example. I recognize that in order to have lived this comedic life, you were both on your own as young adults. And while I am sorry about that, I'm very proud of you both for making it on your own.

Saving the best for last, **Paxton and Norah:** you are the reward for being married when I should have been single. Because of you, I experience the greatest love of all. And now that I'm a grandmother, maybe it's time to stop writing about sex, maybe write something you're allowed to read.

ABOUT THE AUTHOR

Judi Lee Goshen

 Judi has a Fiction Writing degree from Columbia College. As a Moth-winning storyteller, she has written and told hundreds of stories, including the stage production of "Fornicationally Challenged," directed by Mark Travis, which had successful runs in Los Angeles and New York.

Judi has been a stage actor since the age of seventeen. In her twenties, she was in an improv group after graduating from The Second City. Her thirties were spent doing dozens of national TV commercials, and most recently, she portrayed a doctor on "Chicago Med."

In her day job, she works for the University of Chicago. On the weekends, she plays with her grandchildren. She still writes, tells stories, and lives in a Chicago condo overlooking Lake Michigan.

BOOKS BY THIS AUTHOR

Chicago Strorytellers From Stage To Page

From the time humans first developed language, there have been stories. And since then, storytellers have used their words to entertain, warn, instruct, and amuse—but most of all, to connect with other people. The craft has evolved from tales spun around an open fire to a live performance art. Chicago's thriving storytelling community, for instance, shares their words via club shows, festivals, and podcasts. Chicago Storytellers from Stage to Page brings you twenty-five entertaining, personal stories, honed in performance by some of the city's most accomplished storytellers but now available in written form for the first time. Some will make you laugh out loud: a man seeking the sexiest way to deal with Chicago's notoriously bad winters, or a woman returning to ballet class only to find she has gravely misjudged her experience level. Other tales may bring a tear to your eye: a woman struggling to support her sister through a terminal illness, or a daughter dealing with her father's loss by taking care of his favorite cat. There are stories of lost buses and missed planes, workplace triumphs and family traditions, first love and final legacies. Together, Chicago Storytellers from Stage to Page provides ample evidence of the power of story to reveal what it means to be human.